to Bill & Julie Mas[...]
with best wish

[signature]

12/19/08

JACKSONVILLE

The Florida History and Culture Series

UNIVERSITY PRESS OF FLORIDA
STATE UNIVERSITY SYSTEM

Florida A&M University, Tallahassee
Florida Atlantic University, Boca Raton
Florida Gulf Coast University, Ft. Myers
Florida International University, Miami
Florida State University, Tallahassee
University of Central Florida, Orlando
University of Florida, Gainesville
University of North Florida, Jacksonville
University of South Florida, Tampa
University of West Florida, Pensacola

THE FLORIDA HISTORY AND CULTURE SERIES

Al Burt's Florida: Snowbirds, Sand Castles, and Self-Rising Crackers, by Al Burt (1997)

Black Miami in the Twentieth Century, by Marvin Dunn (1997)

Gladesmen: Gator Hunters, Moonshiners, and Skiffers, by Glen Simmons
   and Laura Ogden (1998)

*"Come to My Sunland": Letters of Julia Daniels Moseley from the Florida Frontier,
   1882–1886,* by Julia Winifred Moseley and Betty Powers Crislip (1998)

The Enduring Seminoles: From Alligator Wrestling to Ecotourism, by Patsy West (1998)

Government in the Sunshine State: Florida since Statehood, by David R. Colburn
   and Lance deHaven-Smith (1999)

The Everglades: An Environmental History, by David McCally (1999),
   first paperback edition, 2001

Beechers, Stowes, and Yankee Strangers: The Transformation of Florida,
   by John T. Foster Jr. and Sarah Whitmer Foster (1999)

The Tropic of Cracker, by Al Burt (1999)

Balancing Evils Judiciously: The Proslavery Writings of Zephaniah Kingsley,
   edited and annotated by Daniel W. Stowell (1999)

Hitler's Soldiers in the Sunshine State: German POWs in Florida,
   by Robert D. Billinger Jr. (2000)

Cassadaga: The South's Oldest Spiritualist Community, edited by John J. Guthrie,
   Phillip Charles Lucas, and Gary Monroe (2000)

Claude Pepper and Ed Ball: Politics, Purpose, and Power, by Tracy E. Danese (2000)

Pensacola during the Civil War: A Thorn in the Side of the Confederacy,
   by George F. Pearce (2000)

 **James B. Crooks**

Foreword by Raymond Arsenault and Gary R. Mormino, Series Editors

University Press of Florida

GAINESVILLE TALLAHASSEE TAMPA BOCA RATON
PENSACOLA ORLANDO MIAMI JACKSONVILLE FT. MYERS

JACKSONVILLE

The Consolidation Story, from Civil Rights to the Jaguars

09 08 07 06 05 04   6 5 4 3 2 1

Library of Congress Cataloging-in-Publication Data
Crooks, James B.
Jacksonville: the consolidation story, from civil rights to the Jaguars / James B. Crooks;
foreword by Raymond Arsenault and Gary R. Mormino.
p. cm.– (The Florida history and culture series)
Includes bibliographical references and index.
ISBN 0-8130-2708-X (acid-free paper)
1. Jacksonville (Fla.)–Politics and government–20th century. 2. Metropolitan government–
Florida–Jacksonville Region–History–20th century. 3. Jacksonville (Fla.)–Race relations. 4.
Jacksonville (Fla.)–Social conditions–20th century. 5. Social problems–Florida–Jacksonville–
History–20th century. 6. Jacksonville (Fla.)–Environmental conditions. I. Title. II. Series.

F319.J1C765 2004
975.9'12043–dc22   2003066587

The University Press of Florida is the scholarly publishing agency for the State University
System of Florida, comprising Florida A&M University, Florida Atlantic University, Florida
Gulf Coast University, Florida International University, Florida State University, University
of Central Florida, University of Florida, University of North Florida, University of South
Florida, and University of West Florida.

University Press of Florida
15 Northwest 15th Street
Gainesville, FL 32611-2079
http://www.upf.com

Contents

ILLUSTRATIONS

TABLES

FOREWORD

Jacksonville: The Consolidation Story, from Civil Rights to the Jaguars is the twenty-ninth volume in a series devoted to the study of Florida history and culture. During the past half century, the burgeoning population and increased national and international visibility of Florida have sparked a great deal of popular interest in the state's past, present, and future. As the favorite destination of hordes of tourists and as the new home for millions of retirees and other migrants, modern Florida has become a demographic, political, and cultural bellwether.

Unfortunately, the quantity and quality of the literature on Florida's distinctive heritage and character have not kept pace with the Sunshine State's enhanced status. In an effort to remedy this situation—to provide an accessible and attractive format for the publication of Florida-related books—the University Press of Florida has established the Florida History and Culture series.

As coeditors of the series, we are committed to the creation of an eclectic but carefully crafted set of books that will provide the field of Florida studies with a new focus and that will encourage Florida researchers and writers to consider the broader implications and context of their work. The series includes standard academic monographs, works of synthesis, memoirs, and anthologies. And, while the series features books of historical interest, we encourage authors researching Florida's environment, politics, literature, and popular or material culture to submit their manuscripts as well. We want each book to retain a distinct personality and voice, but at the same time we hope to foster a sense of community and collaboration among Florida scholars.

Jacksonville: The Consolidation Story explores the recent history of one of modern Florida's most important communities. As James B. Crooks demonstrates in this groundbreaking study, the historic and sprawling city at the mouth of the St. Johns River has undergone a remarkable set of transformations during the past four decades. The city's preeminent scholar and the author of *Jacksonville before the Fire* (1991), Crooks is able to draw upon more than thirty years of primary research and personal observation in his wide-ranging analysis of a complex and distinctive urban environment. Much of the book deals with the aftermath and legacy of the city-county consolidation of 1967, which established Jacksonville—all 840 square miles of it—as the largest city in the continental United States.

Crooks's study also examines the difficult years that immediately preceded consolidation. During the early and mid-1960s, Jacksonville was a city in decline with an unenviable reputation for bitter race relations, poor schools, polluted air and water, and an outdated and crumbling urban infrastructure. How the city's political and business leaders, including the regional power broker Ed Ball, convinced the leaders and inhabitants of Duval County's overwhelmingly white suburbs to accept consolidation is a remarkable story of negotiation and persuasion—a story that Crooks relates in fascinating detail.

In the years since consolidation, Jacksonville has experienced explosive growth and increased visibility in the American urban hierarchy. But no one, prior to Crooks, had taken the time to examine the inner workings of the city's regenerative growth and expansion, placing them in the evolving and interrelated contexts of cultural, political, and economic change. By tracing these changes through a series of mayoral regimes, city plans, economic growth schemes, and corporate comings and goings, Crooks provides us with a carefully balanced, in-depth analysis of the accomplishments and failures of an important Sunbelt city. During the first decade of the twenty-first century, the challenges posed by urban sprawl, inadequate zoning, poverty, environmental pollution, and racial discrimination remain serious concerns for all Floridians, and the choices made in recent decades continue to influence our present quality of life as well as our prospects for the future. With this in mind, we would be well advised to turn our attention to *Jacksonville: The Consolidation Story*, the latest addition to the growing and increasingly sophisticated historical literature on urban and suburban Florida.

Raymond Arsenault and Gary R. Mormino, Series Editors
University of South Florida, St. Petersburg

PREFACE AND ACKNOWLEDGMENTS

This book evolved from my four-year experience as historian in residence during Mayor Tommy Hazouri's administration in Jacksonville from 1987 to 1991. At the beginning of Hazouri's term, I approached the University of North Florida's president, Curtis McCray, and the mayor about the possibility of observing firsthand operations at city hall in a manner roughly modeled after historian Arthur Schlesinger Jr.'s position as a member of President John F. Kennedy's staff from 1961 to 1963. Afterward, of course, Schlesinger wrote about his experience with the president in *A Thousand Days*. Hazouri and McCray agreed to my proposal, though my role was not that of a staff member but primarily as an observer with access to public meetings, documents, and members of the administration. My initial goal was to write a history of the Hazouri administration, but subsequently I expanded my effort to write a history of Jacksonville's city-county consolidation. What follows is the result.

Shortly after beginning the research, Duane Atkinson of the city's Public Information Division called to tell me he had found a cache of mayoral files in the mezzanine of the old city hall parking garage. There were forty-four file cabinets full of letters, memoranda, and reports from the Haydon Burns, Louis Ritter, Hans Tanzler, and Jake Godbold administrations. This collection, covered with dust and grime, became the most important source of research materials for this book. I secured permission from Ivan Clare, then director of public information, and Lex Hester, the city's chief administrative officer, to read and make copies of relevant documents. Duane and I lugged filthy cabinet drawer after cabinet drawer to a sixth-floor desk where I worked.

A major concern became the quantity of papers from each mayoral administration. As practitioners and observers of urban governance know, cities are tremendously complex organizations, with responsibilities that include law enforcement, public safety, schools, civil and criminal justice, water, sewers, roads, public housing, health care, welfare, parks, playgrounds, and state and federal relations. The list could go on in Jacksonville to include providing electric power, managing ports and airports, providing public transportation, staffing a city-owned radio station, and overseeing a large river system and oceanfront. To research all of these issues from the 1960s to the 1990s would have taken me well into the twenty-first century. To write about all of them with meaning and style would have approached the impossible. Thus I made decisions to narrow my topic.

I have two goals for this book. First, I want to examine the story of consolidation of Jacksonville with Duval County, Florida. I want to describe what preconsolidated Jacksonville looked like, how consolidation came about, and how consolidation was carried out under four mayors,[1] and to assess the experience of consolidation in terms of the changes that took place in Jacksonville over twenty-five years. I also want to compare Jacksonville's experience with other cities, particularly Tampa, which chose not to consolidate with surrounding Hillsborough County in the year Jacksonville chose to do so.

My second goal is to examine historically three major challenges confronting contemporary urban society, using Jacksonville as a case study. These challenges are race relations, the environment, and the fate of downtown areas in the context of suburban sprawl. The plight of the downtown has been an issue at least since the suburban expansion after World War II. Race relations came to the forefront in the 1950s and 1960s for all Americans, although of course they were an issue for African American communities long before that time. American concerns about the natural environment began with the conservation/preservation movement more than a century ago, but environmental concerns became focused in cities and suburbs beginning in the 1960s and 1970s. How Jacksonvillians—citizens and leaders—dealt with those three challenges is a story that I felt worth telling. How elected officials and citizens continue to deal with all three challenges will affect the character of Jacksonville and other American cities for the foreseeable future.

The book begins with an introduction to preconsolidation Jacksonville of the 1960s. On the surface, initiatives by Mayor Burns had cleaned up the waterfront, attracted major business investment, and built new public facilities. But beneath the surface, all was not well. African Americans challenged racial segregation. The Southern Association of Colleges and Schools had disaccredited the public high schools. The St. Johns River and its tributaries were heavily polluted. Critics described city government as boss ridden, expensive, and corrupt.

Chapter 2 looks at the response to these conditions in the formation of the Local Government Study Commission, which drafted the charter for a new Jacksonville. It proposed to consolidate the city with its surrounding Duval County. Local voters endorsed this charter by an almost two-to-one majority in August 1967.

Chapter 3 examines the experience of the first consolidation mayor of the Bold New City, Hans Tanzler Jr., beginning October 1, 1968. It places special emphasis on his efforts to clean up the river, ease racial tensions, and revitalize downtown with the help of federal urban renewal dollars.

Chapter 4 shifts the focus to race relations in Jacksonville during the 1970s: civil disturbances and their aftermath; well-intended efforts by the interracial Council of Leadership for Community Advancement (COLCA); investigations into local police-community relations by the Florida Advisory Committee to the U.S. Commission on Civil Rights; and an assessment at the end of decade by the Jacksonville Urban League of race relations in the city.

Chapter 5 examines the 1970s from an economic perspective. The difficult years of inflation, oil embargo, recession, and stagflation on the national level limited the momentum of consolidation locally for the Bold New City. The attempt by Offshore Power Systems to build two floating nuclear-power plants challenged the environment and eventually the fiscal capacity of the Jacksonville Electric Authority and city to fund them. Yet the decade was not all hard times. Opening of the University of North Florida, private support for the arts and education, and the creation of new initiatives like the Jacksonville Community Council, Inc. (JCCI) and Hubbard House served the city well.

Chapter 6 focuses on Mayor Godbold's two terms in office with his substantial achievements in downtown development, efforts to address environmental problems, and overtures for improving race relations. In chapter 7, Mayor Hazouri's one term in office is examined with regard to his achievements in ending automobile tolls and curbing odors, the latter overcoming a major negative Jacksonville image. His failure at reelection led to the Austin years described in chapter 8. Mayor Austin's one term focused primarily on downtown development, climaxing in the acquisition of the Jacksonville Jaguars National Football League franchise. His administration also resolved the garbage crisis carried over from his predecessor's term, and had a mixed record in race relations.

The concluding chapter, chapter 9, assesses the effects of twenty-five years of consolidation on Jacksonville's African American population, the environment, and the downtown. It compares consolidated Jacksonville with Tampa and Hillsborough County, which turned down consolidation in 1967. Finally, the chapter briefly addresses the effects of urban growth upon city governance nationally, with concluding thoughts about Jacksonville's experience.

In this study, I admit up front to a bias in favor of racial justice, a healthy environment, and a thriving downtown. I have tried to understand the nature of race relations in this city. I have described the fragile character of the local environment, environmental threats, and the city's response to them. I have described the deterioration of downtown and the efforts to revitalize it. Finally, I have tried to present my story fairly, though some readers may disagree.

Acknowledgments

I have benefited from the assistance of many people on this project. First, I am grateful to President Curtis McCray for freeing me from part of my duties in the classroom at the University of North Florida, and to Mayor Tommy Hazouri for permission to observe Jacksonville governance firsthand for four years. I also am very grateful to Duane Atkinson for discovering the cache of documents, calling me, and assisting with their recovery. Thanks, too, go to Ivan Clare and the late Lex Hester for their cooperation.

Also at city hall during the Hazouri administration, Tommy's chief administrative officer, Mitchell Atalla, and his assistant, Ann Shorstein, were particularly helpful, as were many mayoral aides and department heads.

Dr. Pat Cowdery, then head of public health, provided generous access to documents relating to bio-environmental issues. R. B. Johnson, then executive director of the Human Relations Commission, shared his agency's limited archives.

Beyond city hall, Hans Tanzler provided scrapbooks and interviews. So did Jake Godbold, whose wife, Jean, shared the mayor's scrapbooks and provided space at Gateway Chemical for me to read and take notes. Tommy Hazouri donated his scrapbooks to the University of North Florida archives, which I read, and he talked many times with me. Matt Carlucci donated his father's papers to the same archives in response to my request. At the University of North Florida, documents librarian Bruce Latimer and archivist Eileen Brady were particularly helpful, as was Marianne Roberts, the history department's office manager. History department chairs David Courtwright, Don Schafer, and Dale Clifford were also very supportive of this work. Carol Grimes provided the files of her late husband, Bob, compiled during his tenure as a member of the Environmental Protection Board. The Rev. Charles W. McGehee, pastor of the local Unitarian-Universalist Church during the 1960s, before his death sent me documents from his days as an activist supporting civil rights in Jacksonville. Nathan Wilson, first chair of the Jacksonville Human Relations Commission, also shared materials before his death. A sabbatical leave from the university for the 1992–93 academic year provided a substantial kick start to my research efforts. Grants from the Jacksonville History Project of the UNF endowment fund provided support for transcribing interviews, assembling scrapbooks, and preparing photos for publication.

I have asked individuals to read and critique chapters, papers, and related articles. My thanks for this effort go to Dr. Joan Carver, Alton Yates, Gerry Wilson, Hans Tanzler, Dr. Sherry Magill, Dr. Arnette Girardeau, Wendell Holmes, Shep Bryan, Nathan Wilson, Dave Foster, and Mark Middlebrook. Any errors that remain in the text are my responsibility, not theirs.

Portions of chapters 1 and 3 were published in the *Florida Historical Quarterly* as "Jacksonville before Consolidation" (fall 1998) and "Jacksonville's Consolidation Mayor: Hans G. Tanzler Jr." (fall 2001).

My thanks also go to the three dozen people I interviewed, who are listed in the bibliography; to Carolyn Wilson and Trish Putnam, who transcribed many of the oral interviews; and to Janice Fluegel, who assembled scrapbooks from newspaper clippings.

Finally, as always, I owe my greatest thanks to my special friend, listener, and life mate, Laura, for her support and encouragement. To my children, Peter and Sarah, who grew up in consolidated Jacksonville, I dedicate this book.

CHAPTER 1

JACKSONVILLE BEFORE CONSOLIDATION

The Jacksonville Story

A delegation of businessmen from Beaumont, Texas, visited Jacksonville during the summer of 1963 to see how local community leaders had dealt with their urban problems. Most impressive to them was the cleanup of the downtown waterfront along the St. Johns River. From the River Club, then atop the new Prudential Insurance Company's southeast regional headquarters building on the south bank, the Texans looked across the river and saw the new retaining walls that had replaced the old rotting wharves on the north bank. Beyond the bulkheads, a new roadway provided a river view for motorists and pedestrians. Nearby stood the new fifteen-story Atlantic Coast Line Railroad home office (the ACL Building). The railroad had recently moved its corporate headquarters to Jacksonville from Wilmington, North Carolina. Adjacent to the ACL Building was the new civic auditorium with an exhibition hall. Beyond, Sears Roebuck had built a large retail outlet covering two city blocks, expressing its confidence in downtown renewal. East of the Main Street Bridge, a new city hall, county courthouse, and jail looked out over the river. Also downtown, a new Robert Meyer Hotel, Florida National Bank, Barnett Bank, and Independent Life Insurance home office confirmed the city center's vitality. All of this new construction and urban renewal reflected what community leaders liked to call "Jacksonville's Decade of Progress," under the mayoral leadership of W. Haydon Burns.[1]

First elected mayor in 1949 on a reform ticket that challenged increased bus fares, the thirty-seven-year-old Burns began a political career that resulted in five terms in office and a successful campaign for governor in 1964. As mayor and one of five commissioners serving as the city's executive branch of government, Burns controlled the police and fire departments as well as building and plumbing inspection, signals and traffic control, and housing. A shrewd politician, he built political alliances through patronage with the other commissioners and city employees. He campaigned for votes in the African American community and appointed the first black police officers in 1950. He won reelection by wide margins.[2]

But Burns was more than just a successful politician. He saw himself as a city builder determined to revitalize a decaying downtown. He liked to tell "The Jacksonville Story" with illustrated lectures to local and out-of-town audiences. The story began in the years following World War II. Burns described the waterfront then as "probably the worst eyesore of any major American city," with its rat-infested, dilapidated warehouses and wharves. Most shipping had long since departed to the newer Talleyrand docks. Main Street and Broad Street, the two north-south highways through downtown, were choked with bumper-to-bumper traffic. Main Street in particular, once a prosperous shopping district, had declined rapidly due to the congestion of trucks, buses, military vehicles, and motorcars following the opening in 1941 of the John T. Alsop Bridge (known as the Main Street Bridge). Beyond the waterfront and crowded thoroughfares, downtown looked old and tired, in part due to the absence of any substantial new construction during the depression decade of the 1930s and the war years of the 1940s.[3]

Burns's vision for the city began with the goal of renewing the ugly north-bank riverfront on either side of the Main Street Bridge. He secured state authorization for $4 million in Parking Lot Certificate bonds, condemned, cleared, and filled land, constructed parking lots, and by 1955 had eliminated his first major eyesore.[4]

Next the Duval County Commission cleared land east of the parking lots for a new courthouse. In 1958, Burns secured passage of a $30 million bond issue for capital improvements to build the city hall, coliseum, and civic auditorium, as well as the Buckman Sewage Treatment Plant, belatedly beginning construction of a sanitary sewage system for Jacksonville. He lobbied the Atlantic Coast Line Railroad to move its home office to Jacksonville, supported the development of the Jacksonville Expressway System, and worked for the growth of the insurance industry. It was Burns

Fig. 1. Haydon Burns, mayor of Jacksonville, 1949–1965. By permission of Eleanor Watkins, Jacksonville.

as promoter of "The Jacksonville Story," with his slide shows and bus tours for local Rotarians and visiting dignitaries, who left a legacy of downtown development during Jacksonville's Decade of Progress.[5]

Not all Jacksonville residents felt positively about Burns. He came from a lower-middle-class background that folks from Jacksonville's elite Ortega neighborhood frequently snubbed. Growing up on the north side, Burns graduated from Andrew Jackson High School, attended Babson College near Boston, served in World War II as a commissioned officer and naval aeronautics salvage specialist, and, on the eve of his first election, worked in public relations. Burns worked hard at presenting himself as a business-oriented public official, but lax financial management practices of the day convinced some observers that political patronage edged over into corruption. One person who knew Burns well claimed this was untrue.[6]

At the beginning of the civil rights movement in the 1960s, Burns reflected the predominantly southern white attitudes that opposed peaceful picketing and demonstrations. He was not a rabid segregationist like Alabama's George Wallace. At the same time, despite his earlier ties with the

African American community, he refused to intervene or mediate between black activists and downtown merchants, and he took a hard line enforcing law and order. His leadership in rebuilding downtown did not carry over into race relations.

Burns's two years in Tallahassee also drew mixed reviews, and he lost his bid for reelection in the bitter campaign of 1966. Still, city council honored Burns's substantial contributions to Jacksonville by naming the new city library after him in 1965. Burns was a successful mayor during the more lax, business-oriented, pre–civil rights, Eisenhower era of the 1950s. Attitudes changed in the following decade, leaving mixed memories of him.[7]

While Haydon Burns went to Tallahassee following his election as governor in 1964, Jacksonville's development continued. Gulf Life Insurance Company began building its new home office on the river's south bank, flanked by the Sheraton–Jacksonville Hotel. The General Services Administration completed a new federal building on Bay Street. City commissioners began planning to replace the overcrowded, run-down Imeson Airport and build the new central city library to be named after Burns.

Meanwhile, the Jacksonville Port Authority (JPA) began a major upgrading and expansion of its facilities. Created by the Florida legislature in 1963, the JPA assumed control of the municipally owned docks and terminals built in 1915 along Talleyrand Avenue. Vernon McDaniel, a staff member at JPA, remembered conditions:

> It was terrible. . . . To tell the truth, there wasn't much there. There were old finger piers on Slip 1 where the coffee was unloaded. Slip 2 was unusable; it had silted in so much a ship couldn't get in there. And the old wooden wharf had fallen into the slip anyway. . . . When one of those big Grace Line banana ships arrived—and those were big ones, 400 feet long—and a tanker also came in, something had to give. We had to move somebody to get both ships unloaded.[8]

While the three municipal docks were in poor condition, the private sector's docks flourished, handling imported oil, autos, coffee, and other goods. Port tonnage had tripled since the end of World War II. Under the direction of Daniel G. Rawls, JPA modernized existing docks, deepened the river channel from 34 to 38 feet, and began to develop Blount Island as a major terminus downriver closer to the Atlantic Ocean. It also assumed responsibility for the new Jacksonville International Airport that opened in 1968. An often unsung commercial giant, the Jacksonville port became a major contributor to the city's growth and development in the 1960s.[9]

Beyond the city limits during the decade, developers continued their postwar suburban housing construction in Arlington, Southside, and other parts of Duval County. In the sand dunes east of Arlington, developer Martin Stein began building a major regional enclosed shopping center at Regency Square. Gateway and Roosevelt Malls opened on the north side and west side, respectively. On the south side, Ira Koger's Boulevard Center became one of the first suburban office parks in the nation. As a result, suburban homeowners began to shift their working and shopping patterns to nearby malls and office parks at the expense of downtown.[10]

Jacksonville's development expanded beyond suburban and commercial growth. In the old Riverside neighborhood, the Cummer Museum opened in 1961 as the result of a generous bequest by Ninah Holden Cummer, art collector and member of one of Jacksonville's most prominent families. In the same neighborhood, board members of the Jacksonville Children's Museum sought to expand their collection and programs beyond their crowded quarters. They combined a $100,000 gift from the Junior League with a 99-year lease from the city in a new park on the south bank of the St. Johns River. Architect William Morgan designed an award-winning building that was subsequently expanded to become the Museum of Science and History. Next, the trustees of the Jacksonville Art Museum began plans to move from its crowded Riverside location. Land was donated at the new Boulevard Center office park on the south side by the Koger family, and the architectural firm of Reynolds, Smith, and Hills provided designs for construction of a new facility that opened in 1968. It later became the Jacksonville Museum of Modern Art and moved to downtown in the 1990s.[11]

During the same decade, the Duval legislative delegation in Tallahassee secured authorization to establish a junior college and later a state university in Jacksonville. In Washington, Congressman Charles Bennett obtained funding to build Fort Caroline National Monument, a replica of the original European settlement on the banks of the St. Johns River. For city boosters, Jacksonville's efforts were comparable to the great reconstruction efforts after the 1901 fire. Downtown renewal, expanded transportation facilities, suburban growth, and new or expanding cultural and educational institutions were substantial steps forward.[12]

Several key factors contributed to Jacksonville's Decade of Progress, beginning in the 1950s. First was the $100 million expressway system to divert through traffic around the congested streets of downtown while providing commuter access from the suburbs and beaches. The Florida legislature established the Jacksonville Expressway Authority (later renamed the Jacksonville Transportation Authority) in 1955 following a decade of frustration and delays in the planning, funding, and construction of bridges and highways. Characteristic of the problem was the Fuller Warren Bridge, later to become part of I-95 in the interstate highway system. Its purpose was to relieve traffic on the overcrowded Acosta and Main Street Bridges. However, failure to plan for adequate approaches at either end resulted in the dumping of vehicular traffic into the narrow streets of Riverside and San Marco. The creation of the JEA, initiated by the Chamber of Commerce and the Duval delegation to the Florida legislature, led to Governor LeRoy Collins's appointment of Lucius A. Buck as chairman of the authority. Buck's choice of county engineer Arthur N. Sollee as executive director, and the subsequent floating of an initial $70 million bond issue, provided the direction and resources to plan and construct a comprehensive system. It included the Fuller Warren and John E. Mathews Bridges, connected to expressways and major highways bypassing downtown and heading out of the city. By the mid-1960s, JEA had begun to work on a fifth bridge across the river downtown (Hart), a beltway bridge south of the city (Buckman), a new expressway to the beach communities (Butler Boulevard), and improvements to feeder roads into the system. As a result of these developments, Jacksonville motorists in the later 1960s traveled the highways of their metropolitan area relatively free of congestion.[13]

A second factor influencing Jacksonville's growth followed passage by the 1953 Florida legislature of the Regional Home Office Law providing tax benefits attractive to out-of-state insurance companies. Subsequently, Prudential established its southeast (later to become south-central) regional home office and the State Farm Group substantially expanded its facilities. Later, Independent Life, Peninsula Life, Gulf Life, Blue Cross and Blue Shield, and the Afro-American Life Insurance Company built new home offices in Jacksonville. By the end of the decade, Jacksonville claimed the title "Insurance Center of the Southeast," with seventeen locally headquartered insurance companies, five regional home offices, and twenty major general insurance agencies. These developments, along with expansion of the Barnett, Florida National, and Atlantic National Banks, provided venture capital for economic expansion locally and across the region. They also provided jobs for both high school and college graduates as clerks, secretaries, sales agents, underwriters, claims personnel, and managers.[14]

Perhaps the most important factor influencing Jacksonville's growth was the Chamber of Commerce. It strongly supported the development of the expressway system, renewal of downtown, and relocation of insurance businesses to the city. In the early 1960s, it went even further in attempting to plan for the future growth of the city and its suburbs. Its 1962 *Jacksonville Workbook for Community Development* reflected the efforts of more than five hundred business and professional men and women under the leadership of Glenn Marshall Jr., president of WJXT-TV and former president of the Chamber. Organized into committees, they examined over a six-month period the issues and opportunities confronting the city, ranging from industry, commerce, and transportation to public health, housing, and education.

They determined that the four most important needs of the city were in public education, public health, port development, and transportation. Seven additional areas of concern included governmental operations, public recreation, industrial development, external affairs (as with the navy), commercial development, housing, and downtown development. Critical to meeting all of these needs, which crossed city-county lines in this preconsolidation era, was the creation of an effective areawide planning board and the city's annexation of adjacent suburbs of Duval County to increase the tax base.[15]

Many of the report's proposals were swiftly implemented. In 1963, with Chamber support, the Florida legislature created the Jacksonville Port Authority. The construction of the Buckman Sewage Treatment Plant became part of a four-phase master plan to build a comprehensive sanitary and storm water sewage system to improve public health. The new airport and continued expansion of the expressway system met transportation needs. Perhaps most important were the Chamber's efforts to remedy the problems of the public school system.

Disaccrediting Duval County High Schools

Conditions in the Duval County public schools were very poor. In 1962, the Chamber of Commerce initiated a citizens' School Bootstrap Committee, chaired by attorney Harry G. Kinkaid and composed of men and women from the business and professional community, League of Women Voters, Junior League, Parent-Teacher Association, and trade unions. It issued a major report in 1963. This was followed by a book-length study two years later, the *Peabody Survey*, undertaken by consultants from George Peabody College of Teachers in Nashville. Both severely criticized the curriculum, physical conditions, administration, and finances of the system. Teachers and students were the primary victims of this inadequate school system.[16]

Highlights of the critiques included Duval County's rank as last among Florida's sixty-seven counties with regard to per pupil funding. Among the twenty largest school systems in the nation (Duval was fifteenth largest), Duval again ranked last.

Teacher salaries were low. Duval County ranked tenth in that category among Florida's ten largest counties. Low salaries contributed to an annual 25 percent turnover rate. Teacher shortages, while a national phenomenon, were particularly acute in Duval County, resulting in many unqualified personnel being hired in the classroom and many teachers teaching out of their field. Working conditions included overcrowded classrooms, with thirty or more students, inadequate instructional tools, lack of any time during the day for preparation or grading of student work, unpaid overloads for extracurricular activities, and the need for one-fourth of the teachers (75 percent of the men) to work second jobs to support themselves or their families. A core of dedicated teachers persisted against the odds in providing quality instruction. But for the majority, teaching was a job with few incentives for professional development and without much satisfaction. The morale was low and the results showed it.[17]

For Duval County students, large classes, outdated or inadequate numbers of textbooks, minimal laboratory, library, and audiovisual equipment, and mediocre instruction inevitably affected their education. The average Duval County student did less well than other Florida high school graduates on college placement exams. The average dropout rate was higher in

Duval County. Only 60 percent of seventh graders completed high school. In the elementary grades, large numbers of students—one-quarter of whites and up to 35 percent of blacks—were overage for their grade. Special-education classes for handicapped children served only a small fraction of the need. Only one teacher taught classes for gifted children. Kindergartens did not yet exist.[18]

Conditions for African American youngsters were worse. Most of the overcrowding occurred in their segregated schools. Physical facilities, ragged hand-me-down textbooks, and minimal laboratory or library materials are still remembered a generation later. Only the most determined young people completed their studies and went on to college, supported by dedicated teachers, coaches, and administrators.[19]

There were also critical deficiencies in the leadership and management of the Duval County public schools. School policies were affected by eight different elected boards with much conflict and overlap. For example, Duval County had school trustees (a body being phased out in other parts of Florida), who could recommend to the superintendent and school board the appointment of teachers and principals. The independently elected Duval Budget Commission (separate from the Duval County Commission) could overrule the school board or superintendent on item expenditures. The popularly elected superintendent, the only elected superintendent among the twenty largest school systems in the nation, had authority independent of and could not be removed by the school board. Because he faced the voters on a regular basis, he rarely made unpopular decisions. The result was a confusing dispersion of power and responsibility, as well as a reluctance on the part of anybody to provide vision or leadership, particularly in programs that might cost money.[20]

Further, Duval County was the only system among the nation's largest without an administrative structure delineating areas of authority and responsibility. Lines of communication were not clear. Decisions large and small were made at the center in a system of 4,842 teachers and 106,370 students. No assistant or area superintendents existed for delegated responsibility. The superintendent even interviewed individual teaching applicants, particularly if they were black. There were rumors that black teachers had to pay kickbacks for their jobs. Appointments to principal or other administrative positions were considered political in nature. Ten years after the Supreme Court's decision in *Brown v. Board of Education,* Duval County still had a separate Division of Negro Education entirely staffed by black personnel.[21]

Overall, the system was characterized by what appeared to be an unquestioning deference to authority at all levels. In the classroom, high school students heard lectures with little opportunity or encouragement to discuss or ask questions. Teachers obeyed their principals who in turn followed the directives of the central administration. An example of how the system worked could be seen in the planning and construction of the new Duncan U. Fletcher High School in Jacksonville Beach, carried out without consulting the teachers who would work there. According to the *Peabody Survey,* the building was acoustically treated, except for areas where it was most needed, such as the music rooms and shops. The science facilities were spread out in different parts of the building, preventing the sharing of supplies, laboratories, or programs. The boys' locker rooms lacked both floor drains and benches in front of lockers. The industrial shop area was poorly designed. The lack of coordination, cooperation, and collegiality across the system was noteworthy.[22]

Of all the problems besetting the Duval County schools, the greatest was financial. The School Bootstrap Committee concluded that the quality of public education suffered severely from lack of financial support. The *Peabody Survey* added, "While adequate financial support does not always guarantee quality education, it is impossible to achieve quality education without adequate support."[23]

Both reports analyzed federal, state, and local tax support for the Duval County public schools, compared the support with that of other Florida counties and large school systems across the country, and concluded that Duval taxpayers were not doing their share. Given relative uniformity of state support in education, the *Peabody Survey* concluded, "The percentage of revenue receipts raised from local sources in Duval County is significantly less than the average of all Florida counties, and this percentage has been decreasing steadily in Duval County during recent years."[24]

Actually, education expenditures had increased 157 percent over the preceding decade, but rising enrollments combined with inflation virtually nullified the increase. The Peabody consultants concluded that in real-dollar terms, the per pupil funding for education at best had seen a negligible increase, and may have been negative.[25]

In comparison with other large Florida counties and large systems nationwide, Duval County ranked substantially below norms in its support for public education. On a per pupil basis, Duval County spent between 20 and 25 percent less than the average of these other jurisdictions. Yet Duval was not a poor county. In the early 1960s, it was third in the state in per capita personal income, third in median family income, and seventh in percent of families with annual incomes of $10,000 or more. Such rankings did not warrant Duval being sixty-seventh among Florida counties in its support of public education.[26]

Still, Duval Countians did pay the twenty-five-mill maximum property tax (including five mills for bond redemption) for their schools, as permitted under the state constitution. The problem lay with property assessments. In 1964, the Duval County Taxpayers Association reported that property was assessed locally at only about 30 percent of true value. On a $15,000 house (decent accommodation in the 1960s), a 30 percent assessment resulted in an assessed value of $4,500. With the Florida homestead exemption then at $5,000 assessed value, the home owner paid no taxes. The Taxpayers Association estimated that of 93,487 households in Duval County in 1963, two-thirds were totally exempt from property taxes. Low taxes, of course, were a home owner's delight. Business leaders also believed low taxes served as an incentive in Jacksonville's efforts to recruit new businesses in competition with other Florida cities. Yet the School Bootstrap Committee concluded that assessments could be increased to 50 or 60 percent without overtaking Dade, Pinellas, or Hillsborough Counties. It also estimated that an increase to a 50 percent assessment at the current tax rate would close much of the funding gap for Duval County's schools.[27]

The 1964 city elections provided an opportunity to begin turning around the deterioration of the public schools. The incumbent property appraiser promised to hold the line on assessments, while his challenger proposed facing the school financial crisis by raising them. After wide media coverage of the issues, the voters gave the incumbent a decisive victory. Low taxes, regardless of educational consequences, were the voters' choice.[28]

One week after the election, the Florida Department of Education stripped state accreditation from eight local schools and warned thirty-seven more. Then the Florida Commission of the Southern Association of

Colleges and Schools (SACS) announced it would recommend disaccreditation of all fifteen high schools. Lack of adequate financial support was a key factor. Belatedly, the Jacksonville community began to awaken. Newspaper editorials blamed local conditions on the "indifference, apathy and selfishness of Duval residents." Prominent citizens worried about the effect of disaccreditation on college-bound students. Leading clergy pointed to the moral responsibility of taxpayers to provide adequate education for the next generation. High school students demonstrated downtown, carrying signs proclaiming, "No accreditation without taxation." The Duval County Taxpayers Association, under the leadership of railroad executive Prime F. Osborne III (who had close ties to the Chamber of Commerce), filed suit seeking a "just valuation" of properties. In early 1965, local circuit court judge William Durden ruled on the taxpayer suit, declaring the assessor had "systematically and deliberately and intentionally under-assessed property." He ordered a full market-value property assessment by July 1, 1965. Conditions slowly began to improve, and increasing numbers of property owners began paying attention to how their property tax dollars were being spent by local government officials.[29]

In the aftermath of the disaccreditation decision, the George Peabody consultants studied how Duval Countians had permitted the situation to develop. They stressed the excessively complex and overlapping governmental structures in which elected officials failed to act. They pointed to the highly politicized nature of the school system in a community where politics was held in low esteem. Another concern was the shortsightedness of Duval voters, who had permitted conditions to deteriorate and still supported an incumbent assessor who promised to keep taxes minimal. After all, wealthy citizens could always send their children to private schools. Blue-collar families, struggling to make ends meet on limited incomes, might conclude that if their children simply finished school as they had done, regardless of the quality of their education, their children were prepared for life. Senior citizens on tight budgets possibly feared the impact of tax increases more than they worried about the character of their community's schools. The willingness of the Chamber of Commerce to confront the school crisis helped focus attention and begin long-overdue change.[30]

Land, Air, and Water Pollution

While the 1962 Chamber of Commerce report helped precipitate major changes in the funding of public education, it had a far less significant impact on public health or land, air, and water pollution in the Greater Jacksonville area. Beyond endorsing the construction of the Buckman Sewage Treatment Plant, a four-stage development of sanitary sewage and storm water drainage systems proposed by consultants and accepted by the city commission in the 1950s, the Chamber saw little to change in the condition of the St. Johns River and its many tributaries, or with regard to land and air pollution. In fact, the Chamber of Commerce report concluded almost smugly: "This great St. Johns River complex forms a natural drainage system, probably unequaled by any area of equal size. The system carries surplus runoff water, sanitary effluent and industrial waste to the ocean where it is purified by nature."[31]

Further, it added: "The price of good employment conditions and industrial development is often a certain amount of water and air pollution. Something less than 100 percent pure air and water (except for domestic use) can be tolerated without any appreciable discomfort. . . . *Complete treatment* of sanitary and industrial waste, before passing it on to the stream or into the air, is *very expensive*" (italics in the report).[32] The reality was substantially different.

By the 1960s, the St. Johns River and its tributaries had become highly polluted. Chicken processing plants, chemical companies, paper mills, fertilizer plants, homes, restaurants, strip shopping centers, and office buildings dumped wastes into local waterways. State board of health officials called McCoy's Creek "so badly polluted that it is just a big open sewer." Other badly polluted waters included sections of the Trout River, Ribault River, Moncrief Creek, Long Branch, Deer Creek, Hogans Creek, Miller Creek, Lake Marco, Craig Creek, Big Fishweir Creek, Cedar River, and Ortega River, plus downtown areas of the St. Johns River, "in other words, most of the natural water resources in the Jacksonville area."[33]

Complicating the picture was the area's flat terrain. Surface drainage was poor. Creeks and streams flowed slowly. Marshes, swamps, and tidal estuaries covered one-third of the county and were susceptible to pollution. The shallow groundwater table made untreated sewage disposal a health hazard. The marine character of the environment, combined with the slow-moving rivers, tidal flux, and flat terrain, resulted in a highly complex and endangered ecosystem threatened by rapid population and economic growth.[34]

Shortly after World War II, the state board of health became concerned about the increasing degradation of the St. Johns River system in Jacksonville and recommended the construction of a sewage treatment plant. In 1953, the city hired Abel Wolman of the Johns Hopkins University, a consulting engineer of international reputation in the field of water pollution, to examine local conditions. An advocate of the cliché that "the solution of pollution is dilution," Wolman concluded that the city did not need waste treatment. Two years later, the Boston consulting firm of Metcalf and Eddy recommended a master plan for city sewers but concluded that cleaning up the St. Johns River by eliminating the discharge of untreated sewage could wait until the final stages of construction.[35]

The state board of health disagreed and threatened to block further development along the river. The city responded by constructing the Buckman Sewage Treatment Plant in 1961, connecting to sewers on the north side of Jacksonville. Yet, except for servicing the Springfield area, this effort did nothing to reduce the flow of raw sewage into the St. Johns River, which by mid-decade totaled fifteen million gallons per day. Only 20 to 25 percent of all raw sewage in Jacksonville passed through a sewage processing plant. Statewide, Jacksonville was responsible for the discharge of 90 percent of all untreated sewage into state rivers.[36]

Passage of the Federal Water Quality Act of 1965 required states to establish water quality standards and classify their rivers. Jacksonville was ordered to clean up its pollution by 1973 to standards for a Class III river suitable for recreation, fish, and wildlife. On the eve of consolidation, the city still faced this major challenge.[37]

Besides water pollution, Jacksonville also had air pollution. Once in 1948, sulphuric acid droplets in the air began to disintegrate nylon stockings on women on the streets of downtown Jacksonville. The episode did not recur, but during the 1950s residents complained at different times about noxious odors, carbon particles, smoke, dust, and pollution clouds hanging over the city. A more serious problem surfaced in 1961 when pollution killed vegetation and damaged paint surfaces in East Jacksonville and Arlington. Complaints led to a study on air pollution but little action. In 1964, another pollution alert resulting from sulfur dioxide and fluoride in the air led to the formation of the Air Improvement Committee of Greater Jacksonville. Predominantly a business group, the association contracted with the Bioenvironmental Engineering Department at the University of Florida for a more substantial study of local conditions. Its report in 1967 analyzed the causes of vegetation damage, paint corrosion, air particulates, visibility impairment, and odor nuisances.[38]

While Jacksonville's air was clearly less polluted than that of Los Angeles and many northern industrial cities, the combination of paper mills, power plants, waste incinerators, chemical companies, and automobiles had created a nuisance bordering on the dangerous. City health and sanitation commissioner Claude Smith Jr. called automobile exhaust the city's number one health problem. Further population growth resulting in more automobiles with their exhaust fumes promised to create greater threats to the public's health.

The greatest nuisance in the Southeast, however, was the odor emanating from two pulp mills and two large chemical companies that processed sulphate turpentines from the pulp mills into perfumes. Their "pervasive rotten cabbage" smell challenged the Gator Bowl as the city's number one claim to fame, or infamy. Private industry made limited efforts to clean up conditions. In 1965, the Florida legislature created the Duval Air Improvement Authority as a first step in confronting Jacksonville's air pollution problems.[39]

The third area of environmental pollution lay on the land in the disposal of solid wastes. In the early 1960s, the principal method of solid waste disposal was the open dump. According to the annual report of Jacksonville's Department of Health, Welfare, and Bio-Environmental Services:

> People living in rural areas simply threw their garbage out on the land. Those in more urban areas dumped it in the yard or on the roadside. Many residential and business areas started organized dumping on the most convenient vacant land. Garbage collection was provided to the most affluent with varying types of service. . . . Collection vehicles usually left about as much garbage and litter at the pick-up sites and along the streets as they collected. Greater numbers of people, for one reason or another, did not have collection services, as opposed to those who did.[40]

The city sanitation department operated eighteen dump sites. Private franchise collectors in the county managed another fifteen. Meanwhile, businesses and private citizens used dozens of illegal dumps throughout the area. Sites included borrow pits, ravines, stream banks, ponds, and open fields, with little regard to air or water pollution, insect or rodent infestation, or appearance. "Scavengers roamed at will on the sites. Fires were purposely set to reduce the volume with little thought of the increased health hazard." Almost no testing took place to assess biological or chemical contaminants. Dr. E. R. Smith, head of the Jacksonville health department in the late 1960s, described flying over rural areas and seeing Duval County as "one huge dump."[41]

The Jacksonville–Duval County experience was not unique. Historian Martin V. Melosi has written about conditions across the country in this era when open dumps and open burning were common occurrences. Still, a *Jacksonville Journal* headline in 1961 warned, "Duval's Garbage Is Threatening Public Health: Worst Sanitation in the State." The article reported on a three-month survey by the county's board of health and the sanitation division of the state board of health. At least one hundred tons of waste each day were being mishandled, and only four of fifteen dump sites had board of health approval. The amount of solid waste was increasing with population growth and prosperity.[42]

The 1965 passage of the Federal Solid Waste Disposal Act recognized disposal as a critical environmental concern and put pressures on local communities to act. Jacksonville's response awaited consolidation with Duval County in 1968.

Much of the community's awareness of Jacksonville's environmental problems unfolded after the 1962 publication of the *Jacksonville Workbook on Community Development*. The Chamber of Commerce's limited awareness reflected the optimistic advice of nationally recognized experts and popular opinion, which was still in its preenvironmental awareness stage. Federal legislation on water quality and solid waste disposal did not pass Congress until three years later, in 1965, as part of Lyndon Johnson's vision for the Great Society. Air quality studies locally were first undertaken the same year. The dismissal of environmental problems by the Chamber of Commerce was not unique for its time. It reflected one more area in which the community's consciousness had to be raised.

Despite the school and environmental problems, Jacksonville in the early 1960s exuded an image of a city on the move. While Jacksonville's population of 201,030 had not grown during the preceding decade, the metropolitan area including all of Duval County had grown rapidly between 1950 and 1960, increasing by 48 percent to 451,411 people. Metro Jacksonville ranked third largest in Florida behind Miami-Dade and Tampa–St. Petersburg, and eighth largest in the Southeast.

Jacksonville's metropolitan area of almost a half million people was recognizably diverse by race, class, and gender. The typical male resident in 1964, however, according to a report in *Jacksonville Magazine,* was a twenty-six-year-old, white, and American-born with a high school diploma. He had a wife and two children, owned a home, and lived in a modest suburb in Duval County, outside the city limits. This typical male was the only full-time wage earner in his household. He worked as a blue-collar craftsman, operator, or service employee in manufacturing or construction work. His salary was less than $6,000 per year. His family owned one car, one television, a radio, and washing machine, but no freezer, clothes dryer, or air conditioner. Microwaves, home computers, compact disc players, and VCRs remained for the future.[43]

The typical wife also was white, American-born, and a high school graduate. She did not work outside the home. Locally only one-fifth of married women worked outside the home, and then usually only until becoming pregnant. Two-income, two-car families were still in the future. Thus, the typical wife worked full time at child rearing, household management, and family shopping. She visited the newer shopping centers on occasion but made major purchases of furniture and appliances at downtown department stores. She bought her groceries in the neighborhood from one of the national retail chains. Watching television was the usual weeknight family entertainment. Major splurges for dinner, a movie, or dancing generally took place at a downtown restaurant, theater, or hotel. Downtown was still the city center for work, shopping, and play.[44]

While this young blue-collar head of family probably was not among the 10 percent of Jacksonville males employed by the navy, there was a good chance he was a veteran and a strong supporter of American military might in the Caribbean, Europe, and Southeast Asia. There also was a good chance that he and his wife were both in their first marriage and assumed it would last for a lifetime; their mortgaged home reflected strong roots in the community; and the family went to church on most Sundays. In effect, the typical Jacksonville family was middle-American: hard working, God fearing, patriotic, and stable, probably unprepared for the tumult of the coming decade.

The Civil Rights Movement Begins

Missing from the 1964 profile of Jacksonville residents, of course, was any description of Jacksonville's diversity: its singles, affluent, elderly, transients, or racial minorities. Within the city, 84,000 African Americans comprised 42 percent of the population (105,000, or 23 percent of the metropolitan area). Most of them were not middle class; they lived in substandard housing, attended overcrowded schools, worked in poorly paid jobs, and were barred from the segregated downtown restaurants, theaters, or hotels.

Still, they had begun to dream of a better world. While the white majority and the Duval County School Board ignored the 1954 United States Supreme Court decision overturning school segregation, the black minority knew about the bus boycotts in Montgomery and the beginning of the civil rights movement. For Janet and Earl Johnson, who moved to Jacksonville in 1959 following Earl's completion of law school at Howard University, the time had come for action. It began during the holiday shopping season between Thanksgiving and Christmas in 1959. Black youths began picketing downtown stores to call attention to segregation. In the new year, a month after the famous Greensboro, North Carolina, sit-ins began, Jacksonville blacks entered F. W. Woolworth, J. C. Penney, W. T. Grant, S. H. Kress, and other stores downtown requesting service at lunch counters that previously had excluded them.[45]

The leader of the sit-in movement was a remarkable, thirty-one-year-old high school social studies teacher named Rutledge H. Pearson. A Jacksonville native and graduate of segregated Stanton High School and Huston-Tillotson College in Austin, Texas, Pearson had played professional baseball briefly. Tall, slim, and brown skinned, Pearson was adviser to the NAACP Youth Council, many of whom had been his students in the

Fig. 2. Rutledge Pearson, Jacksonville's premier civil rights leader. By permission of Mary Ann Pearson, Jacksonville.

Duval County public schools. The young people loved Pearson. Several remembered him as "the Pied Piper of integration," a charismatic man who listened to and respected his young charges, enjoyed their youthful energy and humor, and firmly instilled the principles of nonviolence along with the ideals of freedom's rights.[46]

The youths assembled for their downtown demonstrations at the predominantly black Laura Street Presbyterian Church (the congregation later moved to the suburbs as Woodlawn Presbyterian Church). Some picketed on the sidewalks in front of the stores, calling attention to their exclusion. Others attempted to obtain service at the lunch counters. Progress was slow, often nonexistent. Store managers closed the counters when the youths arrived. Still, the demonstrators persisted daily after school and on weekends, with a sense of mission fondly remembered a generation later.[47]

Spring turned to summer, and downtown merchants began to complain about losing business because of the demonstrations. Their Miami counterparts had already desegregated their lunch counters. Proposals to integrate the lunch counters in Jacksonville, however, required the support of Mayor Burns. As police and fire commissioner, he could control potential white rabble-rousers, who in other cities had attacked demonstrators. Burns refused to give his support, reflecting the southern white attitude opposing desegregation, and the demonstrations continued.[48]

On Saturday, August 27, the NAACP youth gathered again at the Presbyterian church, preparing themselves with song and prayer before preceding down Laura Street to Hemming Park. Spence Perry, a local journalist, described the scene:

> "Get your free axe handle in the park," read the sign crudely lettered, tacked on a palm tree by the bandstand in [the] park. A tough looking, crew-cut red-neck with a beer belly gave out handles from the tailgate of a station wagon. Small Confederate flags fluttered in the breeze, tied to the radio aerials of cars. The Negro pickets paraded silently, almost stoically, in front of Woolworth's. The NAACP Youth Council had asked for police protection from the white mob and was turned down by the police chief. Additional police were sent to the scene but did nothing to protect the colored demonstrators. Just before noon, the whites attacked the Negro marchers.[49]

Alton Yates, an aide to Pearson, remembered assembling at the church. There were reports of whites congregating with axe handles in the park, questions about whether the youths should proceed, and the unanimous decision of some forty young people to do so. One group of youths demonstrated first at Grant's department store three blocks from Hemming Park. Afterward they moved toward the park, where they were confronted by a menacing band of Klansmen. Arnette Girardeau remembered that members of the Boomerang gang from the nearby Blodgett Homes public housing project intervened to challenge the Klansmen, who turned and chased them toward the black business district west of the park. Once there, the Boomerangs rallied support from nearby taverns and pool halls and the conflict escalated, with black demonstrators chasing the Klansmen back toward Hemming Park.[50]

Meanwhile Youth Council demonstrators at Woolworth's faced other armed Klansmen, who attacked them with bats and axe handles. Quillie Jones, one of the demonstrators, believed that the presence of the Boomerangs and their allies probably saved many young blacks from being severely hurt." Their approach also brought two hundred police, squad cars, and fire engines to intervene, separating the antagonists and restoring order. Downtown became quieter, but on neighboring streets random acts of violence by both blacks and whites continued into the night. The expressways, added Perry, "became battlegrounds for racial strife. Cars were shot at, and rocks were thrown at windshields." Black youths in gangs roamed the streets looking for trouble. Rumors of Klan raids spread into black neighborhoods. Black gangs talked about invading the suburbs, and NAACP leaders worked furiously to head them off. The National Guard was alerted, and city officials struggled to regain control.[51]

That Sunday, Rodney Hurst, sixteen-year-old president of the NAACP Youth Council, cancelled further demonstrations and called for a mass meeting at St. Paul's AME Church. Fourteen hundred African Americans heard speakers call for the U.S. Justice Department to intervene in the denial of civil rights for Jacksonville blacks. The NAACP regional director from Tampa appealed for a selective buying campaign at stores not serving blacks. At Cohen Brothers, a major department store downtown, store officials adamantly refused to serve blacks in their lunch room. Yet 500 of Duval County's 894 black teachers had charge accounts there.[52]

Meanwhile, black clergy from the Jacksonville Ministerial Alliance met with the mayor and Duval County sheriff Dale Carson. Burns refused once again to support downtown merchants in a decision to desegregate lunch counters, rejected appeals for the formation of a biracial committee to discuss grievances, and urged all parties, black and white, to keep the peace. Further disruptions, he added, would be met with "swift and firm" action. In response, NAACP attorney Earl M. Johnson blamed the mayor for the violence, saying his failure to do anything to ease the situation despite pleas from black leaders and merchants gave the green light to axe-wielding segregationists.[53]

At the county courthouse on Monday, eighty-three defendants—fifty-seven blacks and twenty-six whites—stood before Judge John E. Santora, "a tough bull-necked man with a streak of grey in his closely cropped hair." Eight whites and thirty-five blacks were charged with various counts of vandalism, assault, and resisting arrest. The judge dealt with them quickly and firmly, imposing fines or jail sentences. One white man who demonstrated with the NAACP particularly incurred Santora's wrath. Charged with vagrancy, Richard F. Parker insisted he was a Florida State University student with money in the bank. When he added that he was from Massachusetts and a member of the NAACP, Santora interrupted and sentenced him to ninety days. Afterward, while Parker was waiting in an anteroom of the courthouse, a white construction worker approached and slugged him, loosening teeth and fracturing his jaw.[54]

On "Axe-Handle Saturday," August 27, 1960, black Jacksonville was mobilized in a broad-based support of the NAACP youth and their nonviolent demonstrations. Their actions caught the attention of white Jacksonville, whose media had largely ignored prior efforts by the young people. The Chamber of Commerce, concerned about the economic consequences of proposed boycotts of downtown stores, became involved. It formed a community advisory committee that met with NAACP leaders, leading to the hiring of two African American public librarians and the desegregation of downtown lunch counters in early 1961. As a result, the civil rights movement had officially begun in this Deep South city.[55]

Sit-ins and demonstrations were not the only tactics of Jacksonville African Americans in 1960. Businessman Frank Hampton went to court to desegregate the city's recreational facilities. A year earlier he had tried to open the city's municipal golf courses for blacks. When federal courts ordered their integration, the city sold them to private parties at bargain prices. Hampton next sued to open all municipally owned and segregated facilities, including the Gator Bowl, civic auditorium, baseball stadium, and parks. On December 7, 1960, federal district judge Bryan Simpson ruled in Hampton's favor. The city could not sell all of these facilities, especially with their bonded debt. Thus, in January, "all over town," reported the *Pittsburgh Courier*, "the 'White' and 'Colored' signs, which have long dominated every aspect of the city's recreational facilities, were torn down and tossed into garbage receptacles." Hampton and his supporters celebrated by taking their children to the Jacksonville zoo and ordering soft drinks at the formerly "white" lunch counter.[56]

Hampton next moved to desegregate facilities in the Duval County Courthouse, hospital, jails, and beaches on an "ask first, sue later" approach. That spring the county commissioners relented, avoiding a court case. They began by desegregating the courthouse rest rooms. They then reassigned inmates at the county prison farm based on crimes rather than race.[57]

Stetson Kennedy, Jacksonville native and award-winning author of books exposing white racism and the Ku Klux Klan, covered the civil rights movement locally for the *Pittsburgh Courier*. Kennedy watched the desegregation of "this deep South city" with some trepidation. After visiting Confederate Park just north of downtown, he wrote:

> I watched as a group of white kids entered the park. There were cries of greetings from the Negroes already there. As all boys will, one of the latter started to tussle with one of the newcomers as a token of affection. The white boy tripped, hurt his hip and began to cry.
>
> Tensely, I waited to see what would happen. Surely this was a situation rife with violence.
>
> Would the other white kids take the matter up?
>
> Would the other Negroes pitch in against them?
>
> Nothing of the sort took place.
>
> Two somewhat older Negro lads, hearing the sobbing, came over, picked the boy up by the seat of his pants, slapped him fondly on the back, and assured him he wasn't hurt.
>
> The boy wiped his eyes on his sleeves, grinned gamely at them—and got into the game.[58]

To Kennedy's knowledge, not a drop of blood was shed when the walls of segregation came down.

In June 1961, less than a month after the more prominent CORE Freedom Riders had completed their violent, victimized journey from Washington, D.C., across the South through Birmingham and Montgomery to Jackson, Mississippi, other Freedom Riders arrived in Jacksonville and successfully desegregated the local bus terminal without incident. That same month, city officials opened public swimming pools on the condition that blacks and whites voluntarily segregate themselves. In response, Frank Hampton led a group of African Americans to a "white" pool. City officials barred their way, and Hampton returned to court. This time the city closed all public swimming pools in Jacksonville for the duration. While middle-class and affluent whites organized pool clubs in the suburbs during the hot Jacksonville summer, poorer black and white children lacked access to the closed city pools.[59]

Desegregating the Public Schools

While Jacksonville's black youth conducted their sit-ins or picketed down-town stores and Frank Hampton challenged the racial barriers in public facilities, Wendell Holmes, a young black mortician chairing the Education Committee of the NAACP, began moving against Duval County's segregated schools.

The background for his efforts lay in the state and county reactions to the Supreme Court's unanimous 1954 decision ruling that separate educational facilities for black children were inherently unequal under the United State Constitution. A year later, the Supreme Court ordered desegregation of public schools on a racially nondiscriminatory basis "with all deliberate speed." The orders were vague and without guidelines, leaving the forty-eight southern U.S. District Court judges and their immediate superiors on the Fourth and Fifth U.S. Circuit Courts of Appeals to oversee the process.

White southerners ranged from moderates willing to obey the Court's school desegregation rulings to extremists seeking to nullify federal jurisdiction on the state level to the point of closing public schools. In Florida, moderates carried the day when Governor LeRoy Collins convened a special session of the state legislature in July 1956 to pass pupil placement laws. These laws authorized county school boards to assign students to schools based on their intellectual ability and scholarship while also considering relevant sociological and psychological factors. Race was not mentioned, but it was understood to be one of the factors. In theory all assignments were to be made based on the identified criteria without discriminating against any child. In practice, however, school boards and administrators established procedures that they believed fulfilled the letter of

Fig. 3. Earl Johnson, civil rights attorney in Jacksonville. By permission of Janet Johnson, Jacksonville.

the law without visibly changing the character of the state's segregated schools.[60]

Four years later, no black students had yet been admitted to a white school in Duval County. On December 6, 1960, local NAACP lawyer Earl M. Johnson filed suit on behalf of seven black parents claiming that their fourteen children had been refused admission to white schools in the county. Johnson argued that the school board operated racially segregated schools and that racial factors were used in determining student placement. In court, school officials acknowledged that all eighty-nine white and twenty-four black schools were totally segregated: students, teachers, and administrators.[61]

On August 21, 1962, U.S. District Court judge Bryan Simpson ordered the school board to develop plans for the total elimination of the segregated school system. The board responded in October, proposing a plan for neighborhood schools open to all students living nearby, integrated initially in the first and second grades beginning in September 1963, and then one additional grade at a time each year thereafter. Children (or their parents) unhappy with their neighborhood school could freely choose to transfer to another school. Attorney Johnson protested that desegregation under this plan would be minimal due to the segregated character of most housing in Duval County. Jacksonville in the 1960s was known as one of the most segregated cities in America. In addition, implementing the process one year at a time would prolong the process, preventing the current plaintiffs from ever attending an integrated school. Despite these protests, Judge Simpson approved the school board plan. He did, however, provide for modifications if in practice the plan did not work.[62]

When the new school year began in September 1962, only thirteen black first graders were enrolled in five previously all-white schools. According to the Jacksonville correspondent of the *Pittsburgh Courier*, "A wave of threatening phone calls to parents . . . succeeded in deterring the integration of other schools." Violence followed. On February 5, 1963, five Ku Klux Klansmen dynamited the home of one of the first graders, who lived with his grandparents, Mr. and Mrs. George R. Gilliam. Fortunately, no one was hurt. One of the men subsequently confessed to FBI agents, implicating his coconspirators. An all-white federal jury, however, acquitted them.[63]

Meanwhile the NAACP returned to court seeking to accelerate the desegregation process to include more than thirteen youngsters per year. Judge Simpson demurred, observing that the school board had broken the ice for integration and further advances would follow. In the fall of 1964, sixty-two black youngsters enrolled in the first and second grades of previously all-white schools. [64]

Frustrated by the snail's pace of both the school board and the court, NAACP leaders, supported by the Interdenominational Ministers Alliance and other groups in the black community, turned to direct action, challenging the system where it might hurt, in the pocketbook. State support for local schools was based on pupil attendance. Students staying home from school would reduce that support. In a carefully organized campaign beginning on Monday, December 7, 17,000 black youngsters skipped school. The next day 10,000 children stayed away, while 7,000 absented themselves on Wednesday. The cost of 34,000 absentees to the county amounted to a significant $75,000 but did not change school board policies. A year later, in 1965, eleven years after the Supreme Court decision, five years after the NAACP went to court locally, and three years after the decision to desegregate, only 137 black students (less than one-half of one percent of the total black student population) attended previously all-white schools. No whites attended all-black schools. The wheels of justice ground slowly.[65]

While NAACP officials confronted the barriers of token integration in the public schools, they continued their efforts in other areas of the civil rights movement. Beginning in January 1963, Rutledge Pearson, by now president of both the local branch and the state chapter of the NAACP, announced a new year's resolution of "Walk first, then talk." He recognized that white community leaders tended to listen only when demonstrators were in the streets. While Mayor Burns had refused to appoint a biracial citizens advisory group, a concerned Chamber of Commerce appointed its own committee to meet periodically with black community leaders. There was fear that downtown demonstrations discouraged shoppers and the new suburban shopping centers were becoming an attractive alternative. There also was concern that Jacksonville might gain a poor national reputation for race relations, undermining efforts to attract new businesses. One result was the desegregation of lunch counters (but not restaurants).[66]

Negotiations, however, led to only a few token jobs and very limited desegregation. NAACP officials felt shortchanged. A proposed Easter boycott in 1963 of downtown stores was canceled when fifteen merchants agreed to provide more jobs. Only five, however, followed through on their promises. That summer, the NAACP picketed the Southern Bell Telephone and Telegraph Company, demanding jobs. When Southern Bell officials claimed they wanted to hire blacks but could find no qualified applicants, NAACP officials identified a dozen candidates, one of whom had been rejected in Jacksonville after having worked successfully for three years as a telephone operator in New York. In September, theater owners agreed to desegregate downtown but then reneged. Hotel proprietors agreed to accept blacks as guests only as part of predominantly white convention delegations. Restaurant owners promised service but later backed down. As a result, NAACP leaders broke off direct talks with the Chamber of Commerce and resumed picketing.[67]

Events escalated at the beginning of 1964. Congress began debating what was to become the Civil Rights Act of 1964. In Jacksonville, youthful demonstrators supported by black clergy sought to desegregate dining rooms at the Robert Meyer Hotel and other downtown restaurants. Management refused to serve them and called the police when the youth re-

Fig. 4. Civil rights demonstrators in Jacksonville. By permission of Mary Ann Pearson, Jacksonville.

fused to leave. In mid-March, the tempo picked up. Young demonstrators moved through downtown and its fringes at rush hour, making their presence felt by walking slowly in front of traffic, singing freedom songs, and calling attention to their demands. Arrests followed, and soon there were more demonstrators, and more youths in jail. On Friday, March 20, two hundred demonstrators led by Pearson assembled in front of the police station to protest the arrests. Various observers feared a violent confrontation over the weekend of March 20–21.[68]

Meanwhile, Mayor Burns was running for governor in a difficult primary. One of his opponents commented about the generally good atmosphere of race relations in Florida, with the exception of Jacksonville. Burns became defensive and decided to end the protests. He arranged for television time on Saturday, March 21, and prepared a statement for the Sunday newspapers. In it he asked for the cooperation of all citizens to restore order. He condemned both the violence of the Klan bombing and the "mob demonstrations" of blacks. Unfortunately, he equated the two activities. He insisted that local laws be enforced. Young blacks, he said, were misled by adults. They did not have a legal or civil right to "force their presence at certain hotels and restaurants." Further demonstrations would not be tolerated. Burns claimed he was not threatening anyone, but he swore in 496 firefighters as special police to assist his 508-member police department in maintaining order. With his 1,000 law enforcement officers, Burns concluded, "peace will prevail."[69]

NAACP officials sent telegrams to the mayor and Justice Department charging that Burns was "interfering with peaceful attempts to end racial segregation in public accommodations in Jacksonville." As across the South, the issue was clear. Civil rights leaders challenged segregation laws they considered to be both immoral and unconstitutional. These laws excluded African Americans from hotels, restaurants, theaters, and other places serving the public. In contrast, Burns, supported by most Southern whites, upheld local segregation laws and customs maintaining that no one had the right to service or access to the private property of segregated businesses. Ironically, congressional debate then underway leading to the passage of the Civil Rights Act of 1964 would overturn these local laws and customs, opening public accommodations to all Americans without regard to race, creed, gender, or color.[70]

The night following Burns's call for law and order, someone firebombed the mayor's campaign headquarters in the black community. Though little damage was done, Burns blamed his political foes. He called the bombing and other racial disturbances "obviously politically motivated by other candidates for governor."[71]

On the following Monday morning, March 23, blacks from the NAACP Youth Council, led by Bob Ingram, and without the authority of Pearson and the parent body, assembled in Hemming Park downtown. The mayor radioed the police from his office with orders to "disperse or arrest them." With their motorcycle engines roaring and sirens screaming, the police dispersed the demonstrators, who headed north to the all-black New Stanton High School. There, about 250 persons entered the grounds apparently to recruit more demonstrators. Within minutes seven squad cars arrived on the scene. Someone pulled a fire alarm, evacuating students and demonstrators alike. By this time, hundreds of people were milling about outside the school. While school officials tried to regain control of their students, other demonstrators moved on to Darnell-Cookman Junior High School. It was no orderly procession, nor was it quite a mob. Police followed, hassling and arresting youths who sassed back or threw bottles and rocks. At Darnell-Cookman, the protesters changed direction again, some heading back to Hemming Park and others to rally students at Matthew Gilbert High School. More hassle, more arrests, and tempers rose on both sides. Bricks and bottles were thrown, epithets shouted, followed by more arrests.[72]

Meanwhile, in other parts of the city, police closed the off-ramps to the expressway entering downtown. Firefighters responded to real and false alarms in the black community. A white assailant shot and killed Ms. Johnnie Mae Chappell, an African American mother of ten, as she looked for her wallet dropped in the street. Other assailants shot at three sailors, two of them black, in their car as it stopped at a barricade. Police raided the NAACP headquarters, claiming people were throwing projectiles out windows onto passing cars. In response, NAACP officials claimed the police had kicked in the doors and confiscated documents. By nightfall, more than two hundred demonstrators had been arrested. Rutledge Pearson went on television urging blacks to refrain from more violence, while black clergy worked with the mayor, trying to restore order. That evening the mayor spoke to the community via television and tried to downplay the seriousness of the protest. It was not a riot, he said, but more of an outburst similar to what occurs following an exciting football game.[73]

The next day, Tuesday, March 24, demonstrations resumed with a bomb hoax at New Stanton High School. Police arrived. Someone threw a rock. A youth vandalizing a bread truck was arrested by a black police officer, J. L. Massey, and placed in a patrol car. While one group distracted the officer, others freed the arrested youth. The officer pulled his revolver and fired warning shots into the air. Instead of quieting the crowd, the shots spurred rumors that a student had been hit. Other youths responded by throwing bricks and bottles. Police reinforcements arrived, including fifteen cars of state troopers. Tensions escalated among the now angry demonstrators. Protesters next threw rocks and bottles at police, news reporters, and bystanders. Several teachers suggested to Assistant Police Chief H. V. "Tiny" Branch that they could restore order and return the students to their classes if the police would leave. Branch wisely chose to withdraw, leaving behind only the bomb squad. After the police left, a smaller group of youths stoned several reporters, including George Harmon, then assistant city editor of the *Jacksonville Journal.* His company car was overturned and burned. A reporter from *Life* magazine was beaten and required hospitalization.[74]

Later Harmon reflected upon the events and concluded the outbursts were more like vandalism than organized protests. Reporter Al Kuettner from United Press International partially agreed. There was little apparent organization, he said, and a lot of "blowing off of pent-up emotions." Pearson condemned the violence and negotiated with youth leaders to relax racial tensions. He reported the young people had organized their protest, "resentful of the police-state policies they've seen the past few days." Meanwhile, the president of the Interdenominational Ministers Alliance, the Rev. J. S. Johnson of St. Stephen's AME Church, blamed Mayor Burns for the earlier unnecessary arrests and his Saturday television ultimatum calling for law and order.[75]

Major national news weeklies covered the Jacksonville disturbances. *Time* saw the Jacksonville riot as one of "spring's first and ugliest," blaming it on a combination of "the numskullery of a politically ambitious mayor and the hooliganism of Negro teenagers." *Newsweek* blamed it on the "restiveness" and frustration of Jacksonville's black population and the absence of "progress toward desegregation of public accommodations." *U.S. News and World Report* emphasized the murder of the African American woman, the angry mobs of black youth, and the frequent use of "molotov cocktails." Of special concern were the "hoodlums" in gangs beyond the control of more-moderate African American civil rights leaders.[76]

The Southern Regional Council in Atlanta took a longer view in a report issued in mid-April. The council voiced concern about the violence, vandalism, and firebombs and asked whether racial issues could still be resolved by peaceful means. The report noted the frustration of blacks making only token progress, and the long-standing tendencies of ghetto gangs, such as the "High Hats," "Boomerangs," and "Untouchables," to take the law into their own hands. As one observer said of the poor, inner-city kids, they just "don't care any more." The gangs took pride in their war stories of 1960 when they challenged both the axe-wielding whites and the city police. The report urged white and black moderates to work together to avoid confrontations spilling over into the streets into the hands of the gangs.[77]

At a Wednesday morning press conference following the riot, Mayor Burns called for the formation of an informal biracial community relations committee to work for racial harmony. Still unwilling to make appointments himself, he offered to cooperate with any privately organized group. Taking the cue, Robert Milius, president of May Cohens department store downtown, went to work. Responding to his calls were Claude J. Yates, vice president and regional manager for Southern Bell, Robert R. Feagin from the Florida Publishing Company, Charles W. Campbell, senior vice president of Prudential Insurance Company, Dr. W. W. Schell, physician and president of the Urban League, J. H. Burney, vice president of Afro-American Life Insurance Company, and Earl M. Johnson, attorney for the NAACP. The committee quickly proposed the voluntary desegregation of all public accommodations and agreed to study ways to provide more and better jobs for blacks.[78]

The Community Relations Committee also called for public hearings, which began in early April. Nine blacks and twenty-seven whites testified under the direction of former circuit court judge William H. Maness. All of the blacks and sixteen of the whites endorsed full desegregation of local facilities. Their statements described the state of race relations in Jacksonville at the time. Witnesses protested the lack of black firefighters, health inspectors, and other governmental employees. They felt the city police department should be fully integrated, rather than segregating black officers in a substation at Blodgett Homes, with blacks having authority only to arrest blacks while white officers were called to arrest white lawbreakers. The group advocated desegregating hospitals as well as hotels, theaters, and restaurants. They pointed out that school desegregation remained token. "Whites only" signs should come down in stores and public agencies along with the abolition of separate rest rooms. The media and businesses should stop referring to blacks only by their first names. Cultural institutions should include blacks, as should the Chamber of Commerce, Jacksonville Bar Association, and Duval Medical Society.[79]

Not all witnesses agreed. One white feared the mongrelization of the race following integration, arguing that "every civilization that has been destroyed, was first integrated." Another saw the civil rights movement as part of the communist conspiracy, with local protests instigated by outside agitators. More typical of the white opposition to desegregation, however, was the belief that downtown businesses should have the freedom to choose whom they served. Still, some white opinion was open to change as seen in the integrated League of Women Voters. In sum, white views ranged widely from totally segregationist to highly supportive of racial integration.[80]

Unfortunately, the report, which called for the elimination of all forms of racial discrimination in Jacksonville and for leadership from the Community Relations Committee toward that end, got shelved. While the report was being written, private negotiations to desegregate downtown facilities failed. Restaurant owners would cooperate only if all local hotels and restaurants cooperated. but not all would desegregate. They feared losing the patronage of white customers by serving blacks. In frustration, the white committee members tried to divert the agenda to more and better jobs for African Americans. Pearson and the NAACP saw through the maneuver and protested the failure to take a stand on desegregation, the issue that had brought the committee together. Maness as chair of the hearings agreed. Frustrated, the four white business leaders on the committee—Milius, Feagin, Yates, and Campbell—resigned. So did the African Americans. Maness, now virtually alone, tried to breathe life back into the committee, but lacking the support of the white business leadership, the organization expired in December 1964.[81]

Meanwhile, Congress passed and President Lyndon Baines Johnson signed the Civil Rights Act of 1964 in July. Hotels, restaurants, theaters, and other facilities serving the public in Jacksonville desegregated without incident. Forced by the federal government, Jacksonville began to change.

Clearly Jacksonville had major problems with its environment, schools, and race relations. Underlying them, wrote Jacksonville native Spence W. Perry in his 1963 senior honors thesis at Harvard University, were certain major cultural deficiencies. His thesis compared conditions in Jacksonville with those in Atlanta, a city often seen as a model for Jacksonville's growth and development.[82]

First was the virtual absence of higher education in Jacksonville. Before Jacksonville Junior College became Jacksonville University in 1956, the city was the largest in the country without a bachelor's degree–granting institution. Changing names, however, did not immediately create a university. The college had just moved to its suburban Arlington site on the St. Johns River. Its academic standards in the early years, according to the university's historian, George Hallam, were "pitifully low." Its first bachelor's degrees were not granted until 1959, followed by accreditation two years later. While visiting scholars like Nobel laureate Selman A. Waksman and historian Arnold Toynbee began to attract attention to the university in the early 1960s, the impact of Jacksonville University upon the city had only just begun.[83]

Across the river, tiny Edward Waters College was not yet accredited and did not belong to the first rank of African American institutions funded by the United Negro College Fund. Florida Junior College (later Florida Community College at Jacksonville) began classes only in 1966, and the University of North Florida did not open its doors until 1972. Early efforts to attract a state medical school in 1958 and a law school two years later were discouraged. Comparing Jacksonville's situation with Atlanta's array of private and public postsecondary institutions, the Florida metropolis ranked far behind. The result was an absence of intellectual leadership locally along with the leavening cultural influence colleges and universities bring to communities.[84]

A second cultural weakness, according to Perry, was the fragmentation of Jacksonville's business leadership. There were many strong individuals, such as Florida National Bank's Ed Ball, Winn-Dixie's Davis brothers, and Carl Swisher from King Edward Cigars, but they rarely pulled together for the benefit of Jacksonville in the manner of Atlanta's business leaders. Still, change had begun locally with publication of the Chamber of Commerce's 1962 *Workbook for Community Development* and the School Bootstrap Committee's examination of the public schools. But these efforts reflected in part the impact of business leadership coming from outside of Jacksonville at Prudential, Atlantic Coast Line, and Southern Bell.[85]

A third weakness focused on community attitudes toward politics and local government. Where Atlantans took pride in mayors like William Hartsfield and Ivan Allen who sought to build a biracial city "too busy to hate," Jacksonville residents condoned the petty partisan manipulations of their city and county commissioners blocking black aspirations for desegregation, neglecting public education, and ignoring the worsening conditions of the St. Johns River and its tributaries. The bulk of the white elite tolerated these conditions as long as business prospered. Much of the middle class moved to the suburbs and avoided the issues. Many working-class voters joined others in believing that politics was dirty and one simply should not get involved. Thus, despite Haydon Burns's efforts at downtown renewal, overall at mid-decade, city government lacked the respect and support of the Jacksonville community.[86]

Finally, Perry compared the press in Atlanta and Jacksonville. In Atlanta, editor Ralph McGill at the *Constitution* achieved national prominence through his strong leadership, especially in the area of race relations. By contrast, the two Jacksonville dailies, the *Florida Times-Union* and the *Jacksonville Journal,* provided minimal coverage, failed to move beyond traditional segregationist calls for law and order, and offered little leadership to enlighten the community.[87]

Jacksonville in the decade from 1955 to 1965 had begun to change. Downtown and along the waterfront, the port authority and the expressway system presented the veneer of the modern city. The national phenomenon of suburban growth and shopping malls gave further evidence of change. But beneath the veneer, in its heart Jacksonville remained a conservative southern town, segregated by race. Its support of Jim Crow along with its past neglect of schools and environment reflected regional prejudice and ignorance. People were friendly. They pulled together in the private sector to create museums, churches, clubs, and private schools. They also worked with the Chamber of Commerce when business leaders brought issues to their attention. But Jacksonville lacked a well-educated citizenry and strong business and political leadership concerned about the community's overall quality of life. It also lacked media support to move beyond the bricks and mortar of city building to include all of the people in making Jacksonville the city it could become.

CHAPTER 2

CONSOLIDATION

It started at the top. Claude J. Yates had just retired as vice president and general manager of Florida operations for Southern Bell Telephone and Telegraph Company and assumed the presidency of the Chamber of Commerce. On January 19, 1965, he convened twenty-three Jacksonville business and professional leaders for lunch at the Robert Meyer Hotel. Among them were Ed Ball, Jacksonville's leading financier, Jacob F. Bryan III, president of Independent Life Insurance Company, Charles W. Campbell, vice president and general manager of Prudential Insurance Company's south-central home office, J. T. Lane, president of Atlantic National Bank, James R. Stockton and Joseph W. Davin from Stockton, Whatley, Davin and Company, the city's leading real estate developer, and more. It was a blue ribbon group, and in less than an hour, the participants signed a petition to the Florida legislature that read:

> We, the undersigned, respectfully request the Duval County Delegation to the Florida Legislature to prepare an enabling act calling for the citizens of Duval County to vote on the consolidation of government within Duval to secure more efficient and effective government under one governmental body.[1]

A series of events led to the petition. First was the rapid population growth in Duval County after World War II. The population had grown from 304,029 in 1950 to an estimated 525,000 by 1965, an increase over fifteen years of 73 percent. Duval County was one of the fastest growing counties in the nation. By contrast, the city of Jacksonville had declined in population after 1950, from 204,517 to an estimated 198,000. Duval

County, once known for its dairy farms, had become increasingly suburban.[2]

Rapid population growth required more police protection, firefighters, roads, sewers, water, schools, parks, refuse disposal, and other governmental services. While most metropolitan areas across the country were experiencing similar growth and pressure to provide increased governmental services, Duval County was exceptional in its inability to respond.

Its five-member Board of County Commissioners was but one of many governing bodies. An elected Board of Public Instruction, elected superintendent, and elected Board of School Trustees ran the public schools. Elected county judges, small claims court judges, juvenile court judges, criminal court judges, and circuit court judges, plus justices of the peace, sheriff, state's attorney, and public defender controlled the criminal justice system. Appointed authorities oversaw the expressways, port, planning, air quality, county hospital, and welfare. An elected tax assessor estimated property values. The county commissioners could set the tax rate, but an elected Budget Commission could revise it. New legislation to handle suburban growth came not from the county commissioners but from the Florida legislature. The legislature passed local laws in Tallahassee on a biennial basis introduced by the county delegation. Meanwhile, volunteers fought fires; private firms collected garbage and dumped it wherever they established unsupervised landfills; and private contractors dug septic tanks or built inadequate sewage disposal systems in new suburban subdivisions. In sum, there were too many hands overseeing county affairs and too few services adequately provided. Clearly county governance was part of the problem confronting Claude Yates and his associates.[3]

If local leaders were unhappy with county government, they were equally displeased about the city. Jacksonville probably had the most unwieldy structural form of government of any city in the United States. Where most large cities had mayor-council forms and many smaller cities had commissions or council-managers, Jacksonville had a nine-member city council to legislate, and a five-member executive-branch city commission, both elected at large. Each commissioner administered his own area (no women had ever been elected). The mayor as lead commissioner supervised the police, the firefighters, and the airports. The finance commissioner oversaw purchasing, auditing, parks, and the prison farm. The health and sanitation commissioner looked after not only public health, garbage, and street cleaning but also the motor pool, coliseum, civic auditorium, Gator Bowl, and baseball parks. The highways and sewers commissioner took care of sewers and roads. The public service commissioner ran the city-owned electric power plant, water department, and radio station. The divisions of authority had substantial overlap. One commissioner looked after parks and another the Gator Bowl, and a separately appointed recreation board controlled the Department of Recreation.[4]

In addition, while each commissioner had authority in his own area, no one had overall responsibility. Commissioners deferred to one another on issues within each other's domain while a weak mayor lacked authority to intervene. Council members seeking patronage or favors from commissioners also deferred to them. The result was not only an excessively complex and cumbersome government but also an expensive one. The city's 3,241 full-time employees were the most numerous for any city its size in the country. Its monthly payroll also was the highest. The city purchased vehicles without competitive bids. It spent more on insurance than Miami, Tampa, and St. Petersburg combined. Departments had their own legal counsel and periodically sued one another over jurisdictional issues at taxpayer expense. The list went on.[5]

Adding to the governmental complexity and cost was the political climate of the city. A Miami journalist described it as a "tight-knit, ward-boss machine," where friends got the city's business, often without competitive bids, and the government made decisions, behind closed doors, that were then rubber-stamped at public meetings. Mayors like Haydon Burns had emerged to speak for the system and work with the business community. Behind the scenes, attorney C. Daughtry Towers was the acknowledged leader shaping major political decisions. According to one observer, one either joined the system or lost out to the system. Business leaders kept hands off, permitting the political process to continue. Among the city commissioners, city council members, county commissioners, school board members, school superintendent, and other local officials in both city and county, politics and patronage dominated local affairs at the expense of efficiency, economy, honesty, and good government.[6]

Adding in the failure of governmental officials to respond adequately to school disaccreditation, tax inequities, environmental pollution, and racial demands, Jacksonville in 1965 had a full-fledged crisis at hand.

The business leaders at the January luncheon petitioned the Duval delegation for consolidation in part because earlier attempts at annexation had failed. The Chamber of Commerce had made annexation a priority in its 1962 report. In 1963 and again the following year, the Florida legislature had authorized a local annexation referendum to enable the city to incorporate suburban subdivisions in order to provide better police, fire, waste removal, and other services to those neighborhoods. Most suburban residents, however, wanted no part of inclusion in Jacksonville's city government and voted against each referendum. Their opposition was not unlike that of suburbanites across America who wanted little to do with central cities that were too corrupt, expensive, and dangerous.[7]

In addition, cities were home to poor people and racial minorities, also not wanted in white, middle-class suburbia. Jacksonville had a large poor population, and by mid-decade, an estimated 42 percent of its residents were African American. Whether the fear of Jacksonville becoming a predominantly black city was a strong motivating factor in the consolidation of city and county remains unclear. It certainly played a part in some voters' minds, but there were other important reasons as well.[8]

In the wake of the latest annexation defeat in 1964, the Yates Manifesto of January 1965, handwritten on a sheet of paper at the January luncheon, petitioned the Duval delegation to pass local legislation to secure a referendum on consolidation. The Duval delegation, headed by state senator John E. Mathews Jr., was generally sympathetic to the issue. Mathews's bill, SB 1502, received support and was passed by the Florida legislature in the closing days of the 1965 session.[9]

The Study Commission Creates a Charter

The law created a fifty-member study commission selected by the Duval delegation. It excluded anyone holding or expecting to hold public office, in order to minimize political maneuvering. The Study Commission's members had a heavy downtown business and professional orientation. Yet, along with the bankers, lawyers, and insurance executives, there were also labor leaders, architects, the president of Jacksonville University, six women, and four African Americans. It was a respectably diverse group. The law also provided for an advisory committee of representatives chosen by the local bar association, medical society, realtors, Chamber of Commerce, trade unions, ministerial association, Junior League, Federation of Women's Clubs, garden clubs, League of Women Voters, Urban League, NAACP, Civic Round Table, Taxpayers Association, and various city and county governmental bodies. Funding came from both public and private sources. The Duval delegation set March 1, 1967, for the presentation of the commission's recommendations.[10]

The law designated James B. Lumpkin, a local banker, as chairman of the commission, as a concession to a legislator opposed to James Jacqueline Daniel, the choice of Yates, Mathews, and others. Lumpkin resigned at the first commission meeting, however, and the commissioners elected Daniel to replace him. As much as anyone, J. J. Daniel was the key to consolidation's success. A member of an old and illustrious Jacksonville family, Daniel was also a successful lawyer and businessman and was president of Stockton, Whatley, Davin and Company. He had a long record of civic leadership on local and state levels. His many contributions included a major role in establishing the state university system of higher education. Daniel had played football at Princeton, commanded a PT boat during World War II, and led a squadron in the D-day invasion of Normandy. A tough-minded person, Daniel described for journalist-historian Richard Martin the kind of people he respected:

> People who have ideas. People who are stimulating in their conversation. People who can get a job done and have a killer instinct when necessary. People who are doers, who are decisive. People you can depend upon, to whom you can assign responsibility and feel that what you require will be carried out immediately without any further cause for worry.[11]

Daniel appointed Lewis Alexander "Lex" Hester as executive director of the Study Commission. The thirty-year-old Hester, a native of Washington, D.C., had grown up in Duval County, graduating from Florida State University with bachelor's and master's degrees in public administration. In 1965, he was working in Jacksonville as an investigator with the Wage and Hour Division of the U.S. Department of Labor. Richard Martin, in his book on consolidation, described Hester as brilliant and articulate, a master of detail. "Hester read books about governmental trends and urban problems with the same enthusiasm other people devoted to best-selling fiction." Hester's dedication, single-mindedness, and no-nonsense approach to consolidation led to impatience with opponents and procrastinators. He made enemies as well as friends. Yet his work was also crucial to the success of the consolidation effort.[12]

Early in its deliberations, the Study Commission decided that local citizens, rather than outside consultants, should do the study. That way, Hester later remembered, commission members would have a greater stake in its results and would be stronger in their advocacy to the community.[13]

In January 1966, the commission established six task forces to gather data and prepare recommendations for reform. The areas of coverage were broad. Attorney James C. Rinaman Jr. chaired a task force that examined airports, the electric utility, library service, port, radio station, streets and highways, drainage, water, and sewage. Dr. Harlan Johnston chaired a task force looking at agriculture, child care, fire protection, garbage, health, hospitals, recreation, and schools. Advertising executive Kenneth Friedman's task force focused on building inspection, civil service, motor vehicles and motor pool, planning, property maintenance, purchasing, and tax assessing and collecting. Attorney W. E. Grisset Jr. headed a task force that covered courts, law enforcement, legal services, probation and parole, public defender, state's attorney, veterans' affairs, and weights and measures. Banker Martin E. Sweet's task force researched budgeting, the budget commission, fund custody, and finance. Finally, Chairman Daniel's task force analyzed the data from the other five groups and developed proposals for organizational structure, authorities, Duval County, municipalities, and special districts.[14]

Each task force collected data, interviewed relevant witnesses, and made recommendations for reform. Hester attended all interview sessions and took minutes, which he had typed, copied, and distributed to task force members. Almost all governmental officials cooperated, but many only to a limited extent. They were beginning to fear for their jobs. One of the most cooperative was Mayor Louis H. Ritter, successor to Haydon Burns when Burns moved to Tallahassee as governor in January 1965. Ritter endorsed the consolidation of firefighting services, tax assessment and recreational services, partial consolidation of police functions, more areawide planning, stronger home rule, and a strong mayor to replace the city commission.[15]

The commission heard from numerous outside experts. Of particular significance were consultants from Nashville–Davidson County in Tennessee, which had adopted consolidation in 1962. In the summer of 1966, the commission held public hearings and heard opposition to consolidation from the beach communities and Baldwin municipalities. That fall, Daniel's task force drafted its plan. On November 23, in the new Haydon Burns Library downtown, Daniel presented the commission's recommendations for a countywide government under a strong mayor who appointed all department heads including the sheriff. There would be a twenty-one-member nonsalaried city council, each member representing an election district. The county commission and all five municipal governments, including the city commission, would be abolished. All the traditionally elected offices of sheriff, tax collector, tax assessor, civil service board, and supervisor of elections would become appointive. The eight county courts would be consolidated into two. Voters would choose only the mayor, their council representative, school board members, judges, state's attorney, public defender, and clerk of courts. Following Daniel's explanation, commission member Franklin Russell moved adoption of the plan, which passed unanimously. A team of lawyers led by attorney John Chambers began drafting the new city charter for the Duval delegation and the 1967 legislative session.[16]

The Media Uncovers Corruption

While the Study Commission gathered data for its proposals during 1966, Jacksonville voters awoke to discover news of major governmental corruption locally, presented in a series of television investigative news stories and grand jury reports. The television exposures came first, beginning in 1965 on WJXT, a local station owned by the Washington Post–Newsweek Corporation. Its news and public affairs director, Bill Grove, felt that other local media "were glossing over the essential problems of the metropolitan area by generally ignoring them in their editorials, and by contenting themselves with superficial reports on their news pages." WJXT chose to investigate. It reported the purchase of luxury automobiles for city officials without competitive bids, excessive insurance costs, and lawsuits resulting from jurisdictional disputes between city council and the city commission. In February 1966, WJXT called for a grand jury investigation of political and governmental abuse.[17]

Criminal court judge Marion W. Gooding responded to the call at the beginning of the court's spring term. In forming a new grand jury, he challenged the jurors to either prove or disprove the allegations of WJXT. That summer and fall, the jury heard testimony from local officials. Periodically, it issued reports.[18]

The first report, on June 30, condemned the city commission's practice of doling out insurance contracts to "friends and political allies" without regard to "cost, coverage, need or sound business practices." The absence of competitive bids and the failure to consolidate similar coverages cost Jacksonville taxpayers hundreds of thousands of dollars per year.[19]

The second presentment, on July 22, indicted city council members W. O. Mattox Jr. and Cecil F. Lowe, and George G. Robinson Sr., a former official in the recreation department, on grand larceny, conspiracy, and perjury charges. Thirteen indictments charged the three men with purchasing televisions, watches, jewelry, and electric blankets from a sporting goods store and charging them to the city recreation department.[20]

An August 12 report focused on the purchase of 168 automobiles over the preceding five years from one dealer without competitive bids. The city paid maximum list price for each car. City commissioners relied on subordinates to make purchases. Department heads signed off on the purchases but claimed the commissioners had authorized them. Purchasing agents and auditors said they simply followed orders. No one seemed to be responsible. Meanwhile, city officials used their luxury sedans for private as well as public transportation, charging the cost of fuel on city credit cards. Copies of the charge slips secured from the oil companies lacked signatures, yet the city paid the bills.[21]

Next, city commissioner Dallas L. Thomas, a twelve-year veteran of city council, after whom a riverfront park had recently been named, resigned over charges that the city had paid for labor and building materials for work on his private property. He submitted a check to the city for $8,872.01, pleading ignorance of the whole affair. Subsequently the grand jury indicted him on forty counts of grand larceny.[22]

Over the succeeding months, indictments followed against city auditor John W. Hollister Jr., city council members Lemuel Sharp and Clyde C. "Red" Cannon, and city commissioner Claude Smith Jr. By the end of the six-month term in November, the grand jury had indicted two of five city commissioners, four of nine city council members, and two other ranking officials in city government. A ninth official, tax assessor W. F. Wilson, resigned.[23]

Not all of the indictments led to convictions, but the grand jury's report verified what many Jacksonville voters had long believed. Local government was corrupt. It was not corruption on the grand scale of a Tammany Hall boss like William Marcy Tweed, who stole millions of dollars from the City of New York. Rather, it was a more common "nickel and dime" corruption as seen in many boss-ridden American cities where officeholders and contractors used public funds for private perks (a television set here, home improvements there), and special interests kicked back a small portion of their profits in campaign contributions to reelect their "friends" to office. The practice was not unique to Jacksonville. Many Florida city and county governments had become entrenched and ripe for reform.[24]

In its final report, the grand jury called for a range of reforms including the substantial restructuring of local government:

> In brief, it is our view that the structure of the government of the City of Jacksonville has permitted waste and the misuse of public funds. Such governmental structure, together with the fact that through the years there has been no effective check on municipal activities in general and no effective audits thereof, either internally or externally, has resulted in the truly shocking conditions reflected by our findings and actions during the past five months. . . .
>
> Again and again in our investigations, we encountered substantiated and rumored reports of persons who are, or who have been, on the payroll of the City of Jacksonville, but who do not and have not performed services for the city. . . .
>
> We recommend a complete revision of the governmental structure of the City of Jacksonville.[25]

The report, along with the television and newspaper coverage of events, helped prepare Jacksonville voters to support the Study Commission's proposal for consolidated government issued three weeks later.

The next step toward consolidation came in December 1966 with the formation of the Citizens Committee for Government Study Recommendations, Inc., later shortened to the more manageable Citizens for Better

Government. The group, under the leadership of Claude Yates, who drafted the original petition for change, began the campaign for the new consolidation charter.

But first, the Duval delegation to the Florida legislature had to approve the charter and authorize a referendum vote. It planned to hold public hearings in January, but a U.S. Supreme Court decision striking down the legislature's reapportionment plan postponed them until March. When the hearings convened, J. J. Daniel from the Citizens for Better Government spoke for the new charter's advantages. It would make a consolidated Jacksonville more competitive in attracting new businesses; end duplication of services by two governments; combine city and county into one efficient, economical structure; and provide responsible government with one person, the mayor, in charge.[26]

The next day the opposition appeared. Walter D. Smith, a local mortgage banker and, more importantly, a power in the Duval County Democratic Executive Committee, spoke on behalf of Better Government for Duval County. Smith claimed to support reform, but in a more limited way. He recognized how the mood of the community had changed over the preceding year. Yet the Study Commission went too far. Smith believed the beach and Baldwin communities must retain their autonomy. He feared the centralization of authority and the excessive powers of a strong mayor. He also predicted that taxes under consolidation would be more than double the Study Commission's estimates. Smith's proposals for reform maintained the existing governmental forms while focusing on consolidating a limited number of governmental services.[27]

Following a series of hearings across the county, the Duval delegation moved into legislative session in Tallahassee. All of the delegation's five state senators—Democrats John Mathews Jr. and Verle Pope (of St. Augustine) and Republicans Tom Slade, John Fisher, and William T. Stockton Jr.—supported the Study Commission's charter. The House's eleven representatives were split. Five—Fred Schultz, Don Nichols, Joseph Kennelly, John Crider, and Dan Scarborough—supported the proposal, but six—George Stallings, Ted Alvarez, Lewis Brantley, Gifford Grange, Gordon Blalock, and Lynwood Arnold—opposed it. Passage of the charter required a majority vote in both houses.[28]

According to Senator Slade in a subsequent interview, the House opponents were linked to the entrenched political organization. They had been "elected by the traditional means of going to the city and county employees and Daughtry Towers." Consolidation threatened the power of the Democratic organization and the jobs of governmental employees.[29]

Over the next two months, the Duval delegation negotiated a revised consolidation charter. Proponents of consolidation, known through the media as the "White Hats," offered concessions to the opponents, who were known as the "Black Hats." The White Hats recognized that limited changes in the charter were better than losing the entire package. Thus they agreed to autonomy for the beach and Baldwin communities. They reduced the powers of the mayor, albeit reluctantly, permitting an elected sheriff rather than an appointed one. They knew that no city over 250,000 population had an elected law enforcement chief. Maintaining order was a fundamental mayoral responsibility, even in preconsolidation Jacksonville. But elected county sheriffs in Florida were popular. The White Hats conceded. They also accepted election of tax assessors, tax collectors, supervisors of elections, and the seven-member civil service board. They gave council power to confirm or veto mayoral appointees. They limited the tax millage rate and reduced the mayor's annual salary from $35,000 to $30,000.[30]

The makeup of the city council posed another problem. The White Hats accepted an amendment to reduce the council size from twenty-one members to nineteen, fourteen from separate districts and five elected at large. They also removed provisions barring political activity by city employees on their own time.[31]

Maintaining momentum while negotiating concessions became a struggle. House opponents used delaying tactics, hoping the legislative session would end before work on the consolidation charter was completed. Such an event would postpone a referendum for at least a year and possibly forever. Charter proponents countered by threatening to bypass the Black Hats in the delegation and introduce the bill on the floor of the House. It already had passed the Senate. Supporters from Jacksonville traveled repeatedly to Tallahassee to lobby for the bill. The media, both television and newspapers, maintained pressure in support of consolidation. The delegation's attorneys, appointed by Mathews and led by James C. Rinaman Jr., a strong advocate, worked behind the scenes anticipating problems, maneuvering compromises, and keeping abreast, if not one step ahead, of the process. Finally, concessions permitting political activity by city employees and election of the civil service board broke the impasse. Alvarez, Arnold, and Brantley finally supported the bill. The House delegation approved the amended consolidation charter; the bill passed the House and Senate; and the governor signed it on June 26, 1967. The referendum was set for August 8.[32]

The Old System Begins to Reform Itself

While the Duval delegation labored over the new charter, Jacksonville voters began to reform the old system. Five candidates entered the race for mayor-commissioner in the spring of 1967. Leading the pack was forty-one-year-old Louis H. Ritter, the incumbent and a fifteen-year veteran of city government. Ritter played the game of Jacksonville politics very well. After graduating from the University of Florida with a degree in public administration, he ran successfully for city council in 1951 at the age of twenty-five. Four years later, he became the youngest man ever elected to the city commission. Twice reelected, he replaced Haydon Burns as mayor when the latter became governor in 1965. While clearly an insider in politics, Ritter avoided indictment in the grand jury hearings. He also worked hard as mayor.[33]

Ritter accepted the changes taking place locally and nationally during the 1960s, especially in the area of race relations. He began talking directly with civil rights leaders and appointed the first African Americans to city policy-making and advisory boards and agencies. The mayor also integrated the police force, closing down the dilapidated substation in Blodgett Homes. He empowered black officers to arrest white as well as black offenders. Ritter never went as far and as fast as Rutledge Pearson and other civil rights leaders wanted in terms of opening city jobs to African Americans, improving the housing stock, paying adequate wages, or integrating recreational facilities. Still, the mayor listened and acted where he felt he could, as in the appointment of Charles E. Simmons Jr., vice president and actuary of the Afro-American Life Insurance Company, to the civil service board.[34]

Ritter especially understood the relationship between race and poverty. An estimated 15,200 families in Jacksonville (30 percent of the population) earned less than the federal standard of $3,000 per year, and two-thirds of

Fig. 5. Louis H. Ritter, mayor of Jacksonville,
1965–1967. By permission of Louis H. Ritter,
Jacksonville.

them were African American. To respond to their needs, in March 1965 the
mayor spearheaded efforts to establish the Greater Jacksonville Economic
Opportunity, Inc., the local branch of President Lyndon Johnson's War on
Poverty. Ritter next secured the inclusion of Jacksonville as one of fourteen
cities in the federal Model Cities Program, leading to the construction of
the Emmett Reed and Robert F. Kennedy Centers as full-service neighborhood facilities on the western and eastern fringes of downtown.[35]

Beyond the War on Poverty, the mayor saw accessing federal dollars for
urban renewal as a major priority. Access required state legislative authorization (which did not occur until 1968) and passage of a minimum standards housing code to regulate the 20,000 units of dilapidated or deteriorated housing in the city. Jacksonville was the only large city in Florida
without a housing code. After extended negotiations with the Board of Realtors and Property Managers Association, along with support from the
Chamber and the NAACP, Ritter secured council action in August 1966,
paving the way for a major effort to clear the notorious slum of Hansontown.[36]

Another major priority for the mayor was to reduce air and water pollution. Ritter appointed a broad-based Citizens Advisory Committee on Water Pollution Control to study and make recommendations. Its fifty-five members spent a year studying the problem, listening to experts, holding public hearings, and drafting recommendations. Its report, released in November 1966, directed the city to educate all citizens, "industrial and business leaders, elected officials and all others," to the serious problem of water pollution; commit to removing all pollution from the major tributaries of the St. Johns River within the city; enforce existing antipollution laws; require existing and new businesses to clean up their waste disposal; budget city funds to complete the current sewage treatment construction program; work with country officials on a comprehensive plan for the entire metropolitan area; and establish a permanent citizens advisory committee to assist in the implementation.[37]

Ritter had ambitious plans for a progressive Jacksonville. In addition to improving race relations, beginning urban renewal, and advocating for environmental reform, he proposed to expand parks and recreational facilities, add public housing, improve transportation, stimulate business expansion, and place a community college campus downtown. The mayor also supported consolidation, having testified at length before the Study Commission. He too saw major structural reform as essential for the city.[38]

Ritter's main opponent in the May 1967 mayoral election was a newcomer to electoral politics, forty-year-old criminal court judge Hans Tanzler Jr. Another University of Florida graduate and a Southeastern Conference basketball star, the six-foot-four-inch Tanzler also had a law degree from the university in Gainesville. He worked briefly as an assistant county solicitor before appointment as judge in 1963. In that position, he followed closely the city corruption proceedings as they unfolded. Urged on by supporters, Tanzler entered the race to run what he called "a real high-level, clean and ethical campaign."[39]

Ritter won a plurality in the three-person first Democratic primary, but in the run-off required by Florida law, Tanzler edged him, 52 to 48 percent. In a third race against a Republican opponent, Tanzler won handily. A week later, the governor signed the consolidation bill calling for an election referendum.[40]

Tanzler's victory over Ritter reflected the strong opposition to partisan politics that had surfaced over the preceding year of grand jury investigations and trials. Yet Ritter was popular and had a substantial record of achievement as mayor. Under normal circumstances he would have won reelection handily. But 1967 was different, and Tanzler epitomized the nonpartisan reformer advocating open and honest government without spoils or patronage. White middle-class residents voted for him in substantial numbers to overcome organized party and African American support for the incumbent.[41]

The reform thrust carried over into the council elections, where eight of nine incumbents lost their seats. Most significant among the races were the victories of two African American candidates, Mary Singleton and Sallye Mathis, elected at large by both black and white voters.

The forty-year-old Singleton was a graduate of Florida A & M University and former schoolteacher and business partner with her husband in five barbecue restaurants. She had entered politics supporting her husband in losing city council election campaigns in 1955 and 1963. Following his death in 1964, she became active in the Duval County Democratic Executive Committee, crossing racial lines and making many white friends. Mary Singleton had a winning personality. Hans Tanzler remembered her as "a dynamic, loveable person. . . . She was at ease with everyone." She also was bright and capable. Mayor Ritter appointed her to the Housing Board of Adjustments and Appeals, where she served as vice chair. She served on the Local Government Study Commission, though she eventually opposed consolidation as not in the best interests of Jacksonville's African Americans. Frank Hampton, prominent black business and political leader, helped persuade her to run for council on the grounds that a black woman might have a better chance of victory than would a black man. Despite recent surgery for breast cancer, she agreed. She campaigned vigorously, winning support from white Catholics (she was a practicing Roman Catholic), Jewish groups, and the 35,000-member (white) Northeast Florida Building and Construction Trades Council. Singleton won decisively in the second primary and had no Republican opposition. The victory was particularly impressive because council candidates, while representing districts, were elected at large by all city voters, black and white.[42]

Where Mary Singleton came from a strongly partisan Democratic background, the fifty-five-year-old Sallye Mathis approached the council campaign more as a civil rights activist with the NAACP and as a nonpartisan community leader with the Jacksonville chapter of the League of Women

Fig. 6. Sallye Mathis and Mary Singleton, first African Americans elected to city council since 1907. (Walch 1990, cover; reprinted by permission.)

Voters. A graduate of Bethune-Cookman College, she too had taught school. She also had counseled students and had been dean of girls at Matthew V. Gilbert Junior-Senior High School. She retired in 1962 following her husband's death and began devoting full time to civic causes. She helped develop strategy and marched for civil rights locally. She observed city council meetings on behalf of the League of Women Voters. She integrated the governing board of the Jacksonville YWCA and helped organize the Jacksonville Opportunities Industrial Council (OIC). She worked with Wendell Holmes on school desegregation, and Mayor Ritter asked her help in developing the city's antipoverty program. Like Mary Singleton, Sallye Mathis had crossed racial lines and had substantial support in the white community, from organized labor and others. Her NAACP colleagues urged her to run, again hoping a black woman might win. During her campaign, her good friend and mentor, NAACP president Rutledge Pearson, was killed in a car accident en route to a speaking engagement for sanitation workers in Memphis, Tennessee. It was a tremendous blow, given his extraordinary leadership, but Holmes, the Reverend Charles A. Dailey, and others carried on. Mathis won her election, defeating opponents in two primaries and the general election.[43]

In the municipal elections of 1967, Jacksonville voters showed a clear desire for change to take place under the old system of government. Tanzler's victory, combined with the council election results, was indicative. The election of Singleton and Mathis, however, suggested something more. White Jacksonville was beginning to accept integration. Racial attitudes were moderating. Nancie Crabb, active with the League of Women Voters, an advocate for consolidation and in the 1970s an elected member of city council, believed the civil rights marches of the 1960s raised the consciousness of whites. Whites began to see blacks as part of the community. Lew Brantley, a conservative Democrat from the Duval legislative delegation and active in the Jacksonville Jaycees, knew that anyone aspiring to community leadership by the late sixties had to look aggressively "to include the whole community rather than exclude anybody. We knew," he said, "we had to work with the black community." This shift in attitudes was also reflected in Mayor-elect Tanzler's declaration that "qualifications, not color of skin" would be his criterion for appointments on city boards, and in Earl Johnson's substantial role in supporting the consolidation referendum.[44]

No one knew what impact the election of a reform-minded mayor and eight new city council members would have upon the efforts for consolidation. It could have blunted the sense of immediacy of the governmental crisis. After all, the "rascals" were defeated. Yet the underlying problems regarding the structure of city government, with its excessive expense, divided powers, and duplication of services, remained.

Passing the Consolidation Referendum

How to arouse the voters to turn out in support of a midsummer referendum became the challenge for Citizens for Better Government. Again Lex Hester coordinated the effort. The League of Women Voters and American Association of University Women provided volunteer campaign workers. Both organizations formally endorsed the referendum. The Chamber of Commerce also endorsed it and, with the downtown business community, supplied funds. Hester appointed Clanzel T. Brown, president of the Jacksonville Urban League, to organize the African American community. New council member Sallye Mathis campaigned with a sound truck. Endorsements were obtained from the Urban League and the Jacksonville branch of the NAACP.[45]

Meanwhile, Duval state senators Slade, Mathews, and Fisher continued their support with speeches and media interviews. Slade also provided the resources of his Duval County political organization to help mobilize voter support. Yates, Daniel, Rinaman, and others spoke repeatedly across the county. Over the course of the six-week campaign, Citizens for Better Government also enlisted endorsements from the Jaycees, bar association, Duval Medical Society, Junior League, Women's Club, Rotary, Kiwanis, Civitan, Jacksonville Ministerial Alliance, Human Relations Council, and the Republican Party Executive Committee. In addition, Governor Claude Kirk, Jacksonville's congressman Charles H. Bennett, and newly elected mayor Tanzler spoke publicly in support of consolidation.[46]

Major assistance came from the media, both the two commercial television stations and the two dailies owned by the Florida Publishing Company and the railroad. The newspapers assigned two top reporters, Richard A. Martin and George Harmon, to the campaign, editorialized regularly, and even "manufactured" news interviews in behalf of consolidation.[47]

Across the city, voters heard the pros and cons of consolidation debated in neighborhood churches, schools, and civic clubs; saw it discussed almost daily on television; and read their fill in the print media. Summertime activities such as out-of-town vacations, trips to the beach, and family picnics doubtless diverted the attention of many potential voters, but the debate over consolidation reached the people who were willing to listen.

Opposition to consolidation came from city and county employees, the city and county Democratic executive committees, the Black Hats of the Duval legislative delegation, and most, but not all, of the elected officials from the old city council, city commission, and county commission. The city employees union feared the impact of consolidation upon jobs. Despite assurances about protection for civil service employees, there were no union guarantees in the new city charter. Where advocates promised that governmental downsizing would come through attrition, union leaders were less sure. After all, much of the support for consolidation came from business leaders not known for their sympathies toward organized labor.[48]

City employees may have feared for their jobs, but council member Mary Singleton had larger concerns about the impact upon the African American community. With approximately 42 percent of Jacksonville's population, black community members saw in consolidation a dilution of their political strength. African Americans would comprise only 25 percent of the consolidated city for the foreseeable future.[49]

Initially, Singleton had supported consolidation. Chairman Daniel and the Study Commission's inclusion of African Americans in their deliberations made the prospect of consolidation look promising. Civil rights leader Earl Johnson served as secretary of the commission. Urban League and NAACP representatives took part in the studies as did Singleton and Sallye Mathis. The commission proposed district representation to assure the election of African Americans to city council. Commission members also faced the problems of inner-city slums. Their report recommended providing improved governmental services including piped water, sewers, paved streets and sidewalks, streetlights, drainage, and refuse disposal. Most of these services were nonexistent in much of the black community in 1965 and 1966. Finally, the commission recognized that racial unrest existed in Jacksonville and needed to be dealt with constructively. As a result, most African Americans supported consolidation.[50]

Still, trust in the black community was fragile. Following the city elections of May 1967, someone discovered that the council district boundaries in the new charter included both new black council members in the same district. The highly respected and popular Singleton saw an effort to exclude from office either her or her black colleague, Sallye Mathis. Singleton believed it was a deliberate scheme against her. "If that's not gerrymandering," she said, "I don't know what is."[51]

In response, embarrassed advocates of consolidation claimed the boundary lines reflected only lines from census tracts. The results were unintentional. Fortunately for consolidation, Patrick Caddell, the Bishop Kenny High School senior who had drawn the original lines, provided a solution. He restructured the boundaries while maintaining population size of the districts and ensured that the two council members lived in two different districts. The legislature accepted the amendment, but Singleton was not mollified. She along with Frank Hampton became an opponent of the measure.[52]

Opposition also came from voters who saw consolidation inevitably leading to a larger government with higher taxes. Where proponents promised the elimination of duplicated services and limitations on tax rates, critics remained skeptical. Some were poorer homeowners, such as retirees on social security who felt threatened by the prospect of higher tax rates. Others simply opposed providing local government with the revenues necessary to do its job, as had happened with the Duval County schools.[53]

The low-tax, antigovernment phenomenon had a long history in Jacksonville and Duval County, as across the South, and reflected a strong distrust of local, state, and federal authorities. Voters chose their elected officials but distrusted them nonetheless. They paid minimal taxes and expected few governmental services in return. This attitude reflected in part the values of rural, small-town, and village life of an earlier era when residents volunteered their services and did not have to cope with rush hour traffic, solid waste disposal, community health problems, police and fire protection, urban recreational needs, modern school programs, substantial poverty, and the many other issues confronting a medium-sized American city in the 1960s.

Related to the low-tax phenomenon was the fact that consolidation meant the centralization of power into fewer hands. Some opponents of consolidation saw the layers of government as checks and balances and protection against governmental intrusion into their lives. They did not want their property zoned or their small business regulated; they did not want to be told what to do with their garbage.[54]

In Jacksonville, this low-tax, antigovernment attitude undergirded the weak mayoral system established after the Civil War, and carried over into the council-commission governmental form introduced in 1917. Jacksonville voters had never wanted a strong-mayor form of government. During the referendum campaign, this apprehension about strong government often slipped into a hysterical fear that consolidation would lead to federal control, socialism, or communism. Richard Martin, journalist and author of a history of consolidation, believed that over time this hysterical opposition lent credibility to the advocates of consolidation, who included most of the pillars of the community.[55]

Finally, opposition came from the beach and Baldwin communities concerned about local autonomy, despite charter amendments protecting that autonomy.

On the eve of the election, pollster Patrick Caddell, then a high school student and legislative intern, predicted a 63 to 36 percent vote for consolidation (with 1 percent not identified). Other supporters were less optimis-

Fig. 7. Key players who shaped the new, consolidated Jacksonville: *left to right*, John Mathews Jr., Claude J. Yates, Hans Tanzler Jr., J. J. Daniel, and Ted Grisset Jr. By permission of the *Florida Times-Union*.

tic, but the returns on August 8, 1967, came close to Caddell's prediction. Almost 65 percent of the voters, or 54,493, supported consolidation. Only 29,768 voters opposed it. Not surprisingly, the old city voted for it by a two-to-one margin. Duval County, however, also endorsed it, 64 to 36 percent. The largest margins came from the middle- to high-income, white suburban precincts. Rural Duval Countians proved less enthusiastic, yet still gave consolidation a majority vote. Black Jacksonville supported it, 59 to 41 percent. Even the beach and Baldwin communities voted for consolidation of Jacksonville and Duval County, 52 to 48 percent, while also voting for their own autonomy within the consolidated city, 62 to 38 percent. The returns reflected a 47 percent turnout of 183,000 registered voters.[56]

The business and professional elite had achieved their goal of consolidating Jacksonville and Duval County governments. They also had built bridges across the Greater Jacksonville community in support of consolidation. Though critics still remained, the larger community, including both African Americans and previously reluctant suburbanites, came close to a consensus, a major accomplishment in a city plagued by racial, economic, educational, environmental, and political divisions. Still, among the critics were an undetermined yet substantial number of people who voted against consolidation for the very reason Mary Singleton feared: the dilution of black political power.[57]

This fear, that whites intended for consolidation to dilute black Jacksonville's political power, became a belief among many local African Americans. Historian Abel A. Bartley describes the fears of Frank Hampton, Mary Singleton, and newspaper editor Eric Simpson at the time. Almost thirty-five years later, attorney A. Wellington Barlow and newspaper editor Isiah Williams repeated the concerns.[58]

African American supporters at the time, however, saw a trade-off. They acknowledged white dominance into the foreseeable future with consolidation but accepted the half loaf of guaranteed district seats on city council and the promise of improved urban services so badly needed in the neglected urban core under the old regime. They also saw the possibility that if African Americans did become a majority in the future, state legislators might still annex enough white suburbs to maintain control, without a referendum. As a result, most black leaders "saw consolidation as the lesser of two evils."[59]

Consolidation was also noteworthy when compared with the recent failure of a similar referendum in Tampa and Hillsborough County. Tampa had begun the process in 1963 with legislative authorization to create a local study commission. It recommended a referendum on consolidating the two governments, which took place in 1967. The proposal lost overwhelmingly in a light voter turnout.[60]

Two University of Florida political scientists, Walter A. Rosenbaum and Gladys M. Kammerer, studied conditions in the two cities to see why Jacksonville passed and Tampa rejected consolidation. Conditions in Jacksonville were clearly worse. Where Jacksonville's population had declined during the preceding decade and voters had twice rejected annexation attempts, Tampa had grown due to two successful annexations. Where Jacksonville's median educational levels had declined, Tampa's had increased. Both cities had new downtown skylines, but Jacksonville had more slums, which were growing in comparison to Tampa's. Further, Jacksonville had major pollution problems in the St. Johns River. In contrast, Tampa dumped its wastes into the Gulf of Mexico, which carried them out with the tides.[61]

Not only did Jacksonville have greater economic, social, and environmental problems, it also lacked political leadership compared to Tampa. The Bay-area city worked closely with surrounding Hillsborough County in planning, zoning, health services, and property assessments. Local officials responded to changing metropolitan needs. In Jacksonville and Duval County, none of the many governmental bodies had responded adequately to recent growth. Finally, in Tampa there were no scandals comparable to the grand jury indictments of Jacksonville officials, probably the single most important factor influencing voter support for consolidation.[62]

Besides the absence of governmental crises requiring major change, Tampa also lacked the involvement of the civic establishment, minority community, and media in support of consolidation. Where the Jacksonville newspapers and television stations became advocates, the Tampa media remained lukewarm and divided. The Tampa minority community was largely uninvolved and the business elite split. The result was systemic change in Jacksonville–Duval County and continued incremental change in the Tampa Bay area.[63]

Jacksonville's passage of its consolidation charter represented one response to rapid urban growth in the years after World War II. Another response was annexation. A hundred years earlier, as cities like Chicago expanded, they simply annexed outlying areas. By the 1960s, however, only a few states, such as North Carolina, Tennessee, Texas, and Oklahoma, permitted outright annexation. Most required voter approval, and most suburban voters rejected inclusion in their central cities. The 1963 and 1964 annexation referenda in Jacksonville were good examples of the opposition to central city expansion into residential areas of the county.

With annexation generally not possible, many local governments developed independent authorities to provide specialized services across metropolitan areas. These authorities appointed by the governor or local governments were seen as efficient vehicles to provide business-like operations beyond the reach of the central city's political control. The New York Port Authority became a model for Jacksonville, Miami, and other cities. Locally the Jacksonville Expressway Authority (soon to become the Jacksonville Transportation Authority) served the metropolitan area efficiently without excessive political intrigue.

Regional cooperation was another response to metropolitan growth. In metropolitan Toronto (1953) and Miami–Dade County (1957), voters established two tiers of government. Individual towns and cities maintained local autonomy while a larger metropolitan government provided regional services. Dade County, Miami, Miami Beach, Coral Gables, Homestead, and twenty-three other local governments retained their local identity while ceding authority for water, sewers, transportation, parks, recreation, area planning, urban renewal, property assessments, and tax collection to a new Metro Dade government. Police and fire services generally remained local functions. Libraries were local for some but not all of the communities. The resulting two-tier system of governance gave Miami Metro the authority to tax, plan, and develop urban systems across Dade County, provide new services in unincorporated areas, and set minimum standards for all municipalities.[64]

Jacksonville's consolidation went further than any of these other responses in its creation of one government to serve the metropolitan area. Modeled on Nashville Metro, established in 1962, it replaced both the city and county governments with a consolidated government. In both cases, Nashville and Jacksonville established the mayor-council form. Nashville's mayor, however, had greater power. He appointed both the chief of police and the school board, with approval of city council. In contrast, Jacksonville's voters elected the sheriff and the school board. Jacksonville's charter also maintained the existing transportation, hospital, and port authorities, planning board, and elected civil service board. It also created an electric authority to run the municipal power plant. These actions reflected continued citizen distrust both of political partisanship and strong central government. Both consolidated cities permitted small municipalities like the beach and Baldwin communities to retain their local autonomy.[65]

Though Jacksonville's consolidated government lacked some of the powers of Nashville Metro, its creation marked a major step forward for the city on the St. Johns River. Perhaps most significant, the structural change reinforced the electoral reforms that had taken place earlier in the year, changing the political climate from one of bossism, political intrigue, and patronage to a climate emphasizing honesty, efficiency, and economy in government.[66]

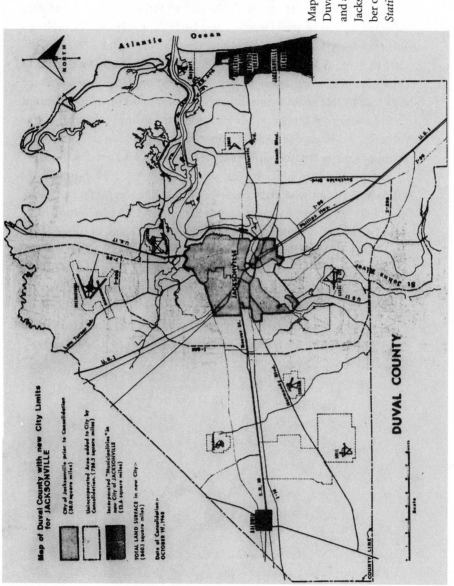

Map 1. Jacksonville–Duval County before and after consolidation. Jacksonville Area Chamber of Commerce 1975, *Statistical Abstract*, 2.

Following the successful consolidation referendum in August, new primary and general elections took place that fall to choose the men and women to implement the new governmental form. Mayor Tanzler ran unopposed to become the consolidated city's first chief executive. The nineteen-member city council held contested races in which an unusually high caliber of candidates participated. Mary Singleton and Sallye Mathis were reelected, as were council members Jake Godbold and Homer Humphries, also chosen in May. In addition, the new council included W. E. "Ted" Grissett Jr., Earl M. Johnson, and I. M. Sulzbacher, strong supporters of consolidation. Particularly noteworthy was Johnson, active throughout the decade as the NAACP's civil rights attorney in support of demonstrations, sit-ins, and school desegregation. He was elected to one of the five at-large council seats. In all, four African Americans were elected to city council, marking a major step forward in race relations for this Deep South city.[67]

The newly elected officials took office on March 1, 1968, but full consolidation did not take place until October 1. The seven-month interim provided time for the mayor, his newly appointed chief administrative officer, Lex Hester, department heads, and citizen advisers to combine the approximately five thousand county employees and five thousand city employees into a totally new organizational structure. They had to endure costly last-minute patronage efforts by lame-duck county and city commissions, which made the transition more difficult. Legal challenges to consolidation required state court rulings, but the voters had acted. Now it became the responsibility of the new mayor and council to make consolidated Jacksonville work.[68]

~

CHAPTER 3

A Bold New City

The elections of 1967 creating a consolidated Jacksonville promised a new day, but that new day would not begin until October 1, 1968. Certain issues could not wait until then. Mayor Hans G. Tanzler had to make the old system work. Shortly after taking office on June 23, 1967, Tanzler met with black community leaders for advice on improving race relations. Their priorities were for more jobs, better police-community relations, good schools, more recreational facilities, and decent housing. The mayor also listened to young African Americans, leaving city hall to engage in sometimes raucous talk sessions with street and neighborhood leaders in pool halls, restaurants, and local hangouts. Those young people had the same priorities: jobs, housing, and more recreational facilities for the black community. Tanzler's public response came on television at the end of July. He announced the opening of city government to minority employment, urged the Chamber of Commerce to help him find jobs, promised to increase housing inspections to upgrade the existing stock, proposed busing inner-city youth to city swimming pools, and noted the opening of a new youth center on West Ashley Street.[1]

On August 9, 1967, the day after Jacksonville and Duval County voters approved the consolidation referendum, the mayor met with eighty of the city's business leaders in the boardroom of the Jacksonville Area Chamber of Commerce. Chamber president W. Ashley Verlander, also president of American Heritage Life Insurance Company, set the agenda: "to discuss racial relations as they exist here in Jacksonville today, and to talk about what we of the business community can do." The mayor spoke about the recent riots in Detroit, Newark, and elsewhere and the possibility for similar turmoil locally. The root problem in the black community, Tanzler said, was the need for jobs. He urged business leaders to support a program to train and provide jobs for African Americans. The mayor noted that H. Rap Brown, one of the nation's most fiery black power advocates, was scheduled to speak that night at a rally at Durkee Field in the black community. No riot resulted, in part because of the mayor's prior efforts in reaching out to the African American community.[2]

The meeting with Verlander and the other business leaders produced immediate results. Tanzler formed what became the Mayor's Advisory Panel on Employment comprising representatives from the Chamber, Urban League, NAACP, Greater Jacksonville Economic Opportunity (GJEO), and the Florida State Employment Service to begin recruiting jobs and job applicants. In the first week at the Chamber offices, 910 applications (80 percent female) were processed, of which 419 were referred to 80 employers. Ninety people were hired.[3]

The gap between applications and hires reflected a variety of problems. Many applicants lacked appropriate job skills. Others had no transportation. Some had unrealistic expectations about job prospects, work requirements, or pay. Some employers had entry barriers that excluded job candidates without high school diplomas or applicants who had had a brush with the law. Recruiting hard-core-unemployed blacks and whites into gainful employment would remain a major challenge for the foreseeable future.[4]

That fall, Tanzler, with funding support from the U.S. Department of Labor, named Edward G. Ballance, plant manager of the local Maxwell House Division of the General Foods Corporation, to chair what became the Jobs for Jacksonville program. Its purpose was "to create, through total community involvement and cooperation, more job opportunities for the disadvantaged citizens of Jacksonville." Ballance sought answers from across the country to the problems of the hard-core unemployed, and he practiced what he learned at his own Maxwell House plant. He recruited twelve persons classified as hard-core unemployed and not only trained the new workers but trained his foremen and supervisors as well in how to motivate the workers. "I told the supervisors," Ballance later explained, "that it doesn't take talent to *fire* somebody, but it does to turn a marginal man into a productive employee."[5]

Fig. 8. Hans G. Tanzler Jr., Jacksonville's first consolidation mayor, 1967–1978. By permission of the City of Jacksonville.

Jobs for Jacksonville was a bold start for the new mayor, even before consolidation went into effect. Yet the challenges were enormous. Promoting Jobs for Jacksonville to a gathering of local businessmen in the spring of 1968, the mayor estimated that 37,000 families locally (26 percent of all Jacksonville families) were earning below the federal poverty level of $3,000 per year. Of these poor families, 21,000 were white (17 percent of all white families), and 16,000 were black (43 percent of all black families). To train and employ these people at decent wages, said Tanzler, was the number one solution for all of the city's ills.[6]

The mayor next proposed establishing a human relations commission to hear grievances and make recommendations for redress. Black leaders, familiar with committees that served as excuses for inaction, were not impressed. Tanzler forged ahead anyway, securing passage that August of legislation to establish the Jacksonville Community Relations Commission. Its purpose was "to promote and encourage fair treatment and equal opportunity for all persons . . . [and] eliminate discrimination against and antagonism between religious, racial and ethnic groups and their members."[7]

That fall, the mayor appointed Nathan H. Wilson as chair of the new commission. Wilson, forty-four, was Florida counsel for Southern Bell Telephone and Telegraph Company and supported better schools, consolidation, and other local reforms. Wilson pledged to "act in the interests of all our people, whatever their race, color, creed or politics." Together with the mayor, Wilson chose the commission members to reflect broadly the community's diversity. When it met for the first time in January 1968, members elected Clanzel Brown, an African American who was executive director of the Jacksonville Urban League, as vice chair and David Adkins from the Duval County Taxpayers Association as interim executive director. The mayor told the commission he did not need to be told that racial inequities existed. He knew that. He wanted concrete solutions. He charged the commissioners to investigate everything from unemployment to police brutality and recommend steps to "overturn one hundred years of prejudice and history."[8]

Meanwhile, the mayor also took steps to expand recreational opportunities and access to social services in the inner city. Building on the efforts of his predecessor, Louis H. Ritter, the mayor presided over the groundbreaking of the first of two city neighborhood centers on the east side and west side of downtown. Jacksonville was one of fourteen cities in the nation, three in the Southeast, to obtain federal funding for what began as a Model Cities program and later became a Pilot City Neighborhood Centers program. The vision behind the program was expansive, serving neighborhoods with a variety of public and private services, enabling residents to obtain health care, job training, and jobs. When Jacksonville's two centers, Emmett Reed and Robert F. Kennedy, opened in 1969, they contained gymnasiums, swimming pools, day care centers, senior citizen centers, health clinics, family planning clinics, meeting halls, and office space for nearly two dozen agencies.[9]

On April 4, 1968, the mayor's efforts to build a biracial community of support on behalf of disadvantaged citizens were confronted by the assassination of Rev. Martin Luther King Jr. Black anger exploded in 122 cities across the nation resulting in the deaths of thirty-eight people and extensive destruction of public and private property. In Jacksonville, there was relative calm. Police responded to scattered rock throwing, fire bombs, and smashed windows. The night following King's funeral, police arrested fifteen youths in twenty-five incidents and briefly imposed a curfew. The Community Relations Commission sponsored a King memorial service on Sunday, April 7, at the civic auditorium for three thousand mourners. Black and white community leaders, including the mayor, took part.[10]

That night, a group of young African Americans hanging out on a south-side street corner were enjoying the return of their friend, Rudolph Hargrett, age 18, home on leave from the United States Air Force. A car of whites passed, circled the block, and returned. A passenger in the back seat sprayed gunfire among the blacks, killing Hargrett. This violent act repeated the random shooting by a young white male of Johnnie Mae Chappell during the 1964 riots.[11]

By October 1, 1968, when consolidation officially began, Mayor Tanzler had spent a full fifteen months actively promoting better race relations in Jacksonville. African Americans had been hired at city hall in white-collar and supervisory positions. New job-training programs had begun under the auspices of the GJEO and Urban League. Four African Americans had been sworn in as members of the newly consolidated city council. The city also had increased enforcement of the minimum standards housing code passed during Mayor Ritter's administration. Further, the Community Relations Commission had investigated numerous discrimination complaints and secured the desegregation of the Fraternal Order of Police. Much more remained to be done, but Jacksonville had acted boldly in promoting better race relations in the consolidated city.[12]

Another issue requiring Mayor Tanzler's attention before consolidation took effect in October 1968 was environmental pollution. Just days before the election of the new government, on December 5, 1967, a letter from the Florida Air and Water Pollution Control Commission and the state board of health arrived at city hall. It ordered the city within ninety days to furnish evidence of plans and an implementation schedule to end the disposal of fifteen million gallons per day of raw sewage into the St. Johns River and its tributaries. Efforts begun under Mayor Burns had resulted in building the Buckman Sewage Treatment Plant that served residents on the north side of downtown, but they were only a fraction of the city's total population. Most Jacksonville residents used septic tanks or pipes carrying wastes directly to the river or one of its tributaries. Efforts accelerated under Mayor Ritter, resulting in a three-phase plan to remove all raw sewage originating in the old city. Implementation of that plan, however, awaited the coming of consolidation. [13]

In the spring of 1968, still before consolidation, Tanzler appointed an advisory committee on pollution to help determine the most effective and economical ways to solve the city's water pollution problems. Committee members learned that in addition to the seventy-two untreated outfalls (later revised to seventy-seven) from homes, hospitals, insurance companies, railroads, city hall, and the county courthouse directly into the St. Johns River, many of the river's tributaries contributed substantial industrial and commercial pollution. Furthermore, 131 miles (later revised to 275 miles) of existing concrete sewer lines built prior to World War II were either collapsing or badly deteriorating. The Buckman Sewage Treatment Plant needed to be doubled in capacity in order to provide secondary as well as primary treatment of wastes.

None of the city's hospitals treated its sewage, although Baptist Hospital had set aside funds to build its own plant. Committee members learned there were more than 125 privately owned sewage treatment plants scattered across Duval County. Most of them were small, unregulated, and of questionable effectiveness. Cost estimates varied, but the committee and mayor saw the need for a sewage user fee to fund revenue bonds for massive construction. In his July budget message, Tanzler recommended the levy. In tax-conscious Jacksonville, this action was a bold step.[14]

A second environmental issue was air pollution. Residents frequently saw a yellow haze over downtown and smelled offensive odors that permeated the working-class east side of the city and often spread across the river to suburban Arlington and beyond. Mildred "Mimi" Adams, a community activist on environmental issues along with her husband, believed Jacksonville faced a severe problem of air pollution due in part to climatic conditions that prevented chemical wastes from dispersing into the atmosphere.

A primary culprit was the municipal power plant burning low-grade, cheap oil that emitted 100 tons of sulfur dioxide into the air daily. She urged a shift to natural gas that would be available from a pipeline currently under construction in northeast Florida. The League of Women Voters, in another study, agreed. The city's electric generating stations were responsible for 75 percent of all sulfur dioxides emitted into the atmosphere, contributing substantially to the air pollution in the community. The league also reported concern about automobile emissions of some twelve tons per square mile per day, a level that could result in eye irritation. The federal government had mandated pollution control devices in all 1968 model new cars, and the league urged local inspections to ensure the devices worked. Shortly after consolidation went into effect, the mayor secured passage of legislation to prohibit excessive air pollution and to create an air pollution control board with delegated powers to establish rules, procedures, and penalties for violations.[15]

Another significant issue before consolidation was that of merging the old city and Duval County governmental services into one new government. While the new city council elected in December did not take office until March 1, 1968, it began meeting informally to establish rules, procedures, and committees. Once in office, the council reviewed mayoral appointees to city positions, including Lex Hester's appointment as chief administrative officer and appointments to the newly created Jacksonville Electric Authority. In July, the council approved the mayor's first consolidated city budget with its provision for sewer and garbage fees. Meanwhile, the administration worked to merge 10,000 city and county employees into one government, establish eight major departments with thirty-two working divisions, ease transitional anxieties among employees fearful of change, and prepare a smooth transition for October 1, 1968.[16]

Meanwhile, the lame-duck county and city commissions challenged and sometimes sabotaged the new government's attempts to consolidate. First, the county commission awarded "a valuable and highly controversial" cable television franchise for thirty years despite the opposition of the incoming government. It then undercut plans of the new government to regulate the nearly three hundred small, privately owned water and sewer utilities in the county by turning them over to the state's Public Service Commission, an agency that had no experience in that field. Next, the

Fig. 9. Jacksonville: "Bold New City of the South." By permission of the *Florida Times-Union.*

commission granted extensive property rezoning petitions during its last weeks in office. Meanwhile, over Tanzler's objections, the city commissioners ordered a reduction in electricity rates and awarded substantial raises to police and firefighters right before the new government took office. Both actions threatened to unbalance the recently passed consolidated city budget.[17]

Consolidated Government Begins

Despite efforts to sabotage the consolidated government, October 1, 1968, came and the new government took command. "An estimated 200,000 people—including school children who had been given the day off—crowded downtown Jacksonville to watch a parade and celebrate . . . their new government as it formally assumed its powers." The momentum carried forward into 1969 when the National Municipal League and *Look* magazine saluted Jacksonville as an All-America City, "the highest and most coveted honor that can be conferred on a community."[18]

High on the agenda of the newly consolidated government was urban renewal. Jacksonville previously had missed the boat on securing federal dollars available for this purpose. First, in the 1950s, the Florida Supreme Court had struck down statewide legislation permitting cities to condemn contiguous blocks of private property for urban renewal. Then, when Tampa and Miami secured local legislation to that end, Jacksonville failed to do likewise. In 1967, Mayor Ritter had lobbied unsuccessfully in Tallahassee for authorization, but he lacked support from his city council and the Duval delegation. Tanzler planned to change that.[19]

Early in 1969, the mayor met with the Duval County legislative delegation. He had only one major request to make of them: "reverse the stagnation and even deterioration of our central city" by securing passage of a statewide law enabling cities to engage in urban renewal. Jacksonville desperately needed it. Within or on the fringes of downtown, 63 percent of the housing was substandard. In one inner-city neighborhood, 53 percent of the families had incomes below the poverty line. Crime rates were disproportionately high. Certain inner-city neighborhoods lacked water and sewer lines, street paving, sidewalks, and streetlights. Urban renewal could help fund needed infrastructure, low-income housing, hospitals, playgrounds, and schools.[20]

Jacksonville had funded its own waterfront redevelopment during the Haydon Burns administrations and currently had bonded for water and sewer construction. But local dollars were limited. Nashville had leveraged $129 million from the federal government for urban renewal. Tampa had secured almost $52 million. Access to federal dollars would enable the consolidated government to greatly enhance its downtown area. Jacksonville was the last major city in the United States to seek the legal authority necessary to participate in federally assisted urban renewal.[21]

Tanzler secured the support of the Duval delegation. He also gained the backing of the new city council and business community. He lobbied in Tallahassee, and in June 1969 the Florida legislature passed statewide enabling legislation for urban renewal. Tanzler moved quickly to implement the new law. He met with federal officials in Atlanta, secured council support for creating a city Department of Housing and Urban Development (city HUD), and hired Herbert Underwood to run the new department. Underwood had experience both on the federal level in Atlanta and on the local level in Miami with Dade County's urban renewal program.[22]

In the fall of 1969, Jacksonville's program began to unfold. City officials targeted two areas. The first began west of Main Street at State Street, extended from downtown north and west along Hogan's Creek to Methodist and University Hospitals (both subsequently part of Shands Jacksonville) and St. Luke's Hospital (which subsequently moved to the suburbs). The Hogan's Creek urban renewal project included what remained of the Hansontown slum, old warehouses, city garages, unkempt parkland and creek, churches, and a handful of substantial homes on Jefferson, Louisiana, and Davis Streets. Plans called for general demolition and a multistage development to include low- and moderate-income housing for 2,000 families, high-rise apartments for elder residents, rebuilding and widening of streets and bridges, flood control on Hogan's Creek, cleanup and expansion of Springfield Park, an expanded campus for Darnell-Cookman Junior High School, neighborhood shops (with a larger shopping area in nearby LaVilla), and a downtown campus for the community college. Physically sound homes and churches could remain. Important to local HUD director Underwood was limiting forced displacement of individuals and families from the neighborhood. "Miami moved acres of people when it built expressways," he said. "The people had no place to go. . . . I don't want Jacksonville to make the same mistakes other cities have made."[23]

The second targeted area also began at Main Street, extended east toward the Haines Street Expressway (later renamed Martin Luther King Jr. Expressway), and south from Eighth Street to the river. It was known as the Neighborhood Development Project. Though less ambitious than the Hogan's Creek project, it sought with greater flexibility to focus on specific

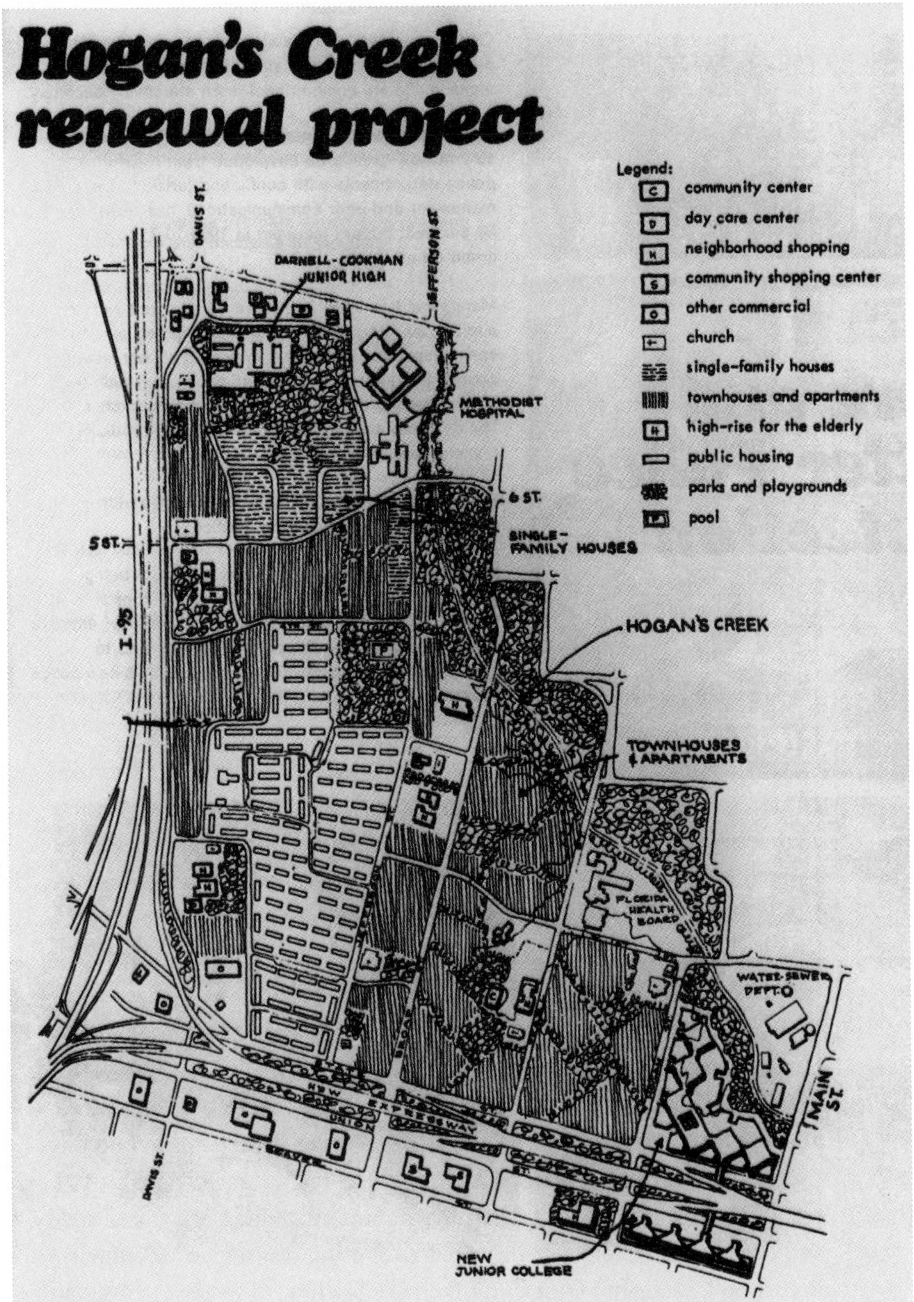

Hogan's Creek renewal project

Legend:
- C community center
- D day care center
- N neighborhood shopping
- S community shopping center
- O other commercial
- + church
-    single-family houses
-    townhouses and apartments
- H high-rise for the elderly
-    public housing
-    parks and playgrounds
- P pool

Map 2. Hogan's Creek renewal project. City of Jacksonville 1971, *Bold View Special Report: Two Years of Consolidated Government*, 19.

projects such as building a new high school, expanding the Cathedral Foundation of Jacksonville's Cathedral Manor elder housing project, replacing existing dilapidated housing with new multifamily units, rehabilitating existing homes, and creating a waterfront park.[24]

A year later in the fall of 1970, the Hogan's Creek project was underway with the demolition of 600 unsafe structures. In February 1971, Florida's U.S. senator Edward Gurney announced the first grant of $7 million in urban renewal funds to renovate Hogan's Creek into "a park-like stream," acquire land for the community college, rebuild wider streets and bridges, install water lines, sewers, curbs, gutters, and sidewalks, and implement plans for a 200-unit high-rise apartment for lower-income elder residents. In subsequent years, Florida Community College at Jacksonville became the southern anchor and the hospitals became the northern end of the Hogan's Creek project. Garden apartments and the high-rise facility were built along with the local HUD offices and the city-state public health center along the north-south axis of Broad Street. A swimming pool, basketball courts, and the park bordering the creek also became part of the area. What did not come to fruition was the neighboring shopping center for residents and new middle-income or affordable housing. The private sector never developed its part of the plan.[25]

East of Main Street, federal funding enabled the smaller Neighborhood Development Project to rehabilitate housing, secure land for a new police station and riverfront park (built under a later administration), and expand facilities around the Gator Bowl (later Alltel Stadium). What did not occur was the construction of a new comprehensive high school (due in part to decisions made following court-ordered desegregation), expansion of the Cathedral Foundation plans for middle-income housing east of Cathedral Towers, or the development of a neighborhood shopping area at First Street and Florida Avenue.[26]

Meanwhile, the city HUD office assumed responsibility for all public housing from the old Jacksonville Housing Authority and began building 970 new units, the first new housing in the core city since World War II. City HUD also began enforcing the minimum standards housing code and began refurbishing the three oldest housing projects in Jacksonville: Brentwood, Blodgett Homes, and Durkeeville. Toward the end of his first term as mayor of consolidated Jacksonville, Tanzler reflected that urban renewal was personally "the most gratifying operation which has been undertaken, and next to the Water and Sewer Bond Program, the closest to my heart."[27]

While the mayor focused on urban renewal on the fringes of the urban core, in the spring of 1968, before consolidation took effect, a Chamber of Commerce committee began to develop an action program "for the improvement, growth and development of the Downtown Area." This Downtown Development Council included both black and white business executives, professionals, and governmental leaders. Initial concerns for increased police patrols, better sanitation and garbage collection, lighting, sign controls, and parking space gave way to a bolder scheme to develop a master plan proposed by the Jacksonville–Duval Area Planning Board. The Downtown Development Council endorsed the proposal and secured city council funding in the spring of 1969.[28]

In 1971, the Baltimore firm of Rogers, Taliaferro, Kostritsky, and Lamb (RTKL), known for its work on the Charles Center in that city, presented the plan. It was impressive. It described an economic profile of Jacksonville, examined space use demand, proposed land and traffic use patterns, considered urban design, and drew up an implementation program and timetable to include the creation of a downtown development authority.[29]

The planners saw the need to rejuvenate retail sales in the department stores and specialty shops that had been losing ground to the newer suburban malls. To encourage retail shopping, they proposed pedestrian walkways extending from Hemming Park (now Hemming Plaza) south along Laura and Hogan Streets to the river. Downtown also needed recreational and cultural facilities other than the civic auditorium and two older, seedy movie houses. There were few attractive restaurants or nightclubs. The plan recommended a riverfront site to provide them. Downtown had only one decent hotel for businesspeople and travelers, and the plan envisioned building at least one more. Housing was limited mostly to senior citizens at Cathedral Towers, and the plan endorsed building affordable and upscale housing nearby and the construction of luxury condominiums on the river. It also urged city council to establish an independent Downtown Development Authority with powers for bonding and eminent domain to implement these ambitious plans over the next ten and twenty years.[30]

As Tanzler began his second term as mayor following his reelection in May 1971, the consolidated city had a blueprint for the future of its downtown. Subsequently city council passed legislation to create the Downtown

Development Authority to implement these ambitious plans, but it met with mixed results. Independent Life, Atlantic National Bank, and Duval Federal Savings and Loan built new home offices. A later mayor oversaw the construction of the Omni Hotel and Jacksonville Landing, the latter a multipurpose restaurant, nightclub, shopping, and entertainment facility on the river. But no pedestrian mall materialized, and the construction of new housing waited for thirty years and the coming of the twenty-first century. Perhaps most damaging of all was the continued erosion of retail trade as department stores closed or moved to suburban malls. The result was a spotty development of downtown that continued into subsequent administrations. Still, in 1971, the city's plans for revitalizing downtown looked bold. [31]

Cleaning Up the Environment

Meanwhile, the city had to expand its water main and sewer construction program to include the newly consolidated county. There were 70 (later 85) subdivision sewer systems and 120 individual water systems of varying quality scattered over its 825 square miles. Many of the sewer systems discharged partially treated effluent in drainage ditches that became odorous, contaminated, and a health hazard. Others had not been adequately expanded to meet subdivision growth. To acquire these utilities would cost $24 million with no price tag yet available on their upgrades. Further, the consolidated city needed to provide sewers for expanding suburbs. Septic tanks could serve in some areas, but shopping centers, apartments complexes, motels, and restaurants needed access to the city system. [32]

Adding to pollution from the discharge of fifteen million gallons per day of raw sewage into the St. Johns River was the industrial pollution of the city's waterways. St. Regis Paper Company alone dumped ninety million gallons of waste into the river daily. Alton Box Company added another fifteen million gallons per day. The Ribault River, a tributary of the Trout and St. Johns Rivers, collected three million gallons per day from Union Camp and was described as "little more than a large, convenient sewer for industrial waste and sewage plants." Moncrief Creek collected 216,000 gallons of chemical effluent daily from the Glidden Company, "the equivalent to the sewage produced by . . . 35,800 people." McCoys, Pottsburg, and Cedar Creeks were comparably polluted. To their credit, St. Regis, Alton Box, Union Camp, and Glidden had begun cleanup efforts, but as the St. Regis plant manager admitted on television, "I think it highly unlikely that St. Regis or any other company would do this on a voluntary basis."[33]

The challenge for consolidated government, sometimes supported, sometime prodded, and sometimes thwarted by state and federal regulators, was to clean up the mistakes of the past, build a metropolitan water and sewer system for the future, and regulate business and industrial wastes to end their contamination of the environment. Initial cost estimates mushroomed from $90 million to $200 million, then $300 million and finally $400 million to complete the task in phases over the next twenty years. Growing price inflation nationally and increasing interest rates on bond issues subsequently would more than double that cost.[34]

Following consolidation in October 1968, the city engaged Flood and Associates, a consulting firm that had worked with the city before, to update past studies to include the newly combined city and county. Their plan (the 1990 Comprehensive Plan for Water and Sewage Systems for the City of Jacksonville), completed in July 1969, had an eight-phase master water and sewage treatment improvement program designed to meet the needs of the consolidated city to the year 1990. The city next hired Sverdrop and Parcel and Associates to draw up an engineering implementation plan that was completed in May 1970. A financial plan developed by Smith, Barney and Company led to the sale of $52 million in excise revenue bonds, the first of three bond issues needed to "merely bring the city's water and sewer facilities up to date—to a level where they can realistically meet the needs of the city with a 1970 population."[35]

Unfortunately, the best-laid plans often do go astray. Funding was a continual problem. The federal Environmental Protection Agency (EPA) changed guidelines, which caused funding delays. At one point, President Richard Nixon froze funding for all federal projects, again delaying Jacksonville's efforts. State policies actually penalized the city for its initiative to abate pollution, allocating funds instead to cities that had taken longer to get started on pollution control. Consequently, the city had to raise water and sewer taxes again in 1973, shift federal revenue-sharing funds from other programs to sewer construction, and divert tax dollars from the general fund in order to complete the work.[36]

When workers started to replace the crumbling sewer lines, they found conditions worse than anticipated. Costs rose, and the rebuilding program was extended to fifteen years. Only 75 of 200 miles of sewer lines were rebuilt by September 1973. In the suburbs, the city began by purchasing the first thirty-four private systems for $11 million but then discovered the cost of the remaining systems had skyrocketed from $10 million to $50 million. The city was forced to reassess its plan to own the entire metropolitan system. New sources of river pollution became apparent in runoffs from 58 dairies and hog farms, 12 sanitary landfills, 450 small-package sewage treatment plants (for motels, apartments, restaurants, and other businesses that could not connect to existing sewer lines), and a substantial number of the city's 48,600 septic tanks.[37]

The city pushed forward despite these problems. In March 1973, a press release announced that the St. Johns River south of the naval air station to the Duval County line at Julington Creek had been deemed safe for water contact sports. Four years later, almost a decade after the state's original ultimatum, the city closed the last of the outfalls. Just after noon on June 18, 1977, Mayor Tanzler stood on the riverfront and announced the completion of the St. Johns River cleanup and the start of the St. Johns River Day festival. The mayor then donned water skis and joined performers from Cypress Gardens on the river. More than 25,000 citizens celebrated with a flotilla of yachts, navy jets overhead, stunt flyers and parachute jumpers, hot air balloons, free helicopter rides, and whistle blowers and bell ringers to mark the closing of the seventy-seven outfalls, finally making the river safe for recreational use. Within months, there were reports of speckled trout, mullet, bream, perch, catfish, red bass, sea cows, and other aquatic life returning to the river. Phases one and two of the water and sewage improvement program, connecting 66,000 homes and businesses to sanitary sewage service, was completed at a cost of $153 million. For Hans Tanzler, the event marked the most visible achievement of his administration.[38]

While the consolidated city worked to clean up its waterways, it also confronted its air pollution problems. The mayor appointed attorney Morton A. Kessler to chair the newly created Air Pollution Control Board. Beginning in 1969, it challenged open burning at construction sites across the county. The board recommended shutting down the Wilson-Toomer fertilizer company, a manufacturer of sulfuric acid, unless it immediately

Fig. 10. Mayor Tanzler and Cypress Gardens water skiers celebrate the cleanup of the St. Johns River. By permission of the *Florida Times-Union.*

ceased its dense smokestack pollution. It closed July 1, 1971. The board listened to citizen concerns about air pollution and oversaw the efforts of the Bio-Environmental Services Division to establish local standards.[39]

Pollution came in two forms. First, there were the emissions targeted by the Environmental Protection Agency and the Florida Pollution Control Board for six major pollutants: sulfur dioxide, particulate matter, carbon monoxide, photochemical oxidants (ozone), hydrocarbons, and nitrogen oxides. Automobile emissions were the biggest problem. The number of cars in the now consolidated city had increased by 79 percent over the previous decade, to 248,000 vehicles, compared to a population growth of 13 percent. Their emissions in 1970 produced an estimated 83 percent of the city's air pollution. The Jacksonville Electric Authority's three municipal power plants were the major stationary polluters, followed by the paper mills and chemical plants. In 1970 both JEA and industry began using 1 percent sulfur content oil (a 50 percent reduction), resulting in a dramatic dip over the next three years in the sulfur dioxide content of the atmosphere. Federal regulations on auto emissions resulted in Jacksonville air quality generally meeting EPA standards from 1970 to 1974. Beginning in 1973, the energy crisis led to increased gasoline prices and electricity costs, resulting in further reduced consumption and pollution. Meanwhile, local industries made substantial investments to reduce their pollutants. By 1977, all were either in compliance with city and state regulations or had presented satisfactory schedules for compliance.[40]

Still, as Jacksonville residents were well aware, there were days of substantial air pollution, especially when temperature inversions in the atmosphere suspended particulates, sulfur, and nitrogen oxides to create ozone or smog. Increasing downtown vehicular congestion and rush hour traffic added to these conditions. Passage of the Federal Clean Air Act Amendments in 1977 raised standards, and Jacksonville was designated as one of "107 oxidant non attainment areas in the nation," one of nine in Florida. Again, the automobile was the major culprit and would continue to threaten air quality in succeeding years.[41]

More upsetting than the visible smog to local residents, however, was the second form of air pollution: notably offensive odors that caused eye irritation and nausea. They came primarily from two large paper mills and two chemical plants. No governmental agency at the local, state, or federal level had the ability to measure their impact or propose solutions to reduce their effect.[42]

In November 1971, the Air Pollution Control Board held public hearings regarding odors from Glidden Chemical Company (later Glidden-Durkee Division of SCM Corporation). One woman testified that there were some days when it was "almost impossible to breathe because of the odors" from the plant. A man claimed he could not "open his windows and enjoy fresh air [or] yard." A neighbor of the plant said the odors gave her headaches and smelled like a "polecat boiled in sauerkraut." Another claimed the smell was "embedded in his furniture and clothes." Still another claimed the odors made her feel sick and that her friends would not visit her at home because of them. The odors spread beyond the neighborhood. Motorists on nearby I-95 closed car windows crossing the Trout River Bridge to avoid the smell.[43]

Glidden's vice president, Robert P. T. Young, claimed the company had taken major strides in becoming a good corporate citizen since his arrival in Jacksonville in 1960. He had directed the cleanup of the neighborhood, including wastes dumped in Moncrief Creek. The chemical company had switched fuels from oil to natural gas to reduce sulfate pollution and installed new boilers with the latest technology. Young sincerely believed that "air in the vicinity of the Jacksonville factory was as safe as it was in 1909, before the plant was built." Yet he also acknowledged that he had not yet succeeded in eliminating the offensive odors, particularly those associated with sulfate turpentines. But he was working on it and had spent $2 million to date on environmental improvements. The effort would take another twenty years.[44]

Solid waste disposal was the third major area of environmental concern. At the time of consolidation, as mentioned earlier, the principal method of disposal was the use of open dumps, though one antiquated, air-polluting garbage incinerator also operated. The city and county mismanaged some thirty-three dumps without adequate compacting and cover. Residents and businesses dumped additional debris into borrow pits, ravines, stream banks, wooded areas, and open fields. Aerial and ground inspections revealed enormous amounts of untreated raw garbage and trash. Scavengers roamed at will over the sites. Fires were purposely set to reduce volume. There was little evidence of concern for the resulting pollution or health hazards.[45]

The Tanzler administration began free garbage pickups to discourage residents from dumping their trash. It hired Reynolds, Smith, and Hills, engineering consultants, to examine existing conditions and develop plans for an efficient, economical, and sanitary solid waste disposal system. Their report in 1971 led city officials to shut down the old incinerator, close illegal trash sites, and convert others for use by 15,000 homes and businesses not previously served.

The process was slow. The city initially lacked adequate equipment to spread, compact, and cover wastes at its major Imeson landfill. New sites were needed, but residents did not want them in their neighborhoods. Illegal dumping continued along with roadside littering. Yet by 1973, the Community Planning Council could report that refuse collection was being done "as efficiently as possible" at three trash and two sanitary landfills, collecting 1,500 tons of waste per day. A subsequent League of Women Voters study agreed. The Jacksonville Area Planning Board was less sanguine, seeing landfills as a short-term solution. Its members believed future population growth combined with an increasing amount of con-

Fig. 11. Open dump sites in Jacksonville. From Environmental Protection Board 1985, *Annual Environmental Status Report for the Year Ending September 30, 1985* (Jacksonville).

sumer throwaway goods eventually could result in a scarcity of land near urban areas available for waste disposal. The board saw energy resource recovery through incineration as the preferable long-range alternative.[46]

Creating the Jacksonville Transportation Authority

Another challenge confronting the newly consolidated city was transportation. As in other cities across America, automobiles choked local roads. A 1969 Chamber of Commerce seminar focused on the topic, and a year later the mayor spoke at a Florida State University conference on the problems of "metropolitan transportation." Where the population had increased by 12.8 percent from 1960 to 1970, the number of automobiles had increased 78.5 percent. The average number of daily trips within the city increased by 117.5 percent, and downtown trips by 127 percent—more than doubling the traffic level of a decade earlier. The resulting increased traffic congestion worked against opening downtown to development and encouraged suburban sprawl. Meanwhile mass transit use had been declining from 15.4 million revenue passengers in 1961 to 13.6 million in 1969. The privately owned Jacksonville Coach Company lost money in 1971 and recognized that rate increases would only reduce further its number of paying passengers.[47]

In 1971, Tanzler directed general counsel James C. Rinaman Jr. and Jacksonville Expressway Authority attorney Earl Hadlow to find ways of expanding the Expressway Authority's role to include mass transit. The result was the formation of the Jacksonville Transportation Authority by the state legislature. In January 1972, both the mayor and the new JTA asked city council for funds to purchase the Jacksonville Coach Company. Funding assistance came from both state and federal dollars, and ownership of the city's mass transit system passed from private to public hands. The purchase of the bus company did not solve Jacksonville's transportation problems (though ridership initially increased substantially), but it did reflect the consolidated city's bold decision to take over an ineffective private transit system as a first step toward a mass transportation policy.[48]

Other significant steps taken by the consolidated government in its early years included:

- creation of Kathryn Abbey Hanna Park, a 450-acre multipurpose recreational area with a one-and-one-half-mile beachfront on the Atlantic Ocean at Seminole Beach in 1971;
- development of an emergency ambulance service with special cardiac units, giving Jacksonville the reputation of being the safest city in America in which to have a heart attack;
- construction of ten neighborhood health clinics, five swimming pools, two community centers, and five new public housing projects (with three more in the planning stages), mostly at inner-city sites, plus two new suburban libraries;
- reaccreditation of Duval County's public high schools (disaccredited since 1965);
- consolidation and expansion of paid city and volunteer county firefighters into one department providing service across the consolidated city and county, resulting in reduced fire insurance rates;
- consolidation and expansion of city police and county sheriff's deputies into one department, contributing to a reduced crime rate in 1971; and
- reduced property tax rates resulting from a combination of new construction, user fees, increased state gas and cigarette taxes, higher property assessments, and increased Jacksonville Electric Authority revenues in the city budget.[49]

John Fischer, veteran reporter and acting editor in chief of *Harper's Magazine,* described the bold spirit of the consolidated Jacksonville following the spring elections of 1971. Mayor Tanzler had easily defeated former governor and ex-mayor Haydon Burns for reelection. In an era of urban crises in cities ranging from New York and Newark to Detroit, Cleveland, and Los Angeles, Fischer saw Jacksonville as a city confronting its multiple problems believing it could solve them. The cleanup of the air and waterways was the most dramatic, but adding 16,500 streetlights improved visibility and safety in both new and older neighborhoods. New industry brought more jobs. Urban renewal led Independent Life Insurance Company to announce plans to build a new thirty-five-story headquarters downtown. Further, progress in paving streets, opening job opportunities, building low-income housing, improving garbage collection, and introducing neighborhood health clinics, added Fischer, had "led to a marked relaxation of racial bitterness." Earl Johnson, the city's most influential African American leader, agreed. He had recently been reelected to an at-large seat on city council by a predominantly white electorate. "We still have a long way to go," he said, "but we have come a long way too."[50]

This optimism, to be manifested again at the end of the twentieth century, did not last through the 1970s. Racial confrontations, energy crises, economic stagflation (a slowdown in the economy combined with continuing price inflation), and governmental cutbacks slowed the momentum of sewer construction, urban renewal, park expansion, and other Tanzler administration programs over the rest of the decade. Still, consolidated government had gotten off to a good start. Hans Tanzler was a key player in using the new form of governance to make Jacksonville, at least temporarily, "the bold new city" of the South.

CHAPTER 4

RACE MATTERS

The optimism of the bold new city met its first setback in the area of race relations as a result of the Halloween riot of 1969. According to a preliminary report of the Jacksonville Community Relations Commission:

> A few minutes before 4 P.M. on Friday, October 31, a white cigarette salesman/delivery driver parked his truck on Florida Avenue between Phelps and First Street, and went into a store to make a delivery. Through the window of the store, he allegedly saw one or more black youths on the street attempting to steal from his truck. The white driver hastened into the street, pulled a gun, and shot one youth in the leg. A crowd quickly gathered as a result of this shooting incident, and the word spread in the community that a white man had shot a young black man.[1]

Police arrived on the scene and arrested the white man. An ambulance was called to take the youth to Duval Medical Center. The crowd grew, and small groups of youths began moving down Florida Avenue shouting threats and throwing bricks and rocks into store windows. At 5 P.M., Sheriff Dale Carson executed the city's new and heretofore unused Emergency Control Plan. Flaws in its design and execution resulted in an hour passing before its implementation. Meanwhile, rioters spread out over an eight-block area along Florida Avenue, throwing bricks at display windows and firebombs at four stores, most of which were white-owned businesses. At 6 P.M., a large force of police officers finally arrived in riot gear with helmets and shotguns and began marching in force down Florida Avenue. By 7 P.M., the streets were clear. On Saturday morning, fresh disturbances, including the looting of liquor and furniture stores, brought the police back in force to restore order. Over the two days, one shopkeeper died of a heart attack, three individuals received physical injuries, four buildings were damaged by fire, and thirteen arrests were made.[2]

While the sheriff's department had immediate responsibility for restoring order, Mayor Hans Tanzler also had a role to play. Responding to a letter from Arnette E. Girardeau, chairman of the Community Urban Development Council, he requested the Jacksonville Community Relations Commission to conduct a complete investigation of the events to determine causes, assess the city's response, and propose remedial actions "to prevent the recurrence of future outbreaks." The Community Urban Development Council, representing lower-income minority residents, saw the incident as one more piece of evidence in the "polarization of races," which included the recent presidential election where third-party segregationist candidate George Wallace won a plurality of the votes in Jacksonville.[3]

The Community Relations Commission formed a Civil Disorder Task Force with representation from a wide range of community groups. They included the sheriff's office, ministerial alliance, bar association, League of Women Voters, Area Planning Board, Community Urban Development Council, Edward Waters College, Jacksonville University, Urban League, Community Planning Council, and Greater Jacksonville Economic Opportunity, Inc. The task force in turn created five committees focusing on law enforcement and communication, environmental conditions, business practices, community participation, and community-wide understanding. An estimated one hundred citizens took part in the study.[4]

In its report, the Law Enforcement and Communications Committee concluded that the riot was a spontaneous action on the part of the eastside community, and it commended the sheriff's department for its "generally satisfactory and restrained response" to the disorder. At the same time, it identified poor police relations with the black community, especially with low-income black youth, as a problem. It reported that African Americans believed that their treatment at the hands of police officers was inequitable, including verbal and physical abuse. The committee recommended intensive and repeated human relations training for police and ongoing police communication efforts with people in inner-city neighborhoods.[5]

The committee also addressed media reports of the riot. It saw them as generally accurate but also as superficial and sensational. It recommended greater restraint without compromising accuracy, plus ongoing efforts to increase journalistic and wider community understanding of the underlying causes for minority discontent.[6]

The Environmental Conditions Committee sought to understand why neighborhoods like East Jacksonville might explode. It described the neighborhood as a slum with substandard housing, abandoned buildings, junk-filled yards, inadequate municipal services (including garbage collections and police protection), and poor recreational facilities. Residents had to leave the area for jobs, shopping, medical attention, or entertainment. There were no supermarkets, movie houses, or attractive shops. Many residents felt powerless regarding decisions made in their lives, especially decisions by city government. Past promises to build new schools, repair roads, or improve public services frequently had been unfulfilled. Residents resented their conditions and were frustrated about being unable to do anything to change them. Children growing up in the neighborhood could easily develop a sense of hopelessness, which could be converted by a spark or incident to anger and violence. Ghettoes like East Jacksonville, said the committee, produced attitudes in individuals that were "supported and enforced by racism in this society." Quoting the report of the National Commission on Civil Disorders, popularly known as the Kerner Commission Report, the committee added, "White society is deeply implicated in the ghetto. White institutions maintain it and white society condones it." Its eradication would come only with the abandonment of white attitudes and practices.[7]

The committee recommended a variety of changes:

- more rent supplement housing and renovated housing;
- a new high school (a major grievance in the community), improved school staffing (counselors), and facilities (libraries and playgrounds);
- manpower training and job development and recruitment to emphasize minority inclusion;
- improved crosstown public transportation;
- more parks and recreational programs of sports, arts, and block parties to channel youthful energies;
- improved drainage, street paving, tree planting, and trash collection; and

- most important, early action on what could be done to obtain community inclusion on decisions to be made, and a willingness on the part of the city to experiment in response to community needs.[8]

The goal of the Business Practices Committee was to determine whether businesses serving the poor in the Florida Avenue neighborhood exploited them and to recommend remedial action. The committee undertook two surveys, one of 409 lower-income residents of East Jacksonville and comparable neighborhoods, and a second of grocery, furniture, and other retail stores that served these communities. The committee learned that residents purchasing groceries at neighborhood stores paid prices comparable to prices paid at convenience stores in the suburbs. Yet in the absence of supermarkets or transportation to supermarkets, they were forced to buy most of their groceries at these neighborhood stores at prices substantially higher than those paid by white shoppers in suburbia. In visiting the stores, committee surveyors saw many of them as crowded, dirty, and dilapidated, with meats and vegetables that probably should have been condemned by the health department. These local stores often provided credit for known customers. They also charged prices that varied depending on whether one bought by cash or credit. The furniture store prices also were higher than in white neighborhoods. Repossessed stock sometimes was sold as new goods, and goods sold on time often carried exorbitant interest rates. The physical conditions of these other neighborhood stores were, like the grocery stores, old, crowded, dirty, and bordering on the dilapidated.[9]

Residents complained to surveyors about their inability to obtain credit, whether due to poor credit histories or discrimination. As a result, they often were victims of loan sharking by businessmen in the neighborhood. They complained of slumlords not maintaining their rental housing or clearing vacant lots, and of local government's failure to pave and clean streets, provide adequate parks and playgrounds, or maintain schools. Finally, the committee recognized that poor people have less money and thus less flexibility to respond to inflationary pressures such as existed in the local and larger economy in the spring of 1970.[10]

The committee's recommendations included encouraging supermarket entry into inner-city neighborhoods, better governmental services including health inspections of shops and housing, consumer education for residents, more affordable housing, and broader media coverage to publicize conditions and improvements.[11]

No record remains of the other two task force committees, but the conclusions and recommendations of the three existing reports provided evidence of a clear community agenda for the mayor and the community if they honestly wanted to confront Jacksonville's racial problems.

No responsible person condoned the riotous behavior on October 31–November 1, 1969, but as a result of the reports, increasing numbers of Jacksonville residents, both black and white, began to understand how the shooting of a black youth by a white adult could spark the pent-up frustration and anger of other black youths into violent, antisocial behavior. They also began to see the size and scope of the inner-city problems that confronted the entire community. One of Jacksonville's challenges as a bold new city became responding to the report and turning the anger, frustration, and despair of increasing numbers of inner-city residents into hope and the achievement of a better quality of life.

Unfortunately, the community response fell short of the needs. In a report to the Community Relations Commission a year later, staff specialist Jerome Glover reported very limited progress. While the sheriff's department had improved the efficiency of its response to community disturbances and had begun efforts to dialogue with community groups, human relations training of police officers remained minimal and recruitment of minorities was still in the planning stages. The media response to recommendations had come from two radio stations and the public television station, not the daily or weekly newspapers or the commercial television stations. Regarding environmental conditions and jobs, only very limited progress had taken place in housing, education, employment, transportation, recreation, or drainage. For the most part, public agencies promised prompt response to individual complaints along with a continuation of existing, often inadequate programs.[12]

Still, efforts to improve conditions in the inner city continued to be a major thrust of the Tanzler administration, with public housing high on the agenda. Federal officials in 1969 had recommended building 2,800 additional units in Jacksonville, and city council had responded with a down payment authorizing 1,500 units. In the spring of 1970, the mayor requested authority from the Duval legislative delegation to abolish the old Jacksonville Housing Authority and replace it with a city department of housing and urban development to better coordinate building inspection, code enforcement, housing rehabilitation, and new construction for the consolidated city. The mayor recognized that Jacksonville had "massive community redevelopment problems which must be reckoned with in the most expeditious manner, and as soon as possible."[13]

Meanwhile, the Jacksonville Community Relations Commission continued its efforts to gather data and to mediate between groups. A report to the civil service board in July 1970 showed that equal employment opportunities for minorities at city hall remained more a vision than a reality. Of some 1,823 city workers in middle pay grades, only 40, or slightly more that 2 percent, were African American.[14]

On the north side of the city, African American home buyers had begun moving into the formerly all-white neighborhood of Sherwood Forest. The commission investigated reports of block busting by real estate agents to scare whites into selling their homes at below-market values. The commission found evidence of the practice, but in a neighborhood survey, it also discovered that 80 to 90 percent of both blacks and whites in June 1970 were quite satisfied with their neighbors. The respondents believed a handful of troublemakers, both black and white, were stirring up anxieties and fears.[15]

Yet another area of concern was the city fire department, which had only two black firefighters among its seven hundred employees at the beginning of 1971. A citizens committee appointed by the mayor selected outside consultants to assess hiring policies. They recommended expanding the tests to include strength and agility criteria along with a civil service exam relevant to firefighting skills, without any cultural biases. Unfortunately, years would pass before entry criteria changes resulted in a substantial increase in minorities fighting fires.[16]

Police-Community Relations Worsen

Despite these and other efforts by the city, another riot erupted in June 1971, reflecting once again continuing frustration and anger in the black community. At 4 A.M. on Thursday, June 10, a white police officer, Frank Fouraker, shot in the back and killed an unarmed, fifteen-year-old African American named Donnie Ray Hall. Fouraker and his partner had been called to investigate two youths and a possible stolen stalled auto. When the police approached, the boys ran. Hall was an escapee from the juvenile detention shelter and probably wanted to avoid being returned there. Fouraker gave chase, first firing warning shots and then shooting Hall. He claimed the boy appeared to be armed. An open knife was found near the body, but Hall's friend and his father did not recognize it as belonging to the boy. The father also reported that he had loaned the car to his son for the evening.[17]

On Wednesday, June 16, some three hundred African Americans, under the leadership of the local NAACP president, James Washington, marched to the courthouse in a peaceful demonstration, carrying a coffin bearing the name "Hall." When the demonstrators subsequently dispersed along Florida Avenue, small groups began entering stores, rifling cash registers and breaking windows. About 6:30 P.M., police stopped a green Ford Mustang for improper tags and arrested the driver. A crowd gathered, blocking police efforts. Bricks were thrown, breaking a windshield and slightly injuring an officer. As darkness came, once again looting and burning spread along Florida Avenue and across the east side. Police responded in riot gear, clearing streets and arresting anyone within reach.[18]

The next day and evening, roving bands of black youths looted and burned in black neighborhoods on both the east and west sides. Police again swept neighborhoods and made arrests. They responded to thrown rocks, bottles, and other missiles with tear gas grenades. They covered the efforts of firefighters attempting to extinguish blazes. They also employed a tank-like vehicle owned by the Florida Highway Patrol to fire tear gas at protestors. Disturbances continued for a third day and night but then subsided following a thunderstorm on Saturday, June 19. Fortunately, no one was killed and injuries were minor. Fires destroyed some $250,000 of property, and more than three hundred African Americans were arrested.[19]

In the aftermath, Sheriff Dale Carson praised the restraint of his men in the face of angry protestors, thrown rocks and bottles, and sporadic sniper fire. African American leaders saw police actions differently, claiming officers made arrests indiscriminately and physically mistreated innocent bystanders.[20]

Clearly there were conflicting points of view. Police saw rioting bands of urban guerillas burning and looting, then moving on to strike again. Black leaders saw a spontaneous uprising reflecting the anger and frustration of black youth. Black leaders condemned the violence but also saw it as triggered by indiscriminate and brutal police actions, sparked by the shooting of Donnie Ray Hall. The sheriff promised to investigate charges of police brutality, but he defended his men as having worked 12-hour shifts the previous three days under conditions of physical abuse and attacks.

Subsequent hearings before the Community Relations Commission produced testimony including that of African American businesswoman Eddie Mae Stewart. On Friday evening, the third night of the riot, she appeared on WJCT–Channel 7's *Feedback* program to discuss black concerns about the city. Afterward she met Dr. Andrew Robinson in the parking lot en route to her car. A few minutes into their conversation, a police car pulled up and an officer asked, "What the hell are you doing?" Dr. Robinson, a member of the Community Relations Commission and assistant dean at the new University of North Florida, identified himself. Other police arrived, and one of them told the two to "get out of the area before we kill somebody. I ain't going to have this shit on Main Street [where WJCT was then located]. I'll kill a nigger first." Another woman who did not get out of her car quickly enough for another police officer was dragged from it, arrested, and charged with disorderly conduct.[21]

Perhaps city councilwoman Sallye Mathis said it best. At the same hearing, she indicated that she had been watching to see if justice was being done. She added, you can't expect people to respect the law unless law enforcement officials respect them. The day is over, she said, when you can walk up to a black person and call him "nigger." Jacksonville's police might as well start to treat African Americans with respect. The alternative, she intimated, was continued violence.[22]

In an attempt to listen and respond to the concerns of the black youth, Mayor Tanzler met with more than one hundred African Americans at the Kennedy Center the week following the violence. Sheriff Carson did not attend but sent deputies. Carson's absence angered the audience. Tanzler listened to the demands of an increasingly hostile group, offered to meet further with a representative delegation, and promised action after conferring with his administration. This response provoked one person in the audience to claim that Tanzler was simply "jiving" them, that he was not sufficiently concerned with police brutality. Shouts followed, and the mayor, unwilling to put up with further disruptions, left. Anger had replaced dialogue, and everyone was the loser.[23]

The June riot began a long, hot summer in Jacksonville's African American community. Arnette Girardeau and the Black Community Coalition began collecting evidence of police harassment and brutality. That September, the coalition requested Florida's governor Reubin Askew to call for a grand jury investigation into police criminal action. Signed affidavits accompanied the request, supplying the following testimony: [24]

On June 17, Eugene Soloman, deacon in the Unity of Faith Spiritual Church, was participating in a religious service at his church. "Police officers in riot helmets and shot-guns drawn rushed in the door and bodily took me from the church," he wrote. After arresting him, police threw a tear gas container into the sanctuary, closed the door, and departed. [25]

On June 19, Brick Mason and the other residents of a rooming house were awakened at 3 A.M. by police firing tear gas into their building. Ordered to evacuate, they all were arrested on grounds of creating a disturbance by firing shots from the building. Subsequent investigations by the Black Community Coalition concluded that the shots were fired from the street near the house. (September 18, 1971, Askew Papers)

On June 24, about 9 P.M., Gloria Jean Leroy had gone to Bubba's Coffee Shop at Broad and Ashley Streets for dinner. There were about fifteen patrons inside when ten to fifteen police officers with shotguns and full riot gear rushed in, pointed their guns, hustled the patrons into waiting vehicles, and closed the restaurant. Ms. Leroy and others were arrested for creating a disturbance and taken to jail. En route, police stopped motorists and arrested them. At the time of the arrests, Ms. Leroy knew of no disturbances in the vicinity of the coffee shop. [26]

On August 8 at the city prison farm, an alleged sexual attack by an African American upon a white prisoner resulted in white prison guards beating up the alleged attacker. Subsequent interracial violence within the cell blocks led to guards stripping young black prisoners of their clothes and confining them in four-by-eight-foot metal isolation cells (popularly known as "the hole") where they existed six to nine persons per cell, unclothed, unable to stand upright, in intense heat, without adequate sanitation, and served only baby food for forty-four hours. [27]

On August 23, police officers came to the home of Mary Mitchell to arrest her son, Perry. An officer entered the house without knocking, pushed Perry out the back door onto the ground, and began hitting him. Mrs. Mitchell protested. One officer pulled his gun and warned her and another son to "get your asses back." The mother pleaded with the officer not to shoot her son. He replied "to get the hell back before I shoot you son of a bitches." The other son, holding his one-month-old nephew in his arms, was told, "Get the hell back or I will shoot you." Perry's crime apparently was to accompany a friend to the Atlantic Department Store on Golfair Boulevard, where the friend was caught shoplifting five dice. When the friend was arrested, Perry had said to the white security guard, "All you do is pick on black people." That led to the call to arrest Perry at home.[28]

On August 29, Andrew Perkins, proprietor of the Bubba Coffee Shop and a member of the Jacksonville Community Relations Commission, stepped outside his restaurant at 1:45 a.m. for a smoke after a hot night in the kitchen. A police car stopped and an officer asked Perkins if he wanted to go to jail. Perkins thought it was a joke. The officer warned him not to be there when he circled the block. Police were "sweeping" the area. Five minutes later, they returned and Perkins was still smoking and was arrested for vagrancy. Perkins asked how he could be a vagrant while standing outside his own business with $700 in his pocket. He showed the officer his American Express card and Jacksonville Community Relations Commission identification. The officer repeated he was under arrest and took him to jail. Perkins was sure there were no street disturbances in the area.[29]

On Labor Day, Bernard Stokes was arrested while leaving his mother's house to walk home. Police warned Stokes to get off the street because of a curfew. Another squad car arrived and these officers jumped Stokes, forced him against the hood of the car with a shotgun barrel to his neck, and began beating him. When Stokes's mother tried to intervene, she too was arrested. Another son, seeing his mother arrested, approached to ask what was the matter. Police struck him in the mouth with a gun barrel, knocked him down, and kicked him. Two daughters came forward pleading on behalf of the others, "but the officers pointed their guns at them and told them to get their asses back into the house." They turned and ran.[30]

On September 9, police stopped 59-year-old Isiah Jones, a deacon at the prestigious Bethel Baptist Institutional Church, for running a red light. When Jones proffered his driver's license, the officer "grabbed my hand just above my wrist and turned my arm behind my back . . . Then he handcuffed my hands behind my back." The contents of Jones's wallet—money, family photos, and credentials—spilled onto the street. Jones asked permission to pick them up and was refused. He was booked for "running a red light, disorderly conduct, creating a disturbance and resisting an arrest without violence."[31]

On September 9, about 2 A.M., Billy Dan Reeves was sitting in a bar with friends when police entered and began questioning him about a shooting on the street. He denied any knowledge, stood up, and left the premises to walk toward home. Two policemen arrested Reeves, grabbed him, and began kicking and choking him. When his brother protested that Reeves had already agreed to go to jail, the sergeant hit him with his club.[32]

On September 16, Rev. John Farmer, director of the Afro-American Cultural Development Center and member of the Jacksonville Community Relations Commission, was arrested for refusing to present his driver's license while sitting in a parked car. Farmer asked why the police officer wanted to see it and received no response. The officer ordered Farmer out of the car, grabbed his belt, and pulled "fiercely." Farmer told him to take his hands off him, "but he continued to manhandle me." Farmer was booked for "opposing and resisting a police officer in the performance of his duty."[33]

On September 17, four black youths were assisting an older white man who had been assaulted and robbed by another white. Two police officers arrived and stopped three of the young men, but the fourth continued chasing the thief. Without questioning anyone, one officer pulled his pistol, aimed, and fired at the black youth, nicking the collar of the youth's shirt. Before firing a second time, the white victim was able to tell the officer that the youth was not the thief but instead was helping the victim. The officer then turned to searching the three remaining youths. He was going to arrest them until another witness intervened.[34]

These eleven incidents and others, including several shootings, were reported to Governor Askew as being representative of "daily occurrences in the lives of black people" in Jacksonville. The Black Community Coalition had believed race relations between blacks and whites had been improving since passage of the Civil Rights Act of 1964. Yet within the past eighteen months, attitudes had hardened on both sides. The community had not yet become polarized, but "the emerging hatred between the police and the black community" could spread to general hostility between blacks and whites. The coalition asked for a grand jury investigation of the sheriff's department, with appropriate charges filed against criminal perpetrators. It also asked for an investigation of attitudes and practices of senior officers; for ongoing meaningful training programs in the area of race relations; and a commission to study the feasibility of putting the police department under the mayor as in most major American cities.[35]

Yet the affidavits were not the whole story. According to the *Jacksonville Journal*, one Labor Day "family squabble" turned into a full-scale riot requiring police intervention. Police were called to the house of Annette Lampkins, who was upset by her son's drunkenness and disrespect for family members and neighboring children. She hoped Thomas would be taken away to sleep and sober up. When Officer R. V. King arrived, he said he was attacked by the son wielding a butcher knife, and he called for backup. In subsequent affidavits, Lampkins' mother, sister, and neighbors all said that Lampkins did not attack King but that King pulled his gun and threatened him. With the arrival of the backup with lights flashing and sirens screaming, the situation escalated. A crowd gathered. Officer King subsequently claimed, "They were screaming, cursing and throwing rocks at us." Mrs. Lampkins remembered it differently. After the police arrested her son and dragged him to a patrol car, she heard the noise of a brick thrown at the departing police car. A neighbor reported that people in the street then began throwing bottles and bricks into the street. The remaining police dispersed the crowd, cordoned off the block, and began to spread tear gas.[36]

Subsequent editions of the paper reported additional violence in the black community: firebombs, gunshots, bricks, and bottles. Violence escalated in late September when a black shot and killed a police officer and wounded another. The next day another police officer was shot and wounded. In a speech at Florida Junior College in mid-September, Mayor Tanzler called the situation the most "frightening and serious problem facing Jacksonville and the nation today. . . . What do you do," he asked, "when there is a segment of the population that has felt oppressed and deprived for a long time?" Solutions of better education, housing, and jobs would take time.[37]

The grand jury that the Black Community Coalition called for met during the fall term of 1971 and issued its report the following April. Assisted by the office of the state's attorney, the grand jury "conducted an exhaustive investigation into each complaint," hearing testimony from nearly sixty witnesses including black community leaders, police officers, civic leaders, and the Community Relations Commission about twenty-five incidents of alleged harassment or brutality. It found the charges "basically unfounded" and not supported by competent evidence. Most incidents involved teenagers and occurred during times of civil disorders. It concluded that the Jacksonville sheriff's office acted "with proper restraint" in "hostile situations." Still the report did recommend improvements in the interest of better police-community relations, including:

- equal enforcement of the law without regard to race, creed, or color
- improved police training and communication between police officers and the black community
- more neighborhood beat officers
- review of guidelines to ensure respectful and courteous treatment of all citizens
- recruitment of more black police officers
- increased special training for police supervisors handling sensitive situations[38]

The grand jury absolved the sheriff's department of criminal misconduct, but in its recommendations it also acknowledged the Black Community Coalition's concerns about the increasing racial polarization taking place in Jacksonville.

Council of Leadership for Community Advancement

While the grand jury met to investigate the charges of police abuse of African Americans, city council member Sallye Mathis and UNF's Andrew Robinson went to see J. J. Daniel, the man who oversaw the successful effort at city-county consolidation. They asked him to convene a group of black and white civic leaders on race relations similar in stature to the group that had produced consolidation. As they and others like Arnette Girardeau saw it, conditions in the black community were reaching a critical point, and something had to be done to avert trouble.[39]

Daniel agreed, and on November 16, 1971, fifteen black and fifteen white community leaders met in a day-long session at Shiloh Metropolitan Baptist Church to hear reports developed by five NAACP task forces. Their leaders, Rodney Hurst, Alton Yates, Clanzel Brown, Jesse Nipper, and Girardeau spoke about the racial barriers confronting African Americans in education, employment, housing, the media, and the sheriff's department. Mayor Tanzler and Sheriff Carson both attended, as did Prime Osborne, president of the Seaboard Coast Line Railroad and president of the Chamber of Commerce, and Chamber president-elect John Buchanan, head of the Prudential Insurance Company's south-central home office. Out of the conference came five biracial task forces to examine the issues, under the overall supervision of Daniel and Robinson as cochairs. Subsequently the group adopted the name Council of Leadership for Community Advancement, or COLCA.[40]

COLCA committees took their assignments seriously, and over the next months, individual task forces met and made recommendations. The Education Committee under Rodney Hurst criticized recent school desegregation policies for closing eight inner-city black schools, institutions that were important to their respective communities. The committee reported that for black youngsters, desegregation meant abandoning neighborhood schools to bus across town for grades one through five and become minorities in predominantly white, presumably superior schools. (White students bused only for grades six and seven.) Black children understood that the burden of desegregation was primarily upon their young shoulders and that their own schools were presumed to be inferior.[41]

The Education Committee also recommended an affirmative action program to recruit black administrators who would serve as role models; creation of a multiethnic curriculum; mandatory in-service training for teachers and administrators working in desegregated schools; and creation of biracial teams to respond to racial incidents.[42]

The employment task force led by Prudential's Buchanan strongly recommended improved workforce preparation in the public schools, realistic federal and local training programs for unskilled workers, and career ladders in business with training to provide opportunities for new entrants into the workforce. Racial discrimination in hiring on construction jobs, at city hall, and elsewhere had to cease. City council should guarantee fair employment practices on all city contracts.[43]

The housing task force, led by Rev. A. Gene Parks, an urban minister of the United Methodist Church, recommended passage of a local fair housing law heretofore rejected by city council, strengthening minimum housing standards, expanding the supply of subsidized housing for lower-income people, and initiating neighborhood cleanup campaigns. It also urged securing the commitment of real estate sales people, housing managers, home builders, and developers to subscribe to nondiscriminatory open housing policies.[44]

Warren Schell's media task force acknowledged positive changes in the media over the preceding decade and recommended that media representatives be included in ongoing dialogues to continue improvement of coverage. Further, the task force recommended that newspeople meet with the summit leadership to identify problems in the media pertaining to race relations, with the goal of correcting them.[45]

The task force on law enforcement led by Rev. Rudolph McKissick withheld its report pending the release of the grand jury's report in April. Still, it noted ongoing incidents in police-black community relations that continued to provoke the African American community. It also discussed plans to increase police communications with black youth and ways to recruit more black police officers.[46]

COLCA's recommendations resulted in relatively few changes in Jacksonville's race relations during the 1970s. In 1971, seventeen years after

Brown v. Board of Education, the Duval County School Board under court order reluctantly implemented full desegregation of the public schools by busing African American youngsters across town to suburban white schools for grades one to five, established sixth and seventh grade centers in the inner city to bus white students, and made marginal changes in redistricting the area's high schools. The results pleased no one. Black parents objected to closing eight inner-city schools. They also had greater difficulty in getting across town to parent conferences and Parent-Teacher Association meetings. If they did not own a car, attendance was virtually impossible. Further, bused children were unable to take part in extracurricular activities. White parents of sixth and seventh graders were equally unhappy with their children's schools; a child between the ages of ten and fourteen attended four different school in four consecutive years. The discontinuity of that experience combined with the mediocrity of the sixth and seventh grade centers led many white parents to withdraw their children and send them to private or parochial schools. This massive busing to the elementary schools and to the sixth and seventh grade centers lasted until the 1990s, affecting the quality and morale of students, parents, and teachers in the system. A 1977 study of school desegregation by the Jacksonville Council on Citizen Involvement (later renamed Jacksonville Community Council, Inc., or JCCI) concluded that a gradual resegregation of the schools had taken place since the court order and that the sixth and seventh grade centers were educationally "unsound." Parent involvement had declined, and school discipline had become a major problem. The schools and county were not committed to providing a high-quality, racially integrated education.[47]

COLCA's second set of recommendations focused on minority employment opportunities, which also faced major barriers. A 1974 report by the Community Planning Council described them. Where Jacksonville's 121,152 African Americans comprised almost 23 percent of the population in 1970, a disproportionate 38.7 percent of households lived in poverty (compared to 12.8 percent of white households). Eighty percent of blacks worked on the bottom rungs of the economic ladder in unskilled or semiskilled jobs, not much changed from Jacksonville at the beginning of the twentieth century. Black median family income was only 53 percent of white family median income ($5,177 compared with $9,666). While Jacksonville had close to full employment in the early 1970s with only a 2 percent unemployment rate, 15 percent of the adult population was under-employed, and an estimated 37 percent of unskilled black laborers did not work.[48]

One approach to overcoming the racial discrepancies in the workforce emphasized educational and vocational training. The median school achievement for African Americans was 9.5 years (compared to 12.2 years for whites), and only 29 percent had high school diplomas (compared to 57 percent for whites). To prepare the next generation for employment, clearly the recently desegregated public school system had a major challenge. For the current generation of adults, vocational programs at the Florida State Employment Service, Florida Junior College, Jacksonville Opportunities Industrialization Center (JOIC), and Jacksonville Urban League existed but served only a small proportion of the need. A Chamber of Commerce study in 1973 led to the creation of the Jacksonville Vocational-Technical Authority to coordinate and expand community programs, but with limited results. Within city government, Mayor Tanzler formed a Manpower Area Planning Committee and a Minority Business Advisory Committee. He implemented a federally funded Jacksonville Youth Employment Program providing summer jobs for economically disadvantaged youth, and a Public Service Employment Program for individuals who had not worked for thirty days preceding application. Unfortunately, these efforts were curtailed during the Nixon administration in the switch from categorical funding grants for manpower training to general revenue sharing. Jacksonville's share in 1973 was cut by 31 percent, or $1,108,880.[49]

Job training, however limited, was only one approach to overcoming barriers to minority employment. Combating governmental and private-sector racial discrimination was another. The Community Planning Council study concluded that while progress had been made in the preceding five years toward more equal opportunity for all Jacksonville residents, the results were "not as significant as they might be." City council had passed an affirmative action plan in 1973 as required by federal law, but three years later city hall had barely begun to enforce it. First, the Jacksonville Community Relations Commission criticized its limitations, and then, more seriously, the federal Office of Revenue Sharing threatened to cut funding for the city based on the failure of the sheriff's office, fire department, and other city agencies to hire and promote minority and female applicants. This threat caught the mayor's attention, leading to the passage by city council in 1977 of a new and stronger affirmative action plan.[50]

Beyond affirmative action was the question of fair employment practices. During the early 1970s complaints to the Jacksonville Community Relations Commission about employment discrimination increased from 65 in 1970 to 911 in 1974. Efforts to obtain city council passage of a fair employment practices ordinance similar to legislation in Dade County, Orlando, Nashville, and Atlanta failed. The city's record in combating discrimination during the Tanzler years showed progress with the hiring of professionals like Alton Yates, Harold Gibson, Betty Holzendorf, and Hugh Wilson, but for blacks moving up through the ranks to supervisory positions in the city's civil service, progress was negligible. In the areas of affirmative action and employment discrimination, the Community Planning Council concluded, community leaders had "not made overcoming [racial] discrimination a priority issue."[51]

In the private sector, while COLCA had made a start toward tackling employment and other problems, interest in its efforts diminished by mid-1972, and the organization was subsequently dissolved. Meanwhile the Community Planning Council surveyed sixteen major Jacksonville employers and reported that only ten had affirmative action plans. Overall, it concluded, "the effort by many local employers has been minimal and ineffective." A decade after the civil rights movement, progress had been made in the job market, but equal opportunity for African Americans still remained a distant dream.[52]

The third area of concern for COLCA was housing. Again, poverty and discrimination were major problems. In its 1974 report, the Community Planning Council observed that in 1960, Jacksonville "was ranked as one of the most highly segregated of United States cities and there is substantial evidence from the 1970 census that present segregation is even greater." Further, a 1976 study reported 43,906 units of substandard housing in Jacksonville, housing characterized by the absence of full indoor plumbing or by being structurally unsafe. This number, roughly 20 percent of the total housing stock of the city, had increased from 24,664 substandard units in 1969. Most of these houses were in the urban core or near northwest side where an estimated 65 percent of all black families occupied 44.5 percent of all substandard homes. In many cases two or more families occupied the same overcrowded, substandard home. The other major occupants of substandard housing were elderly or handicapped residents. Public housing in one form or another served 10,532 Jacksonville residents, 75 percent of whom were African Americans. Its numbers fell far short of the 38,000 low-income residents who needed housing assistance.[53]

The Tanzler administration made a major commitment to improve housing conditions in Jacksonville, beginning with a series of studies to identify the size of the problems, and then with programs. During the 1970s, the city built eight public housing projects, four in predominantly black neighborhoods. Unfortunately, the Nixon administration froze federal funding for HUD-assisted housing in 1973 due to adverse economic conditions. Following passage of the Community Development Act of 1974, Jacksonville began a limited Housing Rehabilitation Loan Program. It targeted nine lower-income neighborhoods with a variety of grants and assistance programs. Clearly the Tanzler administration had good intentions, but in its dependency upon federal funding was limited by decisions made in Washington. Regarding efforts to obtain fair-housing legislation modeled after the 1968 federal law, the city failed to act. Some new private-sector apartments opened their doors to minority residents, but the larger housing market remained substantially segregated.[54]

The fourth area of concern for COLCA was police-community relations, an area that had been addressed by the Community Relations Commission in 1970, the grand jury in 1972, the National Conference of Christians and Jews in 1973, and the Community Planning Council in 1974, with little effect. In January 1972, a formal request to cut off federal funding for the Jacksonville sheriff's office had been submitted to the Law Enforcement Assistance Administration (LEAA) of the U.S. Department of Justice, alleging discriminatory actions against minorities.[55]

In March 1974, the Florida Advisory Committee to the United States Commission on Civil Rights came to Jacksonville to examine police-community relations. It learned the following:[56]

- Of 848 sworn police officers in 1974, 93 percent were white males, 2 percent were white females, 5 percent were black males, and none were black females, in a city whose population was 23 percent African American.

- The number of black officers reflected a decrease from 1969 when 6.4 percent of the sworn force were black males. Apparently the consolidated city's commitment to equal opportunity did not apply to the sheriff's office.
- Despite LEAA requirements that all law enforcement agencies have an affirmative action plan, the Jacksonville sheriff's office had not drafted or implemented one.
- Efforts to recruit African Americans had been made but were largely ineffectual and quite possibly discriminatory.
- Only five African Americans had reached supervisory positions, and the one black chief had no officers assigned to him. He headed the recently created Community Relations Division that dealt with neither public information nor public relations.
- Complaints about police abuse continued, and black community leaders were not exempt from mistreatment. Nathan Wilson, the white chair of the Jacksonville Community Relations Commission, reported that he had personally intervened on behalf of arrested black commission members at least four times in recent years.
- Complaints about police harassment or brutality were directed to the sheriff's internal investigation unit, which handled them in secrecy and did not let the complainant know the outcome. This procedure ran contrary to directions from the state attorney general to operate in the sunshine.
- Attorney (later U.S. District Court judge) Henry Adams reported that when police used excessive force, they frequently charged the arrested person with resisting arrest with violence, a felony carrying a possible five-year penalty. The arrested person then was informed that the charge of resisting arrest with violence would be dropped in return for dropping the complaint against the police officer.
- Although LEAA guidelines called for sixty hours of human relations training for recruits, Jacksonville provided twelve hours for recruits and no ongoing training for veteran officers.
- Black police officers were assigned to work only in the two predominantly black police zones of the city. No black officers patrolled in the predominantly white zones. Black officers were teamed with white officers, with the white officers being assigned the police cruisers that they

could take home and use for personal business while off duty. In effect, black officers were "a token minority force, virtually invisible to the middle class white community, getting second man slots even in the black community."[57]

The report concluded with the Florida Advisory Committee making a series of recommendations to recruit more women and minority officers, revamp civil service criteria for promotions, introduce human relations training for sworn officers, improve police-community relations, especially in minority communities, and open to the public internal investigations hearings for citizen complaints. Perhaps most important in light of the $3 million in federal grants Jacksonville had received under the Omnibus Crime Control and Safe Streets Act was the recommendation that LEAA "withhold further funds from the Office of the Sheriff until implementation of a bona fide affirmative action plan for hiring and promoting minorities and women is demonstrated."[58]

At the end of the Tanzler administration, the Jacksonville Urban League issued its annual report, *Status of Blacks in Jacksonville, 1979*. It described the black unemployment rate as twice that of whites. Affirmative action was "still resisted in both public and private sectors," though some progress had taken place in entry-level jobs. Decent and affordable housing had become even less accessible, in part because of the failure to fully replace demolished and dilapidated housing and in part because the inflationary cost of living of the decade had not been matched by increased wages. Seven years of school desegregation had led to a disproportionate number of African American children being suspended from school and a disproportionate number assigned to one form or another of special-education classes. The sheriff's office had made "a genuine commitment to equal opportunity by its key leaders," following the Florida Advisory Committee's report on police-community relations, but there were doubts about attitudes at the middle and lower ranks. The absence of any minority judges sitting locally was noted.[59]

In his introduction to the report, the Urban League's respected president, Clanzel Brown, focused on three significant concerns. First was that the threat of recession, inflation, and decreasing job opportunities was playing havoc with the black community at the start of 1979. Second was the serious problem of unemployment, especially among young African

Americans. Third was the lack of black participation at the policy-making level, either on private corporate boards or in the public sector, which precluded effective black involvement in the shaping of programs inclusive of the entire community.[60]

Clearly the progress of including African Americans into the larger Jacksonville community on an equitable basis was slow. Twelve years earlier, Mayor Tanzler had recognized the fundamental issue in the black community as decent jobs. It still was. Further, national forces affected local conditions negatively, particularly with the stagnant yet inflationary economy of the 1970s. Another part of the problem was raising the consciousness and overcoming policies of racial exclusion among white Jacksonville employers and managers in hiring and promoting African Americans to both entry-level and supervisory or policy-making positions.

Another part of the problem lay with the nature of the consolidated city. Power was still widely dispersed. The sheriff, responsible for police-community relations, was answerable to the voters, not the mayor. The school board, responsible for the desegregation plan and the quality of education, also answered to the voters, not the mayor. The Tanzler administration had made a priority of creating equal opportunities for all of Jacksonville's citizens, but it was not clear that the white majority supported the administration's efforts. Tanzler also successfully secured major federal dollars for urban renewal, subsidized housing, and manpower training. Funding, however, depended upon the policies of Congress and the Nixon-Ford administrations, and had declined during the stagflation years of the 1970s. The mayor might have offset federal cutbacks with increased local spending, but instead he took credit for reducing property tax rates, returning tax dollars to businesses and home owners that might have helped fund minority programs. As a result, the vision of equal opportunity for all Jacksonville residents remained unfulfilled.

CHAPTER 5

ECONOMIC OBSTACLES
AND COMMUNITY INITIATIVES

The decade of the 1970s provokes a variety of memories for Americans who lived through it. Perhaps most prominent was the cover-up of the Watergate burglary in 1972 that led to the resignation of President Richard Nixon two years later. The war in Vietnam finally ended, and the United States diplomatically recognized the People's Republic of China. Environmental causes enlisted substantial popular and governmental support, as did women's rights, with congressional passage of the Equal Rights Amendment in 1972. The latter, however, also provoked a backlash and never was ratified by a sufficient number of state legislatures. The nation celebrated its two-hundredth birthday in 1976 and agonized over the American hostages held in Tehran in 1979–80. Northern "Rust Belt" cities saw industry and jobs move south and overseas while in the southern and western regions, "Sun Belt" cities grew in population and prosperity. Perhaps most frustrating for cities and citizens alike during the decade were the higher rates of unemployment combined with increasing inflation that eroded paychecks. While motorists faced fuel shortages and escalating gasoline prices following the OPEC oil embargo in 1973, cities like Jacksonville confronted major fiscal problems. New York City teetered on the brink of bankruptcy in 1975, and Cleveland went over the brink three years later. Mid-decade, the nation experienced the worst recession since the Great Depression. Unemployment, which had been below 4 percent for much of the 1960s, climbed to 9 percent and stayed at 6 percent or above thereafter. The consumer price index, which rose less than 3 percent per year during most of the 1960s, climbed to 6 percent by 1973 and to more than 11 percent in 1974 and again in 1979. For American consumers, on average the cost of living more than doubled during the decade of the 1970s.[1]

The Tanzler administration and Jacksonville residents began to feel the inflationary impact early in the decade when the price of oil more than doubled even before the oil embargo. Attention focused on the Jacksonville Electric Authority (JEA), the city-owned electric utility. JEA paid the city each year about $20 million out of its gross revenues in lieu of taxes, for almost 25 percent of the city's budget. It also burned only imported oil to produce power. In 1971, the bid price on oil jumped from $1.90 to $3.96 a barrel at a time when the Nixon administration had ordered a freeze on domestic prices (including electric power) to slow inflation. Unable to pass along to consumers the price increase that cost JEA $16.5 million per year, the only alternative was to reduce payments to the city. Jacksonville faced the prospect of a major tax increase or reduced services resulting from these lower JEA payments. The mayor appealed for an exemption to the federal price freeze to pass on some of the increased cost of electricity to consumers. He also applied to the Florida Pollution Control Board to increase the sulfuric acid content allowable in purchased oil thereby reducing the price per barrel. The administration succeeded in both efforts, but the latter action displeased environmentalists, particularly as they had only recently succeeded in persuading JEA to buy cleaner oil. Still it was a lose-lose situation. If JEA held consumer rates down, it had to cut payments to the city. If it maintained payments to the city, the utility increased the cost of electricity for consumers. Either as taxpayers or consumers, or both, Jacksonville residents paid for the increased cost of oil.[2]

In the fall of 1973, American intervention in support of Israel in the fourth Arab-Israeli war prompted the Arab nations through OPEC to embargo oil shipments to the United States and Europe. Within ninety days the cost of oil purchased by JEA increased from $2.69 a barrel to more than $12. The cost of the nine million barrels imported each year to produce electric power jumped from $24 million to $108 million. This time increased costs were passed on to consumers: home owners, businesses, and city governments. JEA rates, once the lowest among Florida's major cities, became the highest. Within six months, rates doubled. For the 90,000 residents living at or below the poverty line, the increase in the cost of energy, said Mayor Tanzler, "made it extremely difficult for most, and almost impossible for many, to maintain an existence with the basic essentials of food, clothing, household items and shelter."[3]

Homeowners, renters, and businesses began to turn off lights, turn down thermostats in winter for heating, and turn up thermostats in summer for air conditioning. Their success in reducing the consumption of kilowatt hours only partially reduced their electric bills, but cumulatively, it cut JEA's revenues. The result was a $3.8 million reduction in its payments to the city. Meanwhile, at city hall the mayor also ordered thermostats lowered to 68 degrees Fahrenheit in winter and raised to 80 degrees for summer's air conditioning. He limited operating hours for heating or air conditioning at city hall, the courthouse, library, coliseum, and civic auditorium. Most exterior lighting was discontinued unless needed for safety reasons, and the mayor set a speed limit of fifty miles per hour for city vehicles. These conservation efforts cut energy consumption by 21 percent, but still the city's electric bill increased by $3 million in the following year.[4]

Again, however, it was a lose-lose situation. Mayor Tanzler said it well: "The impact of the reduction of JEA revenues, the reduction in its contribution to the City, coupled with the increase in the City's own electric bill, resulted in a twenty million dollar shortfall in the total city budget, and thus a drastic reduction in our programs."[5]

In his city budget for 1973–74, the mayor proposed meeting this deficit by diverting $9 million of federal revenue-sharing funds earmarked for water and sewer improvements; increasing property tax revenues of $7 million from reassessments and new construction; and, for the remainder of the needed funds, dipping into the city's "rainy day fund" reserved for emergencies.[6]

Six months later, in the city's annual report in January 1975, the mayor talked of JEA's "near bankruptcy . . . [and] cash flow problems." He converted city capital-improvement dollars to current operating costs and reduced governmental services. In his budget message in July, Tanzler spoke of a $10 million revenue gap due partly to inflation and partly to the need to meet enhanced federal environmental standards. The mayor proposed increasing water and sewer taxes to fund the latter. Further belt tightening included a hiring freeze on all but essential city employees, such as police or firefighters. Raising property taxes was not yet an option, although Jacksonville had the lowest property tax rate of any major city in Florida.[7]

Offshore Power Systems Comes to Jacksonville

The hard times resulting from the higher cost of electric power prompted the JEA, mayor, Chamber of Commerce, and others to look for alternative, possibly cheaper sources of energy. At about the same time, in August 1971, corporate representatives from Westinghouse Electric Company and Tenneco, Inc., came to Jacksonville to begin discussions about building platform-mounted nuclear-power plants that could be floated out to sea and anchored off the coast to provide another source of electricity. Westinghouse was at the time the nation's leading producer of nuclear reactors. Tenneco was the nation's largest shipbuilder, with its dry docks in Newport News, Virginia.[8]

The advantages to the proposed nuclear-power-plant platforms were several. First, they could be built in rapid assembly line construction. Further, each unit was identical and would not require time-consuming individual permits from the Atomic Energy Commission. Another advantage was savings in land costs since the plants would operate on platforms at sea, providing power by cable to land-based customers. By being located at sea, the plants' discharge of heated wastewaters would not negatively impact local lakes and streams. Discharges into vast currents of seawater, proponents claimed, would have no negative impact. In effect, Westinghouse-Tenneco believed it could construct quicker, cheaper, and safer plants to meet the burgeoning energy needs of the East Coast. Already New Jersey's Public Service Gas and Electric Company had become a prospective buyer of two plants. Westinghouse-Tenneco also believed floating nuclear-power plants would blunt environmental objections to land-based atomic-energy plants. At this time, there was little popular opposition based on environmental dangers as happened following the meltdown at Three Mile Island in 1979, or after the subsequent Chernobyl disaster in the Soviet Union.[9]

For Jacksonville officials, the advantages of building one or two nuclear-power plants per year at Blount Island in the middle of the St. Johns River between downtown and the Atlantic Ocean were clear. Westinghouse and Tenneco incorporated Offshore Power Systems (OPS) to build the plants.

OPS would invest $250 million in construction, employ 8,000–10,000 workers, pump $1.5 billion into the economy, and eventually pay $6.5 million per year in property taxes. It would become the largest employer in Jacksonville, employing 90 percent of its workers locally. It even promised to train hard-core unemployed residents for jobs in construction beginning in 1972. For the mayor, Chamber, JEA, and the media, the proposal looked like a winner.[10]

Opposition to the floating nuclear-power plant surfaced almost immediately. Nationally, the *Wall Street Journal* reported the concerns of an Environmental Protection Agency spokesperson about the impact of shipwrecks, hurricanes, tidal waves, and earthquakes at sea, warning that the utility would have to "demonstrate convincingly" that the thermal discharge would not damage marine life along the rich offshore areas. In response, OPS president Alexander P. "Zeke" Zechella claimed that "responsible" environmentalists agreed that the thermal discharge would not harm fish. Further, Zechella added, the nuclear generator on its 400-foot-square platform would be anchored behind massive concrete breakwaters "strong enough to hold back the roughest seas encountered in the past one hundred years." Still, the New Jersey Senate opposed purchasing two platforms to be sited three miles off the coast of Atlantic City, and the state assembly passed a bill barring any offshore development that would "severely alter or otherwise endanger the ecology."[11]

In Jacksonville, by contrast, the Chamber's Committee of 100 and the two daily newspapers strongly supported OPS. From March 1972, when the plans first publicly surfaced, to May when Westinghouse-Tenneco announced the decision to proceed, the two papers ran 146 stories, including 16 editorials plus full-page ads, building support for the project. Stories critical of or opposing it were buried or suppressed.[12]

A major problem was the condition of Blount Island, the proposed site for the new facility. In the center of the island lay a 250-acre saltwater marsh and estuarine bayou called Back River. It would have to be dredged and filled for construction of the nuclear-power plant. Earlier, in 1969, the Jacksonville Port Authority (JPA) had commissioned Robert Routa, senior staff biologist of the state's Department of Natural Resources, to study Blount Island. He found the bayou to be "exceptionally productive" for marine life and declared that it "should be preserved intact." A subsequent study by a Jacksonville University biologist agreed, concluding that "spoiling of the proposed areas (which included Back River) would be an eco-logical disaster." In April 1972, Routa reported that the proposed OPS project "will have massive adverse effects on the marine biological re-sources of Northeast Florida." He added that "an alternative site should be found for this industrial plant and Back River should be conserved so that it can continue to function as an important part of the St. Johns estuary."[13]

The *Florida Times-Union* challenged the report. It questioned the entire environmental value of Back River, citing a study done for JPA in 1971 by Battelle Memorial Institute of Columbus, Ohio, in preparation for indus-trial development of the island. The report concluded that the site was dy-ing from silt and its contribution to the area was important only on a short-term or limited scale. B. A. Christianson from the University of Flor-ida disagreed. He wrote Routa that the report of the river's "death" in ten to fifteen years referred only to its physical hydraulic system. The report made no reference to the river's ongoing ecosystem. In effect, the island would continue to play a critical role in the environmental health and productiv-ity of the area.[14]

The political process to secure authorization to dredge and fill the Back River began with Jacksonville's city council. Despite opposition from envi-ronmental groups locally, the city council endorsed the project unani-mously. The state's pollution control board followed suit on May 22. Fi-nally, Governor Askew and the state cabinet acting as the Trustees of the Internal Improvement Fund (TIIF) considered the proposal. TIIF's execu-tive director recommended delaying a decision, but in the face of charter-busloads of Jacksonville business and governmental leaders arriving in Tallahassee, the cabinet voted on May 23 for OPS to begin.[15]

With the escalation of oil prices following the embargo in 1973, OPS approached JEA about the purchase of floating nuclear-power plants for the city. OPS reasoned that future supplies and costs of imported oil were unpredictable and nuclear energy was an economical means to meet future energy demands for the region. JEA responded by signing a letter of intent on October 2, 1973, to purchase two power plants at a cost of $2.2 billion.[16]

That following spring, drafts of the proposed contract between JEA and OPS were referred to the city's general counsel for review. Harry Shorstein, recently appointed to that position by Mayor Tanzler, assigned six attor-neys from his office to review the contract. Their analysis found the pro-posed contract to be both deficient and inequitable, jeopardizing "the ability of the JEA to continue to operate the municipal electric system." Clearly, to them the contract was "contrary to public interest."[17]

The basis for this conclusion lay in a 69-page analysis in which the attorneys found:[18]

- The $2.2 billion figure for the power plants was an estimated cost and nowhere spelled out by item, line, or phase of construction. Further, there was no provision for an independent review of the proposed estimate for the total cost of the project.
- There was no independent financial analysis of the proposed revenue bond issue, despite its being "the largest amount of tax exempt debt offered for sale to finance any project in the history of the United States."
- There was no proposed completion date for the project or commitment by OPS to complete the plans by any specific time. Yet bonds were to be issued in advance of completion based on the assumption that nuclear-power revenues would fund them.
- The contract provided for monthly payments by JEA to OPS without any "relationship of payment to actual work performed." JEA could make 90 percent of payments while OPS had completed only 10 percent of the work. Further, there were no penalties for OPS if work was delayed, even if the delay was entirely its fault. Finally, there were no incentives for OPS to minimize costs.
- There was no provision for independent consulting engineers to determine the technical feasibility of building the nuclear-power plants.
- Cost overruns would be assessed to JEA, while cost savings would accrue only to OPS.
- If JEA breached the contract, it paid damages. If OPS did the same, it paid no damages.

The one-sidedness of the contract was obvious. Yet the consequences for JEA and the city were huge. If the $2.2 billion of revenue bonds were issued and the power plants were not completed on time (or at all), both the city and JEA were legally liable for the full amount. The potential liability exceeded the net worth of JEA and could end the utility's $25 million annual payments to the city at the expense of Jacksonville taxpayers.[19]

The general counsel's report blew the whistle on OPS. JEA's letter of intent expired in September. A few days later, New Jersey's Public Service Electric and Gas Company postponed its order. In February 1975, Tenneco sold its partnership to Westinghouse. OPS then unsuccessfully lobbied the Ford administration in Washington for federal support. In the end, no floating nuclear-power plants were built, and the nuclear-power option locally was replaced by JEA's decisions under subsequent management to build natural gas and coal-fired plants in the 1980s. Once again, JEA would become one of the best and cheapest producers of electric power in Florida.[20]

For Jacksonville, the OPS experience was a roller-coaster ride. Initially there was great enthusiasm that blocked any realistic appraisal of environmental or fiscal costs. After the events, a *Columbia Journalism Review* story strongly criticized Jacksonville's two local newspapers for their one-sided presentations. Its author suggested that it might be healthy "to maintain some skepticism or at least some show-me objectivity in the face of development as vast as the OPS project." The newspaper disagreed. J. J. Daniel, on the board of the holding company that owned the *Florida Times-Union,* replied, "I don't think the newspaper should have been critical or skeptical." George Wachendorf, then the paper's business editor, responded, "I did for Westinghouse-Tenneco what a good public relations firm should have done. Maybe I got carried away."[21]

Besides the newspaper's one-sidedness was the "old boy" network operating in behalf of OPS. Officials from the Seaboard Coast Line Railroad had introduced Westinghouse-Tenneco to JEA as a prospective business client. If successful, OPS would have provided increased business and revenues for the railroad. The railroad also owned the newspapers that strongly supported the project. The administrative vice president of Gulf Life Insurance Company was chairman of the JEA board. The group insurance plan for OPS employees would have gone to Gulf Life. Wesley Paxson was chairman of the JTA board. The board shifted priorities on bridge building in Jacksonville in order to construct the Dames Point Bridge providing greater access to Blount Island. The Paxson Electric Company became the major electrical contractor at the OPS site. The port authority guaranteed to buy back the Blount Island land sold to OPS if the project failed. It also offered to sponsor $180 million in industrial bonds for OPS at the lower rate of a public agency, saving OPS an estimated $158 million in loan costs. A JPA board member owned Florida Rock Industries, which received a $4 million contract to supply materials to OPS. None of these connections was illegal. Often the old-boy network worked to advance the economic interests of the city. In this case, however, the network accepted OPS proposals without adequate safeguards. Until Harry Shorstein and the general counsel's office became involved, no one represented the public interest for the JEA, the city, or, ultimately, the Jacksonville taxpayers.[22]

The last years of the Tanzler administration were difficult ones financially. The city's economy did not rebound after the mid-decade recession like the rest of Florida, where increased tourism and an influx of newcomers buying homes stimulated the state's economy. For Jacksonville, unemployment, though less than the national average, continued to be high relative to the early years of the decade. Population growth, which averaged better than 3 percent in 1973 and 1974, slowed the next year and averaged less than 1 percent per year for the rest of the decade. Overall, Jacksonville's population grew 8 percent during the 1970s compared with 11 percent nationwide and 43 percent in Florida. When the University of North Florida opened in rural southeast Jacksonville–Duval County in 1972, the expectation was for rapid residential and commercial growth nearby. That growth did not occur until well into the 1980s.[23]

For the mayor, slower growth meant tighter city budgets and a property tax increase in 1977, the only one in his eleven years as mayor. It also meant a temporary end to city-financed capital improvements. Fortunately, federal dollars picked up some of the slack, funding a senior citizen center, a regional sewage treatment plant, a branch library on the west side, and a shipping terminal on Blount Island. As a fiscal conservative, Tanzler was firm in his commitment to maintain low property taxes and proud that Jacksonville had the lowest tax rate among the thirty largest cities in the nation. He saw low property taxes as protection for fixed-income home owners, many of whom were retired and already threatened by inflation and high utility rates. He also saw low property taxes as an attraction for recruiting new businesses to the city to create a larger tax base for future growth. Less was said about the advantages of low taxes for larger existing businesses and wealthier home owners. Tanzler acknowledged delays in funding capital improvements and building or expanding infrastructure. He recognized that Jacksonville had fewer police per capita than the national average and less parkland. But he hoped federal dollars combined with new growth eventually would meet the needs. The growth, however, was limited in the late 1970s. The federal government exasperated Tanzler in its formulas for federal revenue sharing in which cities with lower tax rates were penalized. The federal formula assumed that lower-taxed communities could make more of an effort in their own behalf. In response, Tanzler argued that the formula rewarded inefficiency and waste. Cities that economized, improved efficiencies, and provided less expensive services were unfairly penalized. Not surprisingly, it was an argument that the mayor could not win.[24]

While city government struggled to maintain the momentum of consolidation, the private sector, which had begun the effort, continued to mobilize citizen participation to develop programs and priorities for the bold new city. An early initiative led to the creation of an independent Community Planning Council in 1968. Under the leadership of David Hicks, Lois Graessle, James P. Smith Jr., and others, it recruited volunteers, studied issues, and published in 1974 a fifteen-volume report on goals and priorities for Jacksonville. The report made multiple recommendations on fifteen community issues. They included: [25]

- Environmental protections for safe water, pure air, and clean streets
- Health care for all citizens
- Decent jobs for everyone
- Learning opportunities for all
- Financial aid available to people in need
- Preservation and strengthening of families
- Adequate public and private resources to meet community needs
- Affordable and decent housing
- Community appreciation of the arts
- Consumer education
- A community where all have a sense of direction and peace of mind
- Safe streets
- Rehabilitation of offenders and reform of the correctional system
- Speedy justice in the criminal justice system
- Prevention of juvenile crime

Parallel with the Community Planning Council's efforts, the Chamber of Commerce began to broaden its focus beyond business growth and development to include emphasis upon "upgrading the quality of life in the total community." To that end, president-elect Fred Schultz organized a three-day Jacksonville Community Planning Conference in June 1974 at Amelia Island Plantation. Conference planners invited a cross section of one hundred community leaders (ninety-one attended) to discuss goals and priorities for the city. They included representatives from business and organized labor, government and the private sector, minorities, and women's groups. Keynote speakers included James Rouse, creator of planned cities and downtown magnets, and Wilbur Thompson, a leading urban economist. Rouse applauded conference participants for their concern about urban issues, noting that people usually came together for such a conference only in a crisis situation. He urged careful management of future growth. Thompson foresaw the abandonment of downtown in the shift of retail trade to suburban shopping centers and urged the development of policies to reclaim the core city. The delegates split into working groups that examined issues of government, the economy, physical development, human enrichment, and human needs. Out of three days of dialogue came ten priorities for Jacksonville:[26]

1. Downtown development
2. Educational excellence
3. An open and affordable housing supply
4. Land use planning
5. Mass transportation
6. Adequate public utilities (water, sewers, electric power, etc.)
7. Job opportunities
8. Adequate public revenues
9. Joint efforts to improve race relations
10. Cultural enrichment

The similarities between the Community Planning Council goals and the Community Planning Conference priorities were remarkable. Variations on both lists would surface and resurface in consolidated Jacksonville over the succeeding decades whenever concerned citizens came together to identify goals and priorities for their city.

Planning for Downtown Development

The number one priority for the city as defined by the Amelia Island community planning conference was downtown development. The conferees concluded that the downtown was "a vital part of the community." They recommended "a substantial increase in scale and scope" of existing plans and "increased public and private sector involvement" to achieve cultural enrichment, aesthetic qualities, increased hotel and convention trade, day and night activities, housing, education, business expansion, and a "workable transportation system."[27]

The Tanzler administration and Downtown Development Authority already had ambitious plans underway for urban renewal and city center revitalization. In the aftermath of the Amelia Island conference, they hired as new consultants Hammer, Sikes, George Associates from Washington, D.C., to prepare additional plans for downtown transportation and redevelopment. In his report to the community in January 1976, consultant Philip Hammer assured his listeners that his firm built on the efforts of prior plans using local, state, federal, and private-sector input. His was not a utopian vision, he said, but a workable plan.[28]

Hammer recognized the considerable renewal activity, both public and private, going on downtown. Yet for each new Independent Life or Blackstone building, there were abandoned buildings downtown or simply land cleared for parking lots. Unoccupied, older buildings blighted entire blocks. The resulting islands of development in downtown in effect were offset by nearby decay. Further, on the fringes of downtown were poor neighborhoods also with deteriorating shops and housing stock. Even the urban renewal project along Hogan's Creek was only partially rebuilt with stretches of open, unoccupied land. To create or recreate an entire downtown was more dream than possibility. Reality was a step-by-step process of renewal that seemingly took almost as many steps backward as forward.[29]

Further, Hammer was concerned about the dispersal of people and institutions downtown. A key factor in maintaining economic viability for retail trade was access. In the past, when downtown was more compact, employees in the old city hall built after the Great Fire of 1901 could walk a few blocks to the major department stores. Shopping during lunch hour and after work was readily accessible. As the governmental center moved further east and the new railroad headquarters was located on the west side of downtown, and hotels, insurance companies, and a hospital were built across the river on the south bank, the department and specialty stores became increasingly inaccessible. Employees postponed their shopping until evenings and weekends at the strip and shopping malls nearer home.

Downtown retail stores and restaurants suffered and many eventually closed.[30]

Meanwhile, suburban commuters faced problems driving to work in the city. As downtown grew and businesses expanded, more workers in more vehicles created more congestion, more demand for parking, and more air pollution. Transportation to and within downtown presented major problems for the city. But transportation problems were but part of the larger issues of urban dispersion and sprawl. People lived in suburbs and commuted downtown, clogging highways. Within downtown, government, retail, and private-sector offices were spread out, with no central core where people could work, shop, or eat. Hammer proposed five major projects to confront this dispersion.[31]

The most dramatic proposal was an elevated people mover system with stations every two or three blocks that could integrate the dispersed areas of downtown, providing access from offices to shops and services. It also would eliminate some of the traffic congestion, parking lots, and air pollution. The proposal built upon a series of studies done under the auspices of the Jacksonville Urban Area Transportation Systems (JUATS) funded by city, state, and federal governments. The people mover would carry commuters parking on the fringes of downtown and transport them quickly to their workplace or other destinations. It would facilitate transportation within downtown from the west side to the north side or across the river to the south side. It could spur a new phase of retail shopping as the downtown customer base expanded with the growth of businesses. Hammer saw the people mover as the most important priority in reintegrating downtown and stimulating retail growth. He also saw funding available from the federal government.[32]

Hammer's second major proposal focused on "gateways" to downtown, which currently ran through some of the most blighted areas of the city, especially along State and Union Streets north and west of downtown. This was the entrance used by visiting dignitaries and business travelers arriving from the airport. Hammer proposed removing the blight and creating boulevards with open, green space between two one-way thoroughfares. A parallel concern was creating a north-south boulevard along Jefferson Street bordering on the western edge of downtown, connecting downtown to Riverside and Avondale.[33]

Hammer called his third proposal a "new high activity center," and it followed the 1971 RTKL plan (see ch. 3) for downtown to develop the riverfront for commercial and entertainment purposes between the civic auditorium and the Main Street Bridge. He also foresaw a major hotel and convention center nearby. Linking the riverfront center with the retail center four and five blocks north, Hammer next envisioned, as his fourth proposal, upper-level pedestrian walkways similar to those in Cincinnati and St. Paul, where shoppers had access to two levels of retail shops and studios. Pedestrian bridges would cross streets, and the entire area would become an in-town shopping center to compete with the malls in the suburbs.[34]

Finally, Hammer saw the importance of what he called "market rate housing" to encourage business and professional people to live downtown. His proposed site on the western edge of downtown in LaVilla called for the city to buy, landscape, and land bank twenty-two blocks along Jefferson, Union, and State Streets, making them available for private developers to build up to 500 units of middle-income townhouses and condominiums.[35]

For Hammer, the key to revitalizing downtown was the people mover. If 10 percent of the 60,000 people working downtown each day stayed after work to shop and dine, downtown would flourish. A flourishing downtown would attract the convention trade and new business investment, which in turn would stimulate more activity. It was an optimistic and costly vision. Hammer saw federal funds as key to mobilizing a public-private partnership starting with the people mover mass-transit project. Given slower growth and limits to federal funding, however, implementation of these ambitious plans lay substantially into the future.

Meanwhile Mayor Tanzler's term of office drew to a close. He resigned the mayoralty in early 1979 to run unsuccessfully for governor. In his almost twelve years as mayor, and in the ten-plus years since consolidation, the face of Jacksonville had changed dramatically. Urban renewal downtown had meant a sparkling, cleaner St. Johns River and slums cleared and replaced by low-income and senior-citizen housing, a community college, and a public-health facility. City council had endorsed plans for the renovation of downtown's Hemming Park into a plaza, a new lease for the PBS station in what would become Metropolitan Park, a new police station, and the downtown people mover. The private sector added the signature thirty-eight-story Independent Life tower (subsequently sold to Modis),

Atlantic National Bank, Florida Blue Cross and Blue Shield home office, Blackstone Building, and 3,600-seat First Baptist Church, and plans for a new hotel on the south bank of the river. Despite the recession, downtown property assessments more than doubled between 1972 and 1978, from $231 to $500 million. At the beach, there was the magnificent new Hanna Park. In city government there were more police and firefighters, lower crime and fire insurance rates, a world-class ambulance service, streetlights increasing the safety of thoroughfares, and special neighborhood programs serving lower-income residents. Particularly significant were the standards of professionalism that characterized the consolidated city government in the chief administrative officer and many department heads.[36]

Beyond city hall, other changes were taking place to improve the quality of life in the consolidated city during the 1970s. In public education, schools were desegregated and reaccredited. Kindergartens were introduced, special-education programs were expanded for gifted and handicapped children, and an increasing number of high school graduates attended college. In higher education, Edward Waters College achieved professional accreditation, Jacksonville University opened a business college, Florida Junior College completed its fourth campus, and the University of North Florida opened its doors, enabling Jacksonville to lose the stigma of being the largest city in the nation without a state university.[37]

In the private sector, the Children's Museum became the Museum of Arts and Sciences (and later the Museum of Science and History); the Jacksonville Art Museum added its Koger wing; the Florida Ballet began public performances; the Jacksonville Symphony recovered from near dissolution in the 1960s, playing at Washington's Kennedy Center and New York's Carnegie Hall; and the Cummer Gallery expanded its offerings. The introduction of noncommercial public radio, WJCT-FM, in 1972 offered an alternative to commercial stations. Dr. Wayne Wood, a local optometrist, sparked the organization of Riverside Avondale Preservation in an older neighborhood concerned about encroaching commercialism and the preservation of traditional housing and urban lifestyle. His efforts were replicated by other neighborhood activists in Springfield, San Marco, and San Jose Estates seeking to enhance their quality of urban life.[38]

Another new beginning was the formation of the Jacksonville Women's Movement (JWM) in 1970. Under the leadership of Vicki Wengrove, JWM began with consciousness raising, moved on to lobbying of Mayor Tanzler to appoint more women to public boards, secured the formation of the Mayor's Advisory Commission on the Status of Women, established self-help clinics to offer abortion counseling—which led to opening the Women's Rape Crisis Center—and, in 1976, opened Hubbard House for battered women, the first such facility in the southeastern United States.[39]

Also during this decade the Jacksonville Council on Citizen Involvement, later renamed Jacksonville Community Council, Inc., or JCCI, was created. It emerged as a result of the three-day Jacksonville Community Planning Conference in June 1974 at Amelia Island. That fall, conference leader Fred Schultz, Jim Rinaman, J. J. Daniel, and others created JCCI as a citizens think tank to study community problems and make recommendations. Subsequently JCCI expanded its role to pursue implementation of study recommendations, with some notable results.[40]

In many ways the first decade of consolidation brought substantial progress in the governance, shape, and character of Jacksonville–Duval County. At the same time, almost as many problems remained as before. The cleanup of the St. Johns River was impressive, but many of its tributaries remained heavily polluted. Landfills were opened, but indiscriminate littering of wastes continued. Polluting power plants and fertilizer factories closed, but other odors remained. African Americans had a greater stake in local government and community, but racism and discrimination persisted in many forms. Downtown plans were ambitious, but most of the plans remained for future implementation. Of major concern was the economy. In a growth mode at the beginning of the decade, it had supported much of the positive change, but at the end of the decade the economy showed stagnation on both local and national levels. The new mayor taking office in January 1979 faced major challenges in providing adequate services, building and rebuilding the physical plant, and enhancing the quality of life for the residents of consolidated Jacksonville.

CHAPTER 6

THE GODBOLD YEARS

When Hans Tanzler resigned the mayoral office on January 1, 1979, to run unsuccessfully for governor, his successor as mayor was president of the Jacksonville City Council, Jake M. Godbold. The new mayor contrasted sharply with his predecessor. Where Tanzler was tall, athletic, polished, and patrician in manner, Godbold was a "good ole boy," short and stocky, with only a high school diploma and a tendency to speak ungrammatically, which troubled more sophisticated voters. He was born on the blue-collar north side of the city; his family lived for a time in public housing in the 1940s. The new mayor graduated from Andrew Jackson High School and worked as a collection agent for Independent Life Insurance Company. Later he established his own industrial chemical and janitorial supply business, Gateway Chemical Company. Outgoing and friendly, Godbold began his political career when elected president of the Jacksonville Jaycees. In 1967, he ran for and won a city council seat in the last election before consolidation. That fall he was elected as an at-large member to the newly consolidated city council and served twice as its president before becoming mayor.[1]

In the May 1979 citywide mayoral election, Goldbold faced opposition from business interests who doubted this good ole boy had the sophistication to work successfully with business and governmental leaders in Tallahassee and Washington. Godbold, however, put together a coalition of blue-collar white and African American voters, and won. Once elected, Godbold reached out to Chamber of Commerce officials, expanded his base of support, and built a government-business coalition that worked well together for most of his eight years in office.[2]

The issues Godbold faced as mayor carried over from the Tanzler years. Downtown development plans remained largely on paper with little recent public or private construction. Environmentally, the St. Johns River flowed more clearly, but the U.S. Environmental Protection Agency was threatening to fine the city over conditions at the aging Buckman Sewage Treatment Plant. In race relations, although Godbold appointed the first African American to head a city department and named numerous blacks to independent authorities and boards, the local NAACP branch charged the city with not implementing the affirmative action plan passed by city council two years earlier.[3]

Tight city budgets combined with reduced state and federal funding explained part of the mayor's problems. In a speech to Downtown Rotary in April 1979, Godbold hinted at future tax increases. "It's been nice to tell people throughout the nation the past few years that we've got the lowest tax rate in the nation," he said in a direct dig at his predecessor. "But our city has paid a heck of a price for it. We've stood still in areas that can't afford to sit [sic] still any longer. It's time to move forward."[4]

Evidence of the city's "standing still" was mixed. The first years of consolidation had resulted in substantial progress in environmental cleanup and downtown urban renewal. At the same time, the economic slowdown from the oil embargo affected both public and private sectors, locally and nationally, resulting in cutbacks in capital programs and city services. These cutbacks continued into Godbold's first term as the nation faced increased inflationary pressures during the Iranian hostage crisis at the end of the 1970s, and a deep recession during the early years of President Reagan's first administration. The result was a ten-year lull in new initiatives in downtown development from the early 1970s to the early 1980s.[5]

Early in Godbold's first term, the EPA called attention to the problems of the aging Buckman Sewage Treatment Plant. Built in the 1950s to handle residential wastes, it now was overwhelmed with untreated industrial wastes, particularly from the Anheuser-Busch brewery. The facility was understaffed, inadequately maintained, and subject to frequent breakdowns. Neighborhood odors were noxious. Funding to fix its problems on a twenty-year plan called for spending $80 million per year. The city spent

Fig. 12. Jake M. Godbold, mayor of Jacksonville, 1979–1987. By permission of the City of Jacksonville.

$30 million. Further, aging sewer lines across the city were not being rebuilt as fast as they collapsed.[6]

Downtown, Godbold criticized the city's past failure to maintain the civic auditorium, coliseum, Gator Bowl, and minor league baseball stadium, charging that the city acted like a slumlord. Public housing lacked adequate maintenance dollars from both the federal government and the city. Parks and recreational funding, already low by national standards, fell further behind in the 1970s. In January 1981, the U.S. District Court held city officials in contempt for violating a court order to end overcrowding in the city jail. In Washington, the Reagan administration cut back the Comprehensive Employee Training Act (CETA) program, eliminating 1,277 jobs locally. Pressures on city hall to find replacements for firefighters, police officers, recreational workers, and other city employees increased. It almost seemed that after more than a decade of consolidation not much progress had occurred, until it was pointed out that the city had spent those years catching up from the shortcomings of the preconsolidation era.[7]

Complicating the issues was a city council more fractious than in the early years of consolidation. It rejected Godbold's $66 million bond program for capital improvements and recreation (though later passing a program one-third the size). Council members rejected new public housing to be sited in their districts, prompting the regional HUD office to cancel a $12 million grant for new construction. Council further let authorization for the Downtown Development Authority lapse, in part because of political disputes with its director. It repeatedly made the capable director of the city's Environmental Protection Board a scapegoat, until he resigned.[8]

The new administration appeared divided and ineffectual. Efforts to implement affirmative action hiring initiated by the mayor met with foot dragging by department heads. At first, the mayor did not respond to NAACP criticism. Then, when he encouraged enforcement, counterpressures by subordinates led to the resignation of his affirmative action officer. Further regulatory efforts slackened. The city had the weakest pollution laws and environmental regulations in the state. Despite a two-mill tax increase in 1980, budgetary restraints led to a reduction in the number of housing inspectors checking conditions of inner-city housing. Polls showed the mayor's popularity in decline. Elected by 56 percent of the voters, his approval rating sank to 44 percent after his first year and to 23 percent by early 1982.[9]

The mayor, however, fought back. Unable to produce immediate concrete results downtown or elsewhere, he turned to Mike Tolbert, his "division chief for fun and games," to organize community celebrations to bring people together and boost morale. The first celebration on the riverfront downtown featured water-skiers, skydivers, navy jets screaming overhead, the Jacksonville Symphony, and fireworks. Another filled the Gator Bowl with 55,000 fans in an attempt to woo the Baltimore Colts to Jacksonville. It failed, but Jacksonville did secure and support a United States Football League franchise in 1984 and the National Football League Jaguars a decade later. Godbold later claimed that "Colt fever was the start of the city believing in itself." More successful was the Mayport Jazz Festival, first staged in October 1980. It subsequently achieved national and international acclaim, moving from the tiny fishing village of Mayport to Metropolitan Park on the river.[10]

In addition, in 1979 Godbold, city officials, and Chamber of Commerce leaders began visiting other U.S. cities to learn how they made progress in downtown development. They started with Baltimore, which at the time had achieved national recognition for its Inner Harbor and Charles Center renewal. Subsequently, Jacksonville officials visited Minneapolis in 1980 to learn about its public-private partnerships and San Antonio in 1981 to see its river walk with nearby tourist attractions and cultural amenities. After each trip the mayor invariably and enthusiastically became an advocate of similar projects for Jacksonville.[11]

Godbold also worked behind the scene, allaying fears about his inability to work with state and federal officials and corporate leaders. He persuaded the EPA to accept a compromise solution to the Buckman Sewage Treatment Plant problems; encouraged Anheuser-Busch to restructure its waste treatment programs to reduce pressures at Buckman; and worked out a compromise with federal HUD officials to locate scatter site public housing on the fringes of downtown. Further, he invited Albert Ernest, president of the Chamber of Commerce, to join together in a public-private partnership to advance downtown and economic development for the city.[12]

Downtown Development Takes Shape

The public-private partnership was crucial for downtown development. Traditional urban renewal programs, such as Hogan's Creek, where land had been cleared for private development that did not take place, were replaced by tax increments. These were incentives to promote private investment. Cities built or rebuilt infrastructure (roads, sewers, even parking garages) to attract businesses, using bonds funded by the increased tax dollars anticipated from the new development. The Downtown Development Authority (DDA) secured tax increment authority for both the north and south banks of the St. Johns River as first steps toward redeveloping both areas.[13]

The city's major private partner in downtown development was Central Jacksonville, Inc. (CJI), an offshoot of the Chamber comprising twenty executives under the leadership of Ernest, a banker. CJI worked closely with the DDA to develop a three-phase, $250 million program on the north bank to include a new Southern Bell office tower, hotel, and convention center across the street from the civic auditorium and a festival marketplace along the river from the civic auditorium to the Main Street Bridge. These plans replaced the downtown proposals of the 1970s. Earlier efforts had focused on developing northward away from the river to the shopping district around Hemming Park. The new plans, resulting in part from the visit to San Antonio, paralleled the riverfront.[14]

The south-bank proposal also focused on riverfront development extending from an expanded Baptist Medical Center east to a new Prudential regional home office, an expanded Museum of Science and History, restaurants, hotel, offices, and shops at St. Johns Place, and twin office buildings at duPont Center. The capstone was a 1.2-mile river walk completed in 1985, extending from the hospital to St. Johns Place, opening the waterfront for the first time to residents and visitors to stroll or jog its length. While the river walk was initially popular, the downtown spotlight subsequently shifted across the river to the Jacksonville Landing, upon its completion in 1987. Publicized as a major tool for economic expansion, the south-bank river walk did not live up to expectations. Shops and cafes did not flourish as promised, until almost a decade later. Plans for riverfront housing did not materialize. By the end of the decade, despite the river walk, two south-bank hotels had lost their national corporate affiliation, and Gulf Life Insurance Company had been sold, with the new owners planning to move the firm from Jacksonville. Tax increments had worked for Prudential but clearly were not a panacea for downtown development.[15]

The north-bank plan was more successful, though it did not proceed smoothly, either. Original DDA and CJI plans in early 1980 called for a hotel/convention center to be located across the street from the civic auditorium (which also had exhibition and conference space) in the site recently vacated by the closure of Sears Roebuck. At about the same time, however, historic preservationists discovered the beauties of the old, no-longer-functioning Union Railroad terminal with its handsome neoclassical facade, located on the western fringes of downtown. The preservationists cleaned up the old building and staged popular one-night festivals. Then a business group led by developer Steve Wilson bought the facility and proposed locating the convention center there.[16]

This proposal split advocates for downtown development. The Downtown Merchants Association opposed moving the convention center away from the proposed core city site. They saw the center as a catalyst for revitalizing the central business district with new restaurants, shops, galleries, and hotels. In contrast, the distant terminal site would stand alone and fragment the efforts of those seeking maximum impact for downtown. The Jacksonville chapter of the American Institute of Architects also supported the core city site. Locating the convention center across from the civic auditorium close to the river would enhance the area. It would concentrate conventioneers, shoppers, tourists, workers, and residents downtown, consistent with earlier plans, maximizing the economic, cultural, and aesthetic impact. Developer Preston Haskell, primary backer of the reopened but still money-losing Holiday Inn City Center (the former Robert Meyer Hotel) also agreed, as did Robert Cockayne, manager of May Cohens, downtown's largest department store, and a member of the DDA.[17]

In contrast, the Jacksonville Historic Landmarks Commission recommended the terminal site not only for its historical and aesthetic value but also because commission members felt there was inadequate space for parking at the proposed core city site. They saw downtown expanding toward the old station. In addition, the old terminal had greater access to the two interstate highways entering Jacksonville.[18]

Normally a historic landmarks commission would be no match for the downtown business leaders, but in this case converting the train station had the support of Wilson, the developer, and half a dozen of the city's major contractors, who had made large contributions to political campaigns. Mayor Godbold sided with them, as did Joe Forshee, president of city council. Godbold liked the historic landmark as a convention center, he said, for "sentimental reasons." He also saw the importance of developing the western fringe of downtown. The DDA and CJI wavered. They had favored the core city site, but four of the seven authority members shifted to support the terminal site. The DDA's executive director, Herb Underwood, attempted to negotiate a compromise with the terminal backers to gain their and the mayor's commitment for the rest of the DDA's downtown agenda, which included renovating the old Florida Theatre, creating a new riverfront Metropolitan Park, and building hotels, marinas, and a festival retail center.[19]

At this point, city council members became restive. They saw the DDA undermining their right as elected officials to make the final decisions about downtown development. The mayor tried to mediate with proposals to build transportation links from the terminal to downtown and a hotel to be located near the restored convention center. In June 1982, council voted to approve the terminal site. Subsequently, half the DDA members resigned in protest against the politicization of the decision. Haskell closed his money-losing hotel and Cockayne began considering the closure of his department store facing Hemming Park. Other downtown department stores and clothiers soon followed suit.[20]

Despite these setbacks, downtown development proceeded, becoming the foremost achievement of Godbold's mayoralty. Developer Steve Wilson brought representatives from the Rouse Company of Columbia, Maryland, to discuss the festival marketplace. Rouse had built the highly successful Quincy Market in Boston and played an instrumental role in Baltimore's Charles Center and Inner Harbor. He had never built in a city of less than one million people, but with the right incentives he was willing to try. The city agreed to cover nearly half the cost of the $43 million project with $10 million of infrastructure improvements, a $10 million second mortgage, and a commitment to build a parking garage. The city also rented the site to Rouse for $100,000 per year and waived the rent for the first five years. Critics said the Jacksonville Landing was overpriced and city subsidies excessive. For Godbold, its opening in June 1987 was the capstone of his downtown efforts that also included the convention center, Florida Theatre restoration, Metropolitan Park, and south-bank river walk.[21]

Godbold's reelection in 1983 by an overwhelming majority accompanied the turnaround in Jacksonville's fortunes downtown. At his inaugural in July, the mayor spoke of the "new spirit of cooperation in the community." Folks no longer were negative about the city but had become "a community of believers." Earlier the United States Conference of Mayors had voted Jacksonville honorable mention as one of eight of the nation's most livable cities. Events of the following months seemed to confirm their decision. That August, city council selected Rouse to build the festival market that became the Jacksonville Landing. President Reagan signed legislation to finance the downtown Automatic Skyway Express. In October, the restored Florida Theatre (built in the 1920s) reopened to a full house, and the jazz festival moved downtown, inaugurating the new Metropolitan Park on the river. Then in November, city council authorized the purchase of the terminal site for the new convention center. When completed, it hosted the world-famous Egyptian Ramses II exhibit. Meanwhile, the Enterprise Center on the old Sears site was built, housing a new Florida National Bank building (later First Union) and Omni Hotel. The mayor liked to call the 1980s "the billion dollar decade" for downtown development, and, clearly, the skyline showed the effects.[22]

Not all of the changes were downtown. The medical community began a major transformation during the decade. Sparked by Winn-Dixie's Davis Brothers donation of the site, the Mayo Clinic established a satellite operation in Jacksonville and began to play a major role in the city's and region's health care. St. Luke's Hospital built a new south-side facility subsequently purchased by Mayo. On the north side of downtown, the University of Florida Medical School established its urban campus at Jacksonville's University Hospital and eventually bought both it and Methodist Medical Center to become Shands Jacksonville. Meanwhile, Baptist Medical Center and St. Vincent's Medical Center expanded their facilities. These changes heralded the beginning of Jacksonville as a regional medical center.[23]

Another sign of the city's turnaround during the Godbold years was consideration of Jacksonville in 1984 for a second All-America City award by the National Municipal League. Jacksonville had first won that coveted award in 1969 for its successful consolidation of city and county. This time, a delegation of fifty civic leaders flew to Baltimore to make the case based on the success of the public-private partnership in downtown/economic development, support for accreditation of the predominantly black Edward Waters College, successful public school accreditation, and the renovation of the historic Florida Theatre.[24]

The quest failed. Jacksonville received only honorable mention. Two reasons stood out: the lack of growth management and problems with odor pollution. "If Jacksonville were to be judged solely on economic development, it would have made the top ten," reported an official from the National Municipal League. "But we all feel that some of the [city's] leadership has a myopic view of development," a go-for-broke attitude that refused to balance growth with the larger concerns of growth management.[25]

Growth management was a relatively new issue in Jacksonville and across the state of Florida. Prior to World War II, incentives for growth had been the norm. They had included draining swamps, providing land, and subsidizing railroads to attract settlers and businesses to this predominantly rural state. After the war, however, tourism, retirees, increased air traffic, interstate highways, and technological innovations like air conditioning led to unprecedented growth. By the 1970s, the state legislature had begun to enact laws to protect the land and water through taxation, regulation, and planning. Implementation was delegated to regional or local authorities, with varying degrees of success.[26]

In Jacksonville, residents and their government preferred growth over management. A 1983 Area Chamber of Commerce study reported 59 percent of area residents preferred growth at its present or a more rapid rate. Only 19 percent wanted it to slow. Part of this attitude reflected lower-income residents desiring more and better jobs on the northern and western sides of the city. Part reflected land-developer and builder interests. Part too reflected an awareness that while Jacksonville was growing, its rate of growth was slower than for much of the rest of the state, especially the more glamorous areas of Miami-Dade, Broward, Orlando, and Tampa–St. Petersburg.[27]

The state's Local Government Comprehensive Planning Act of 1975 required all cities to adopt comprehensive plans. Jacksonville's planning department created the 2005 Comprehensive Plan to meet the city's needs to the year 2005, but city council failed to provide for enforcement. It became a guide rarely used, rather than a tool for managing growth. In its 1984 study of growth management, Jacksonville Community Council, Inc. (JCCI) concluded that the community lacked consensus on the overall issue. Too many influential voices feared interference with individual property rights. The consequences of this attitude were seen most clearly in the south-side suburb of Mandarin, which sprawled with new housing developments and strip malls during the 1970s, and eastward in unplanned growth along Baymeadows, Butler, Beach, and Atlantic Boulevards during the 1980s. It was this unrestrained growth along with zoning conflicts that attracted the attention of the National Municipal League in the spring of 1984.[28]

In response to the JCCI study, Mayor Godbold appointed a Citizens Growth Management Task Force chaired by attorney Dale Joyner to look at impact fees, bridge tolls, sign ordinances, historic districts, and zoning qualifications as they might affect the city's growth. Its report in June 1985 concluded the 2005 plan was ineffective and listed the following problems:[29]

- Growth patterns were haphazard, and the resulting development lacked essential supporting public services.
- Infrastructure, including roads, bridges, sewers, and water services, were underfunded compared with other cities of comparable size.
- Traffic congestion was increasing, causing greater air pollution and potential for accidents.
- Neighborhoods were threatened by thoroughfares constructed through them.

The report supported continued growth for Jacksonville but at the same time recommended stricter subdivision regulations, sign and tree ordinances, increased funding for infrastructure, air and water pollution controls, and impact or user fees.[30]

Impact fees were a major stumbling block. Though all other urban counties in Florida required them, the powerful North Florida Builders Association, comprising local developers and real estate interests, successfully opposed them. They argued that local home buyers would be penalized. Nothing was said about fees as a means to slow the growth of burgeoning strip malls. As often in the past, the developers heavily influenced city council and the issue was tabled. Other recommendations moved slowly and contentiously through council. By the end of Godbold's terms, the media and most residents had shifted their focus from the issue of urban sprawl to celebrating downtown development with the new Jacksonville Landing.[31]

Environmental Problems: Odors and Solid Waste

In addition to concerns for growth management, the issue of air quality helped shape the decision against Jacksonville becoming an All-America City. In April 1984, the local CBS affiliate, WJXT-TV, televised a documentary, "The Smell of Money," and portions were picked up for national distribution. Odors had long been a problem in Jacksonville. The documentary described the odors as a threat to public health and portrayed the unwillingness of the political and business communities to do anything about them. Prime Osborne, chair of CSX Corporation, reflected the view of many local businessmen with his statement that "the odor smells like money," referring to the jobs and profits for Jacksonville.[32]

In response, John Winchester, a professor of atmospheric chemistry at Florida State University, cited high acid air concentrations in Jacksonville from the paper mills and chemical plants. He claimed they contributed to lung cancer rates locally that were 30 percent higher than in the rest of Florida. Meanwhile, city health officials acknowledged the odor nuisance. No other Florida city had two large paper mills and two chemical plants plus a sewage treatment plant polluting the atmosphere. Yet they could find no evidence to show a direct causation between the odors and sickness. Individuals repeatedly reported headaches, skin rashes, and respiratory problems that they blamed on the odors, but the evidence was anecdotal.[33]

Godbold was well aware of the odor concerns. Earlier, in the closing months of the Tanzler administration, the city had responded to citizen groups concerned about objectionable odors by funding an odor study undertaken by Environmental Science and Engineering, a consulting firm from Gainesville. They sought to identify odor sources, evaluate health effects, determine thresholds of objectionable odors, and develop methods to abate or eliminate them. In their 1980 report, the consultants identified the sources of most complaints as St. Regis Paper Company, SCM Organics, Alton Box Board Company, and Union Camp Chemical Company.[34]

The consultants then randomly surveyed residents from five odor-prominent census tracts and learned that odor was their principal community concern. One in five respondents reported that odors made them physically ill. One in six left his or her neighborhood for leisure or recreational activities because of the odors. Still, in assessing the toxicity of chemical compounds in the air, the consultants found none to be in concentrations sufficient to negatively affect the public's health. As a result they recommended continued efforts to control odors but were vague in how to achieve that goal.[35]

While the study was underway, the Bio-Environmental Services Division (BESD), under its competent, tough-minded division chief, Walter W. Honour, of Jacksonville's Department of Health, Welfare, and Bio-Environmental Services, proceeded to enforce existing air and odor standards with Alton Box, Union Camp, and St. Regis Paper Company. Its efforts were undercut, however, in 1980 by city council passage of an ordinance prohibiting Jacksonville from exceeding state standards for enforcement. The state regulated chemical pollutants in the air, but not odors. Subsequent budget cutbacks further limited BESD's effectiveness. Honour publicly protested the cutbacks, was suspended, and then resigned. The result, according to the WJXT report, was a decline in environmental enforcement efforts locally, particularly in contrast to cities like Tampa. The mayor saw himself on the horns of a dilemma. Could Jacksonville be both clean and prosperous? "I don't want the reputation of a dirty, don't care about the environment, city," he said, "but I don't want to be harassing industry either."[36]

The television documentary in 1984 became a wake-up call to the Godbold administration. The mayor formed a citizens commission representing both industry and environmentalists to find solutions. It recommended repealing earlier legislation and toughening standards to be enforced by the Environmental Protection Board (EPB). St. Regis, with its emissions of hydrogen sulfide fumes smelling like rotten eggs wafting over suburban Arlington and beyond, protested it could not afford the cost of modernizing its forty-year-old plant. Ironically, it already had retrofitted a plant in Pensacola with state-of-the-art technology, resulting in both greater production and profits.[37]

In the fall of 1984, the mayor submitted an omnibus bill to city council that he hoped would resolve the city's multiple pollution problems. With regard to odor prevention, the bill provided for a four-step enforcement process beginning with an EPB citation. If ignored, EPB could file a complaint requiring a public hearing. If still no reaction, EPB could issue a ruling requiring compliance. Finally it could fine a polluter up to a maximum of $5,000 for failure to comply. Unless the polluters voluntarily complied, the process could be dragged on for months. For larger polluters, the fines were a mere slap on the hand.[38]

Despite its participation in drafting the bill, Alton Packaging Corporation (formerly Alton Box Board) began arguing that EPB enforcement moved oversight from city council to the mayor and was undemocratic. Jacksonville Kraft Paper (successor to St. Regis) agreed. They claimed the executive branch would have too much power. These efforts played upon possible city council fears of relinquishing legislative authority to the mayor. For a while, it looked like they might succeed, but council eventually voted the odor bill into law. Three years later, however, odor standards had yet to be enforced. Effective odor controls would have to await another mayor and a new city council.[39]

The consolidated city's next major environmental challenge became the disposal of solid wastes. The Tanzler administration had begun closing private unregulated landfills and limiting waste sites, but aerial views in the early 1980s still showed Duval County littered with trash. "You can fly over this city," said Godbold, "and it looks like one big garbage dump. There are old couches, broken refrigerators, food lying on just about any empty piece of land you can find."[40]

Having closed a heavily polluting solid waste incinerator in the 1970s, Jacksonville had four sanitary landfills, one in each quadrant of the city. Despite free residential pickups, illegal dumping along the side of roads and in woods continued. Small businesses, which had to pay a fee to dump at the landfills, were major culprits. The city tried to crack down on them, but it was a slow process.[41]

Meanwhile, residents near landfills complained about rats, odors, and the noise of vehicles at the sites. Protests about the landfill located on the suburban south side prompted the mayor to promise to close it within two years. Foul conditions at the west-side landfill led city council to close it in 1984, resulting in increased illegal dumping by businesses unwilling to truck their refuse to more distant sites.[42]

Complicating the situation was the increased amount of refuse being produced by Jacksonville residents and businesses. In 1978, Godbold's first year in office, the city transported about 1,500 tons per day. Nine years later, the city was disposing of 2,500 tons of residential garbage and refuse daily, reflecting the increased population, prosperity, and trash of a throwaway society. On a per capita basis, garbage disposal increased from five pounds to eight pounds per person during this period. This almost two-thirds increase in solid waste coincided with the closing and promised closing of two of the city's four landfills.[43]

The mayor anticipated this potential crisis in early 1982 by hiring Flood Architects-Engineers-Planners, Inc. to develop a disposal plan to last until 2010. Its report recommended a $300 million resource recovery incinerator to provide energy to JEA by burning up to 2,200 tons of refuse daily.

Landfills then would be used essentially for the resulting ash. Both Dade and Pinellas Counties had mass-burn facilities, and Pinellas sold power from its plant to the local electric utility.[44]

The mayor also hired a second consulting group, Camp, Dresser, and McKee, to locate new landfill sites. Their report recommended six environmentally safe locations, including one south-side property owned by DDI, a land management corporation connected to Winn-Dixie's Davis family. That site brought opposition from the family and the likelihood of extended lawsuits to delay action. The city backed down, and the Davises offered another site close to Durbin Creek on the St. Johns county line that the city accepted after a brief site visit.[45]

Nearby residents and St. Johns County officials voiced concerns about groundwater contamination on the 150 acres along Durbin Creek. City officials met with residents and assured them their fears were unnecessary. Only 300 acres of the 868-acre site would be used, and the latest technology of landfill liners made likelihood of groundwater contamination almost nonexistent. The residents remained unpersuaded. The Godbold administration ended before this conflict could be resolved.[46]

Further complicating the environmental picture during the Godbold years was the growing awareness of hazardous waste sites and spills; storm water runoffs from roads and parking lots, polluting waterways; PCBs and other chemicals settling on river bottoms; leaks from 80,000–90,000 septic tanks; ulcerated fish in the St. Johns River and its tributaries; asbestos fiber contaminants in older buildings; and the discovery of the disease-spreading Asian tiger mosquitoes hatching eggs in scrap car and truck tires at storage sites. Environmental problems, it seemed, could never be resolved once and forever. They could be counted on to confront in old and new forms each administration taking office.[47]

Affirmative Action and Minority Set-Asides

It seemed that racial problems could not be resolved once and forever, either. Despite passage of an affirmative action hiring policy by city council in 1977, little change had taken place. While fully 29 percent of city employees were African Americans, most worked at the lower pay scales as maintenance or clerical workers, skilled craftsmen, or paraprofessionals, or in protective services. In the higher paying categories, blacks made up only 15.7 percent of technicians, 11.7 percent of professionals, and 7.7 percent of administrators. The goal was 21 percent in each category, half male and half female. Four years later, blacks had made gains, but virtually all of the gains were made by women. Black men had actually lost ground among professionals and administrators during that time. Equal employment opportunity coordinator John Farmer attributed the limited progress to the instability of the national and local economies that were only then emerging from the Reagan recession. For budgetary reasons, the city had been forced to freeze all but essential hiring and otherwise reduce employment rolls. Further, the federal CETA program had been ended. Clearly one could not hire new employees when there were cutbacks rather than vacancies or employment growth. Black city council member Rodney Hurst agreed.[48]

Three years later, however, with the national and local economies once more on the upswing, a Jacksonville Community Relations Commission report still saw little progress in the city's efforts to implement affirmative action. Executive director Alton Yates's agency looked only at new hires in the upper salary ranges over the preceding years and found that African Americans comprised only 5.4 percent in that category. A few departments made reasonable progress—recreation, human resources, and city housing and urban development—but most, like public works, the sheriff's office, public safety (firefighters), Jacksonville Electric Authority, and central services, did not. Yates recommended strengthened recruitment efforts by the city, holding administrators responsible for affirmative action hiring and changing the Rule of One.[49]

The Rule of One was a civil service promotions policy whereby applicants took a test and the individual scoring the highest score got the job. Credit was given for seniority, which benefited long-term employees, usually white males. A candidate's work record, interview, or appropriateness for the position could not be considered. To do so, argued supporters of the rule, would be to open promotions to possible individual biases by supervisors at the expense of the exam system supposedly based solely on merit. The exams, however, were never tested to ensure that high test scores were a predictor of future job performance. Efforts to expand the rule to include the top three candidates in order to give supervisors some discretion were repeatedly blocked by the civil service board, city council, and the city's director of personnel. Mayor Godbold spoke in behalf of changing the rule, and over time even the civil service board changed its position, but the rule continued in force into the next mayoral administration. Insiders believed the opposition of the politically powerful firefighters was the major reason for the mayor's inaction.[50]

The challenge confronting African Americans entering city employment could be seen in the case of firefighter Winston Nash. First hired by the city only after the federal courts forced the department to employ African Americans, Nash after seven years applied to become an engineer. His record was excellent. He had served in the U.S. Air Force, earned an associate's degree in fire science from the community college and a bachelor's degree in business at the University of North Florida, worked effectively as a firefighter, and lived in the community. Nash was rejected. He grieved unsuccessfully with the mayor's office and then went to court challenging the promotion tests as discriminatory. Rejected first by the U.S. District Court, Nash won on appeal and again eventually in the U.S. Supreme Court. In all it took ten years to fully confirm Nash's promotion. His case was not typical, but it reflected what happened when a department was determined to maintain the Rule of One resulting in the exclusion of minorities in its upper ranks. No municipal authority was willing to force its change.[51]

Meanwhile, in January 1984 city council passed and Mayor Godbold signed legislation establishing a minority set-aside enterprise program to guarantee women and minorities at least 10 percent of city contracts. Supporters anticipated their securing $1–2 million in construction contracts, where blacks previously had none, and $7–8 million in service contracts, doubling current efforts. The plan was modeled after a Boston ordinance and went into effect the following October. In the first year, the city awarded fifty contracts totaling $2.25 million, with about 60 percent going to black-owned businesses and the rest to women and Hispanics. Over its first three years, $11 million in contracts were awarded, although the 10 percent goal was never reached.[52]

Of concern was the fudging of minority and female ownership. The law provided for 50 percent ownership for eligibility, which could enable a husband-wife partnership to bid. In one case a construction company receiving a $750,000 contract was owned by a woman but operated by her sons. Another concern was that 10 percent was too small a set-aside to cover both women and minorities and that there should be a 25 percent goal for both groups.[53]

Protests arose in the bypassing of the ordinance in the construction of the Prime Osborne Convention Center. To speed the process with private contractors, normal purchasing procedures were waived, resulting in the exclusion of minority contractors. Their protests prompted the city and developers to make last-minute adjustments, with five of six contracts going to women. The experience left a bad feeling in the black business community.[54]

Ronnie Ferguson, the respected executive director of the Jacksonville Urban League, sent a letter to the mayor in September 1985. "In recent months," he wrote, "I have noticed a growing amount of concern in the Black community resulting from their feelings of exclusion.... Many people have expressed to me that they felt we were taken in as a community by rhetoric and campaign promises. There is the feeling that when things really count we are left out and involved after the fact." Ferguson urged a meeting to discuss set-asides, affirmative action, minority jobs in the construction of the Rouse festival marketplace (future Jacksonville Landing), and the "expenditure of governmental dollars on major projects while cutting back services for the poor and disadvantaged."[55]

Still another issue was police-community relations. While not directly the mayor's responsibility (the sheriff was an elected official under the city's charter), their relations could either brighten or tarnish the city's image. In 1981, the Jacksonville Urban League issued a report on police-community relations in which an independent survey showed almost 83 percent of Jacksonville African Americans experienced police treating black males more harshly and violently than white males. Ninety percent believed the police treated black females worse than white females. Ninety-four percent believed the police would more likely shoot a black person than a white, and 76 percent believed that police officers were prone "to take action first and ask questions later, especially where minorities are concerned." These negative perceptions were partially offset by two-thirds of the respondents believing that only a small minority of police officers were unnecessarily brutal or violent toward people being arrested.[56]

In a series of community forums, also organized by the Urban League, participants urged the hiring of more black officers (8.7 percent of the force at the time) and more opportunities for black advancement. They strongly opposed the "fleeing felon" law whereby police could use all legitimate force, including shooting to kill, in capturing a fugitive regardless of whether the potential felon was armed or a physical threat to the officer. Other community participants suggested that white policemen had difficulty handling situations in the black community "allowing their tempers to flare up," leading to violence. Chief Jerome Spates, the only high-ranking black officer in the sheriff's department, agreed. White police did have a difficult time relating to the black community, and he supported recommendations for a continuing program of training in stress management and community and race relations.[57]

A seminar of black clergy urged an end to police stereotyping of African Americans, yet the clergy recognized the need for the black community to become more fully involved in crime prevention. They too urged sensitivity training for the police and a proactive role by the sheriff to improve police-community relations. Their vision was for a relationship in which African Americans could look upon the police as "friend" rather than "foe," something that currently did not exist.[58]

Rev. R. B. Holmes Jr., president of the Jacksonville branch of the NAACP, summed up the report by acknowledging that Jacksonville needed "strong law enforcement because of the moral disorders and criminal elements that are raging in the community. . . . On the one side of the coin, we are positive about the police department because we have one of the best in the state. On the other side, we are extremely negative toward the force because black folk are abused much too often." He saw the need to reduce tensions between the police and community and the need to control police misconduct. To reduce the negative perceptions of the police, Holmes urged establishing a police review board to handle citizen complaints; full integration of the police force to reflect the community's population; and relaxation of the fleeing-felon law that "give[s] officers the right to be judge, prosecutor, executioner, and jury at the same time." The shooting of people in the back of the head who weighed under 120 pounds and were unarmed, Holmes said, was "totally ridiculous."[59]

On August 20, 1983, police tried to stop an African American motorcyclist, Michael Joseph Alexander, for a traffic violation. For whatever reason, Alexander fled. After a seven-and-one-half mile chase, he was shot to death by the officer. The sheriff's department justified the shooting under the fleeing-felon law whereby police could use all legitimate force in capturing a fugitive. A grand jury upheld that view. In response the black community, led by the Interdenominational Ministers Alliance, angrily protested the excessive use of force in a minor traffic violation. To his credit, Mayor Godbold acted to appoint a special committee to investigate the situation. Chaired by developer Charles A. "Bucky" Clarkson and comprising five African Americans, the director of services for the sheriff's office, director of public safety, president of the Chamber of Commerce, and two other leading businessmen among its eleven members, the committee looked for ways to prevent such incidents in the future rather than to assign blame.[60]

Committee members, if they did not already know, learned of the deep divide within the Jacksonville community over the sheriff's department. Alton Yates, executive director of the Jacksonville Community Relations Commission, reflecting the Urban League report of two years earlier, told the committee about the "almost total and complete distrust of the police" and said that "many black folks would rather take their chances with the criminals than with the police." Chamber president James Winston suggested the need for special training in race relations for police recruits. At a public hearing in November, witnesses reported physical abuse of blacks by white officers as common. Blacks feared the police. Yet, as others testified, white police officers also feared blacks. The racial gulf was wide and deep.[61]

In its report to the mayor in February 1984, the Clarkson committee avoided a judgmental approach to the issues before it. It clearly heard the complaints of the African American community but also praised the sheriff's office for its efficiency and general professionalism. Despite very limited funding and overextended manpower, it had received national recognition for its overall performance.[62]

At the same time, there clearly was a "two-way perception problem between the black community and the police force." Blacks viewed the police with suspicion. The police saw blacks as unsupportive and antagonistic to them. To try to bridge the gulf between the parties, the committee made twenty-nine recommendations, including: [63]

- restricting the use of deadly force to suspected violent crimes and self-defense;
- increasing black community support by increasing the number of blacks on the force from the current 8 percent to a goal of 25 percent

within four years, while facilitating opportunities for black advancement;

- increasing in-service human relations training with programs to open dialogue between the police and the black community;
- providing educational opportunities and support for officers to pursue educational goals, setting standards for all recruits to have an associate of arts degree by 1990, with a long-range goal of a bachelor's degree by 1994;
- hiring forty additional officers immediately to reduce current excessive workloads and another fifty officers to meet future community growth;
- upgrading equipment, especially radio systems, enabling officers outside their patrol cars to maintain contact; and
- extending the term of the Clarkson committee for three years to assist in the implementation of its recommendations.

The mayor endorsed the twenty-nine recommendations but reduced the life of the Clarkson committee to a one-year extension. He told Sheriff Dale Carson, "There's some dudes out there that shouldn't be out there and you ought to get rid of them."[64]

Unlike many past studies, the Clarkson Report produced results. In the years that followed and under a new sheriff, James McMillan, who was a member of the Clarkson committee, the department increased its minority hiring to achieve the 25 percent goal, encouraged minority advancement within the department, engaged in dialogues between the police and the black community in public housing projects, introduced educational standards for recruits, and successfully lobbied for additional officers, winning praise from the African American community. In 1988, the Jacksonville Community Relations Commission honored McMillan for his services in building better relations between the police and the black community.[65]

Still, for the city during the Godbold years, support for improving race relations, while real, rarely had top priority on anyone's agenda. Employment opportunities and advancement for qualified applicants remained limited in both the public and private sectors. Education, the responsibility of the independently elected Duval County School Board, continued under a court-ordered desegregation plan. Equally important to Bernard Gregory, an African American community leader, were issues of preschool and after-school child care, the indifference and lack of motivation among a substantial number of students, and the increasing number of dropouts who were disproportionately African American.[66]

Another concern was the lack of affordable housing available to lower-income residents whether black or white. Federal cutbacks during the Reagan years led to inadequate maintenance of existing public housing and the virtual end to building new public housing. Jacksonville had federally owned or subsidized housing for 10,000 residents with another 3,000 on waiting lists. State and local support was minimal. The Florida legislature did pass an affordable-housing bond program to encourage developers to build multifamily units, with the provision that 20 percent of them should be set aside for lower-income persons. It never enforced the requirement. In Jacksonville the Duval County Housing Finance Authority subsidized housing in the suburbs for recent college graduates but never financed a multifamily development in a minority census tract.[67]

Meanwhile, the city had full discretion over spending its federal Community Development Block Grant (CDBG) dollars and put most of them into economic subsidies for business growth and jobs. In 1986, of $8.1 million in CDBG funds, 16 percent went to rehab 300 housing units in the city at a cost of $1.2 million, while $6.9 million went to subsidize the construction of the Rouse-designed festival marketplace at the Jacksonville Landing. This was at a time when one survey estimated 68,000 substandard housing units in the city. In 1987, 12 percent of CDBG funds went for housing. Clearly, affordable housing was not a high priority at city, state, or federal levels for lower-income black or white residents.[68]

The Godbold mayoralty ended in June 1987 under the two-term limitation imposed by the city charter. In some respects, the mayor's eight years in office had been a roller-coaster ride. Early on, the distrust of business leaders, threats of federal environmental and housing penalties, city council bickering, African American protests, federal and state funding cutbacks, and a national recession had challenged the mayor's ability to govern. Polls had reflected disappointment in him. Yet by the time of his reelection in 1983, Godbold had proven to be both popular and capable of overseeing a downtown renaissance, signing a minority set-aside ordinance, supporting the arts in the restoration of both the Florida Theatre and the Prime Osborne Convention Center, and promoting Jacksonville to any and all comers. His enthusiasm for the city knew no bounds, and that enthusiasm resonated with Jacksonville voters. Challenged in the mayoral primary by an African American candidate, Godbold won 71 percent of the vote. Against his Republican opponent in May, he won 75 percent of the vote. At his second inaugural Godbold claimed that Jacksonville was "no longer a city of lost faith, but a community of believers. We believe in ourselves," he said, "and we believe in our community."[69]

This mood was captured by the out-of-town media. The *Miami Herald* headlined, "Jacksonville Mayor Credited with Getting City Back on Track." The *Tampa Tribune* praised Godbold for bringing Jacksonville's downtown "back to life." The *New York Times* covered the October jazz festival at the opening of Metropolitan Park. The *St. Petersburg Times* praised the changes from a backward, politically corrupt city to a city clearly becoming "big league." The *Chattanooga News–Free Press* praised Godbold's civic leadership. He had put "enthusiasm back into the city. He realized the river was the strength of the city. He realized the potential of the city," and he persuaded voters of it. These views were echoed also by the *Atlanta Constitution.*[70]

The river focus was a key ingredient. Neglected prior to the consolidation of city with county, then cleansed of much of its pollution during the Tanzler years, the river became the focal point of the new Jacksonville under Mayor Godbold. On the south bank were the new river walk, restaurants, Prudential Insurance building, and hotel complex. Located on the north bank were the restored railroad terminal, now convention center, Rouse-built festival marketplace at the Jacksonville Landing, and Metropolitan Park, home of the annual jazz festival. The riverfront became, in the *Miami Herald*'s words, "Jacksonville's new showplace."[71]

Yet the roller-coaster experience also had its downside in Godbold's second term. First was the growing list of problems confronting city government. The mayor clearly recognized them. Nasty odors still permeated large sectors of the city from paper mills and chemical plants. Landfills were filling rapidly with city garbage and other solid wastes. The city was under court order to build a new jail. A severely understaffed police force confronted a rising crime rate. The fire department and parks and recreation were also understaffed by both state and national standards. Transportation and affordable-housing needs awaited the next mayor. Governing Jacksonville, like other American cities, was a continuing challenge to play catch-up with urban problems while avoiding community crises.[72]

Fig. 13. The Rouse-built Jacksonville Landing. From Downtown Development Authority 1987, *Annual Report* (Jacksonville).

The second major downer was the exposure of government corruption during the mayor's second term. Godbold, to his credit, was never indicted. The key players were attorney Thomas H. Greene, a boyhood friend of the mayor, and the city's general counsel, Dawson McQuaig.

The corruption scandal had its origins in the kind of political favoritism that had characterized city government before consolidation. Campaign contributors had the inside track on city contracts. Established rules and regulations were waived to serve special interests. Beginning in 1985, Mark Middlebrook and Dave Roman of the *Florida Times-Union* began describing the actions of the city's former general counsel, Dawson McQuaig, who received legal fees from the Jacksonville Electric Authority at three times the going rate. When he was general counsel, McQuaig had recommended that legal work normally done by his office be done by attorney Greene. When JEA began building its $2 billion coal-fired generating plants, Mc-Quaig arranged for Greene to become a co-bond counsel. When Greene began representing the brokerage firm Shearson/American Express (later Shearson–Lehman Brothers), Shearson wound up floating $1.6 billion in bonds. Greene received $3 million in fees and McQuaig $267,000 in a variety of payments from Greene.[73]

State and federal grand juries investigated. The state grand jury did not recommend prosecution but condemned "political favors and game-playing for friends . . . at the expense of . . . the public trust." The federal grand jury, however, indicted Greene for bank fraud, indicted McQuaig initially for conflict of interest and later for perjury, and indicted finance director Ray Clardy and Godbold aide Henry Stout for perjury. All were convicted. Eventually, Greene and McQuaig also confessed to wire and mail fraud conspiracy.[74] The exposure of the political favoritism, fraud, and perjury were devastating to Godbold, a man whose personal honesty was not questioned. He had trusted his friends and colleagues and they had misused him. His first response was to direct his staff to tighten procedures on bond and investment decisions. During the course of the investigations, the grand juries called the mayor and his chief administrative officer, Don McClure, to testify. Much time was taken in response, and day-to-day governance slackened. The mayor was often absent from city hall. Increasingly the mayor's office took on the appearance of a lame-duck administration. In support of the mayor, Godbold's friends surprised him in early 1987 with a standing-room-only reception at a local hotel celebrating his eight years in office. His accomplishments, his friends assured him, far outweighed the mistakes of his friends and colleagues.[75]

And clearly they did. Twenty-four years later, another mayor, then an assistant state's attorney, said it well. Of the "people over the past thirty years [who] have done the most to make us appreciate Jacksonville," there was Jake Godbold, "the perpetual booster, promoter and cheerleader . . . who you knew loved the place and made you love it."[76]

Still, there remained questions that would confront Godbold's successors in their attempts to make consolidated government work. How far does one trust one's aides and friends on city financial matters? Where does the mayor draw the line? Who makes the tough decisions? Godbold wanted clean air, but not at the expense of the major polluters and the jobs they provided. He needed an environmentally safe landfill site, but not over the opposition of the Winn-Dixie interests. He supported affirmative action for minorities and women, but not enough to challenge the firefighters and their support of the civil service Rule of One. He supported growth management, but not at the expense of the builders. These tough decisions were not unique to the Godbold administration nor to consolidated government. His successors would have to make similar decisions in their efforts to make the city work effectively in the best interests of the entire community.

CHAPTER 7

THE HAZOURI YEARS

The next mayor to confront the challenges of making consolidated government work in Jacksonville was forty-two-year-old Tommy Hazouri, a
Democrat with twelve years of experience in the Florida state legislature.
Hazouri's father had immigrated as a child from Lebanon in 1904. His
mother, born in Jacksonville, had Syrian-Lebanese parents. Together they
raised their son to be proud of his Arab heritage. The son grew up in a
downtown neighborhood living with his family over the family grocery
store. He was the first in his family to attend college. While at Jacksonville
University, he served as a legislative intern for Congressman Charles
Bennett, later worked briefly as a research assistant for Mayor Louis Ritter,
was appointed to the Jacksonville Community Relations Commission by
Mayor Hans Tanzler, and then became an administrative assistant to
House majority leader Carl Ogden in Tallahassee. Elected to the Florida
House of Representatives as a Democrat in 1974 at age thirty, Hazouri
lived politics twenty-four hours a day.[1]

His record in the state legislature generally supported the programs and
policies of Democratic governors Reubin Askew and Bob Graham. Anticipating the end of Jake Godbold's mayoralty in 1987 due to the city charter
limitation of two terms, Hazouri opened a campaign account in fall 1985.
Over the succeeding eighteen months, the candidate laid out a platform
that included abolishing tolls on the city's bridges, eliminating the city's
odor problems, meeting water, sewer, and other infrastructure needs, increasing police and fire protection, expanding mass transit, and developing
long-range planning—a grab bag of policies not unlike those of his primary opponents.[2]

Five candidates competing for mayor resulted in no one winning a majority in the first primary. In the runoff, Hazouri defeated his fellow former state legislator John Lewis with 59 percent of the vote. In the general election, Hazouri trounced Republican Henry Cook 88,422 to 30,066, winning 75 percent of the vote. Hazouri's victory, according to one analyst, resulted from greater name recognition, better campaign organization, and his stand on the popular issues of eliminating odor pollution, regulating billboards, and eliminating bridge tolls.[3]

With strong voter support, Hazouri took office on July 1, 1987, and two weeks later he presented his first budget to the Jacksonville City Council. Funding priorities included 104 additional police officers to bring the city up to national standards and 100 new firefighters to improve public safety. Equally important was the mayor's emphasis on a cleaner environment, especially removing "the smell in our air." He also wanted to find solutions for solid waste landfills that were close to capacity, reduce air pollution by eliminating bridge tolls, and strengthen growth management policies to protect the environment. Further, he promised to promote economic growth along with downtown development and hold to a standard of government in which there was "no place for racism, sexism or ageism."[4]

Passing an Odor Ordinance

The first step in passing an odor ordinance came in August 1987 when the mayor declared war on odor pollution. Obnoxious odors were as much a part of Jacksonville's image as the Gator Bowl or the St. Johns River. A CSX executive had once compared them to the smell of money, signifying local prosperity. Local residents thought otherwise. "I love this city," one resident told a reporter, "but I'm embarrassed to bring visitors in from the airport and watch them twitch their noses and ask 'what's that smell?'" Another claimed she could not enjoy her yard due to the odors. "I'm struggling to breathe.... The stuff is unbearable." The most common comparison was to the smell of rotten eggs, with the odor resulting from the discharge of a sulfurous compound produced by the pulp and chemical companies in the city.[5]

The main culprits causing Jacksonville's worst odors were two paper companies—Jefferson Smurfit Corporation (formerly Alton Packaging

Fig. 14. Thomas L. Hazouri, mayor of Jacksonville, 1987–1991. By permission of the City of Jacksonville.

Company) and Seminole Kraft Corporation—and two chemical companies—SCM Glidco Organics and Union Camp Corporation. A fifth odor contributor was the city's Buckman Sewage Treatment Plant. For years the paper mills had cut down pine trees from north Florida and south Georgia and processed them into chips "cooked" into a mixture of wood fibers that eventually became paper. One by-product was a sulfur compound known as total reduced sulfur, or TRS, which was discharged into the atmosphere, emitting a rotten egg smell that drifted across much of the city. Another by-product of the pulp processing was crude sulfite turpentine, or CST, which the chemical companies refined into fragrances for soaps, perfumes, tissues, and processed foods. Glidco was the largest such manufacturer of fragrances in the United States. Union Camp was the second largest. As the CST was unloaded, transferred, stored, and processed, leaks and spills caused the release of sulfur and intense turpentine odors. Residue from the CST was flushed into streams and sewers, flowing untreated into the city's sewage treatment plant, which produced its own noxious odors. The quantity being dumped into the city's waste water system was approximately 180 pounds per day in the summer of 1987. This amount was one hundred times more than the Buckman plant could treat without causing its own odor nuisance. Ninety-five percent of these pollutants came from SCM Glidco.[6]

Executives at both the paper mills and the organic chemical plants acknowledged the existence of the odors and reported investing, or planning to invest, millions of dollars in technology and procedures to reduce them. But the process was slow. City officials had been embarrassed by a 1984 television documentary about the odors (see ch. 6). Subsequently city council, under Mayor Godbold's leadership, passed the Omnibus Environmental Ordinance to control them, but enforcement provisions were minimal. The city and state environmental agencies had reached agreement with the paper companies on a plan to reduce air pollution. Yet in the following three years, only limited change had taken place. Jacksonville remained under the cloud of obnoxious odors that annoyed residents, tourists, and prospective new business clients.[7]

Thus Hazouri's declaration of war on odor pollution was welcomed by the community. To marshal his forces, he appointed his boyhood friend and attorney William C. Gentry as his special counsel on the environment to recommend changes in the law, initiate civil cases in court against noncomplying companies, and report criminal cases to the office of the state's attorney for prosecution. Gentry grew up within blocks of the Jefferson Smurfit pulp mill and knew the odors well. After examining the problem, he concluded that the existing laws lacked sufficient enforcement provisions. "A $500 fine is meaningless to these companies," he said. Tougher regulations and larger fines were needed to move polluters toward compliance.[8]

By October Gentry had a pretty good picture of the problem. The paper mills were making progress toward eliminating odors, but the chemical companies, particularly SCM Glidco, were not. Based on his findings and the reports of the Bio-Environmental Services Division, Gentry determined that SCM Glidco constituted "the single major odor producing source in the community." He concluded that the companies were responsible for their own pollution and taxpayers should not have to foot the cost to clean it up. What was needed, he reported to the mayor, was new legislation enforcing odor standards, with substantial penalties for violators.[9]

In January 1988, the mayor submitted to city council his odor bill as an amendment to the Omnibus Environmental Ordinance. It increased civil penalties for polluters from $500 to a maximum of $10,000 per violation; decreased the number of complaints required to initiate an odor citation from ten to five; established a $500 criminal penalty for violators of pollution laws; and authorized city pollution inspectors to issue $50 fines on the spot for minor infractions.[10]

Executives from the four most affected companies reacted angrily. George Robbins of SCM Glidco challenged the need for the ordinance. He claimed his company already had spent $5 million to reduce odors and planned to spend $1.5 million more to comply with state standards. The proposed new city regulations were unfair. Union Camp executive Don Neighbors also reported major investments in odor reduction and argued that the new standards were too vague. Reducing the number of validated complaints for a citation, he said, "would make it very easy for a small group with any kind of 'ax to grind' to cause a company to be cited." Bob Williams from Jefferson Smurfit said his company, which had 284 complaints against it in 1987, was spending $30 million to have new equipment in place by early 1989 to eliminate all direct emissions. "We support the mayor's effort . . . we are committed to eliminating odors to the extent that technology will permit . . . [but] what I'd like to see is not an adversarial position between the city and the industries, but a partnership to eliminate odors." Frank Lee of Seminole Kraft claimed he had made an agreement with former mayor Godbold when Lee reopened his pulp mill in February 1987. His investment of $75 million in new equipment would eliminate odors by 1992. Now, he added, "a new mayor comes along and says the agreement doesn't count."[11]

Despite the opposition, the administration rallied substantial popular support for the bill. The timing was right. Both the print and electronic media gave the issue substantial coverage. City council members responded to the groundswell and passed it thirteen to four with two members absent. The mayor signed it into law on March 23. A negative consequence was the perceived beginning of an anticorporate attitude on the part of the Hazouri administration in its aggressive pursuit of an effective odor law.[12]

Within weeks after the amended Omnibus Environmental Ordinance became law, the Duval County grand jury completed its eight-month study of odor pollution and indicted all four companies for violating both state and local antipollution laws. It charged the companies with failing to properly police themselves, adversely affecting property values and interfering with residents' health and welfare. According to the report, the city's odor problems were more than an embarrassment to the city. They resulted from criminal negligence.[13]

SCM Glidco's president Robbins called the report "biased, factually deficit and very misleading to the general public." The four companies challenged the law on constitutional grounds. In February 1989, Duval County judge Hugh Fletcher struck down the criminal portions of the law as unconstitutionally vague in the way the law determined when odor pollution became a crime. An appeals court agreed. Yet the civil portions remained.[14]

Meanwhile the city began to validate citizen complaints. Over the summer, the Bio-Environmental Services Division cited Jefferson Smurfit three times. In October, Jefferson Smurfit agreed to pay a $7,500 fine, the first penalty under the new law. The plant also promised to install new odor reduction equipment by May 1989. May came, however, and the odors continued, as did additional citations.[15]

The city also cited Seminole Kraft. This paper mill dragged its feet in court but finally agreed to pay a $30,000 fine in November 1990 and eliminate all offensive odors within two years. Mill executives announced a $100 million conversion of the facility. Instead of using wood chips to make pulp, the mill planned to use recycled cardboard to manufacture liner board for corrugated boxes. This conversion, said the plant manager, would eliminate all pulp mill odors by November 1991.[16]

Meanwhile SCM Glidco continued to challenge the city in court. It paid a $1,500 fine and claimed by January 1990 to have eliminated all sulfur odors as a result of $2 million spent on twenty-seven different projects. Union Camp also paid a fine and agreed to spend $1 million on forty-seven different tasks to reduce its odors.[17]

When Hazouri left the mayor's office at the end of June 1991, there still were odors, but there was noticeable improvement and the promise of more to come. His promise to wage war on polluters had not produced a complete victory, but his efforts clearly accelerated the effort to improve the air quality over Jacksonville. It also brought criticism about his adversarial approach to controlling odors. And it resulted in a political slap in the face by city council when it appointed, over Hazouri's veto, Glidco's

George Robbins to the city's Environmental Protection Board as an industry representative.[18]

Abolishing Tolls

While Hazouri worked to reduce odor pollution in Jacksonville, he also successfully eliminated bridge and highway tolls, fulfilling another campaign promise. The existing tolls began in the 1950s when city and county officials created the Jacksonville Expressway Authority (later renamed the Jacksonville Transportation Authority) to build four toll bridges across the St. Johns River (Mathews, Fuller Warren, Hart, and Dames Point Bridges), one on I-95 over the Trout River, and later toll booths on Butler Boulevard to the beaches. Tolls from the bridges and Butler Boulevard also financed construction of Arlington Expressway, Haines Street (later Martin Luther King) Expressway, Roosevelt Boulevard, Southside Boulevard, and Mayport Road to the naval station. Integrated into the interstate highway system built in the 1950s and 1960s, these roads and bridges provided tourists, truckers, and commuters access into and around the city.[19]

Tolls were a nuisance tax to motorists. They began at fifteen cents, then became twenty-five cents, later thirty cents, and were projected to reach fifty cents within a year. As traffic increased, particularly at the bridges, the toll booths became bottlenecks, frustrating motorists. Increased air pollution from idling vehicles became another consequence. By the early 1980s local politicians began looking for ways to end tolls. Hazouri made it a major campaign promise and in December 1987 introduced legislation to replace the tolls with a half-cent sales tax. Voters would decide the issue by referendum the following March.[20]

Opposition to the change was substantial. Voters had rejected a similar proposal by 54 to 46 percent in a nonbinding straw ballot in 1986, but only 26 percent of registered voters had cast a ballot. Probably the major objection to the Hazouri proposal was the increased sales tax added to the current 6 percent levy. Jacksonville residents were notoriously shy about voting to raise their own taxes. Within weeks of city council passing the mayor's initiative, four influential local businessmen founded Citizens against Sales Tax and began raising funds to defeat the referendum. Additional opposition came from the African American Interdenominational

Ministers Alliance, which opposed the switch from tolls to tax on behalf of lower-income and elderly residents who rarely used the bridges but would nevertheless have to pay an increased sales tax. Likewise, residents on the west side and north side of the city did not cross the river to work downtown, yet they too would have to pay the extra tax without toll relief.[21]

To counter the critics, the popular Hazouri created a Citizens League to End Tolls headed by his former mayoral opponent, John Lewis, and campaigned energetically across the city. He secured the endorsement of the Jacksonville Urban League and local chapter of the Southern Christian Leadership Council to offset the opposition of the ministerial alliance. He promised to freeze bus fares for ten years for lower-income riders. Suburban commuters from Arlington, the south side, and the beach communities who crossed the bridges daily to work downtown also strongly supported him. So too did trade unions and other local businesspeople.[22]

An early *Florida Times-Union* poll showed 56 percent of the voters wanted to abolish the tolls, primarily to relieve traffic congestion. Three weeks later, however, support had slipped to 43 percent for and 41 percent against with the rest undecided, too close to call in either direction.[23]

As election day approached, an angry Hazouri raised the ante. Standing at the Fuller Warren Bridge toll plaza, he lashed out at the opponents of the referendum, charging them with lies and innuendos. "I'm tired of the fat cats of this community sitting behind closed doors and talking about the poor. These fat cats are the same people who would keep the odor in our air, keep the billboards on our streets and keep the tolls on our bridges, and they will do anything to continue to shackle the progress of Jacksonville, Florida." The charge, repeated in newspaper and television ads, added a new dimension to the debate.[24]

On March 8, Jacksonville voters endorsed the tax-for-tolls referendum by the narrow margin of 50.8 percent to 49.2 percent. The west-side and north-side opposition did not mobilize sufficiently to offset the strong support from Arlington, the south side, and the beach communities. Hazouri's strong proactive campaign played a major part. Once again, however, as with the campaign against the corporate odor polluters, Hazouri's harsh words toward opponents would be remembered. Subsequent stories and editorials in the daily paper reminded readers of the "fat cats" charge and the supposed antagonism of the mayor toward a substantial portion of the influential business community.[25]

Fig. 15. Mayor Hazouri and Jacksonville Transportation Authority chairman Chester Stokes watching as the wrecking ball topples the toll booth on the Mathews Bridge. By permission of the *Florida Times-Union.*

On August 11, 1989, the thirty-six-year toll era ended for Jacksonville drivers. The mayor and Jacksonville Transportation Authority chairman Chester Stokes climbed aboard a crane and watched a wrecking ball topple the first toll booth on the Mathews Bridge. Demolition of the other booths followed. So too did unintended consequences. Traffic began to shift from bridges that previously had no tolls (Main Street and Acosta) to congest bridges fed by the interstate highway and expressways where tolls were removed. Air pollution remained a problem in part because of the increased traffic. Yet for Hazouri, removing the tolls remained a major accomplishment of his administration. George Wachendorf, a leading business columnist and no fan of the mayor, acknowledged that he did not see how this first-term mayor could miss becoming a second-termer. "Half-cent sales tax or not, there's something delightfully regal about driving unimpeded through the areas where we used to be nickeled-and-dimed. How can you be mad at the guy who gives you two small apparent victories over the System each and every working day?"[26]

Other Environmental Concerns

Jacksonville's odors and Jacksonville's tolls were among the most important issues of Hazouri's early mayoralty, but not the only ones. Thirty tire dumps in the city contained an estimated 3.5 million discards with an estimated 600,000 tires added each year. These mountains of tires posed a fire hazard; they also became a public health threat when city officials found evidence of Asian tiger mosquitoes inhabiting pockets of water collected in the tires. The mosquitoes were known carriers of dengue fever. Acting as the mayor's point person, deputy chief administrative officer Ann Shorstein initiated court action against the dump owners and oversaw the removal and shredding of the tires.[27]

Another environmental concern was visual pollution. Awareness of it resulted in part from a 1985 Jacksonville Community Council, Inc., study concluding that the city had serious problems. Petitions collected by a newly formed Citizens against Proliferation of Signs led to a charter amendment passed by voters in 1987. Hazouri strongly endorsed the effort, but progress in implementing the initiative was slow. A tree ordinance passed by city council in summer 1988 similarly met opposition from developers, but city officials persevered in its enforcement.[28]

Throughout his four years in office, Hazouri faced multiple environmental challenges: toxic and hazardous wastes, storm water runoffs, leaking septic tanks, privately owned sewage treatment plants polluting the St. Johns River and its tributaries, high ambient ozone levels, and water shortages. The administration sought to identify violators, worked closely with state and federal officials on enforcement, and expanded efforts to raise the consciousness of the community about the importance of protecting the environment.[29]

Landfills and Garbage Taxes

One issue tarnished much of Hazouri's environmental reputation. When he became mayor in July 1987, city officials thought they had solid waste management under control. Since consolidation, Jacksonville had undertaken systematic collection of solid wastes, closed down faulty incinerators, and replaced dumps with sanitary landfills. The rapid population growth and prosperity of the 1980s, however, combined with the proliferation of disposable consumer goods and wrappings, brought new pressures on landfill capacity. Anticipating continued growth, the Godbold administration in the early 1980s undertook two major studies of solid waste disposal that resulted in recommendations to build a 3,000-ton-capacity mass-burn incinerator and a new southeast landfill on the border of St. Johns County. These two additions would replace two rapidly filling landfills on the east and north side of the city.[30]

The Godbold administration chose a landfill site offered by the Winn-Dixie Davis family after the Davises first had rejected the recommendation of the city's environmental consultants. This second choice encompassed 880 acres, including 325 acres of wetlands along Durbin Creek. Fifty-four of the wetland acres were necessary for the landfill. Protests followed. Claims that the latest technology in landfill liners made the likelihood of groundwater contamination almost nonexistent did not persuade neighboring residents or environmentalists. Doug Milne, former mayoral candidate and chair of the northeast Florida group of the Sierra Club, testified before the Environmental Protection Board in opposition to the landfill on environmental grounds. He reported on a University of North Florida study showing that Durbin Creek was the "only remaining unpolluted tributary in the lower St. Johns [River] system" and "many professional proponents of landfills . . . agree even state-of-the-art landfills leak," due to a constant deterioration process ongoing in them. Environmental organizations, heretofore supportive of Hazouri, opposed the landfill due to the potential ecological damage to the area. Meanwhile, a wealthy landowner adjacent to the site, J. T. McCormick, filed suit to stop it. He also encouraged St. Johns County property owners and politicians who did not want a landfill in their backyard to oppose it.[31]

Objections by the federal Environmental Protection Agency in August 1987 that the proposed landfill would harm wetlands, wildlife, and the Floridan Aquifer led to a million-dollar redesign. Then the U.S. Army Corps of Engineers directed the city to show that no other site existed for the landfill. The city hired more consultants, who reported in July 1988 that it was not possible to locate a 350-acre site anywhere in Duval County away from population centers without in some degree affecting wetlands. The report recommended the southeast landfill as "the most acceptable site."[32]

Meanwhile, the city hired Frank Friedman, a prominent local attorney known to support environmental issues, to handle litigation. He negotiated a compromise between the city, county property holders, and, he thought, the St. Johns County commissioners, but it collapsed at a public hearing. Next, hearings before the Florida Department of Environmental Regulation (DER) pitted environmentalist against environmentalist. The city hired Vicki Tschinkel, former head of DER under Democratic governor Bob Graham. She claimed the city actually would improve the site's wetland system. It would remove an existing road, restore wetlands disrupted by logging, create new wetlands, and improve the natural flow of water. These changes, called mitigation, would improve the habitat for birds, frogs, snakes, and other water-dependent life. Another expert agreed, asserting that the city's plans would have no adverse effect and would "drastically improve the wetland system." A third expert testified there was no evidence of threatened or endangered wildlife species at the dump site, though some gopher tortoises would have to be removed.[33]

Opposing environmentalists once again warned about leachates (rainwater filtering through the wastes) penetrating the liner undergirding the landfill and contaminating the soil and aquifer beneath. Possible holes could open in the liner, facilitating this leakage, despite a six-inch layer of clay, twenty-four inches of sand and soil, a geotextile barrier, and a sophisticated leachate drainage system. If the system failed, contaminates could work their way through the wetlands downward into the aquifer or horizontally to the St. Johns River. Other environmentalists argued that wildlife would be endangered, citing various species of alligators, fox squirrels, woodpeckers, eagles, wood storks, sparrows, and kestrels seen in the area.[34]

Seven months later, the DER hearing officer, Robert Benton, advised the DER secretary against the landfill in a 114-page opinion. He claimed it would violate a state mandate requiring that all groundwater be "free from" carcinogenic materials that might be dumped into the landfill. He also ruled against a variance granting permission to build the landfill within 500 feet of a well owned by the McCormick family, though the well had been drilled after the plans for the landfill were announced.[35]

Benton's ruling was not final but merely a recommendation to DER secretary Dale Twachtman. A gubernatorial appointee, he overruled his hearing officer in favor of Jacksonville, approving the landfill. In response, St. Johns County officials appealed the DER decision to Republican governor Bob Martinez and his cabinet. After intense lobbying by Republicans and environmentalists, the governor agreed to hear the appeal and ordered a temporary freeze on construction. Subsequently, following his election defeat by Lawton Chiles, Martinez passed the appeal on to his successor. The new governor with his cabinet decided in February 1991 to rescind permits for the landfill on environmental grounds.[36]

While this costly and ultimately unsuccessful conflict dragged on, the city's two remaining landfills were approaching capacity. Hazouri prematurely closed the east-side Girvin landfill under pressure from neighbors and developers but then had to reopen it when the state ruled the northside landfill was full. The city then negotiated for additional capacity on the north side as a temporary solution, to the displeasure of the landfill's neighbors. When the southeast permits were finally rescinded, four private waste disposal companies offered to build landfills on the west side of Duval County. Hazouri initially opposed private ownership of a city facility, but negotiations led to Waste Management Systems, Inc., operating what became a city-owned landfill opened at Trail Ridge during the next mayoral administration. In the end, the landfill dispute cost Hazouri support among environmentalists. It also raised questions among other voters about an administration unable to implement a policy that cost the city millions of dollars and did not resolve the city's waste management problems.[37]

The second carryover proposal from the Godbold administration was for a refuse-to-energy facility. Hazouri initially endorsed a $400 million, 3,000-ton-per-day, mass-burn unit in a message to city council in the fall of 1988. In addition to the consultant's recommendations, the mayor also had the support of the politically powerful Jacksonville Chamber of Commerce and the city's major daily, the business-oriented *Florida Times-Union*. The paper published articles about successful incinerators in the Tampa Bay area, along with reports of their successful utilization in New Jersey, Connecticut, France, Germany, and Japan. Subsequent environmental investigations, however, documented substantial mercury contamination in the Everglades due in part to the Tampa Bay incinerators. To its credit the paper also reported decisions to postpone mass-burn facilities in Seattle and Los Angeles, as well as stories about the dangers of toxic ash.[38]

Environmentalists from the local Sierra Club and Audubon Society mobilized in opposition. They brought to Jacksonville Professor Paul Connett of St. Lawrence University, a leading national opponent of refuse-to-energy plants who condemned such facilities for their toxic-ash residue and possible links to cancer. The local alternative newspaper, *Folio Weekly,* supported the environmentalists. The city's Environmental Protection Board, under the leadership of its chairman, Robert Grimes, resolved that mass burn was "the least known of the alternatives we have available" for waste disposal and should be considered "only after the integrity of municipal solid waste incineration technology is proven." Concerns for the environment were matched by concerns for the high cost of such a plant. City council members sensitive to costs began backing off their support. The *Florida Times-Union* editorial writers modified their earlier endorsements, and the environmental mayor stopped talking about it. Support for the mass-burn facility disappeared, and the proposed facility was not even mentioned in the adoption of the city's 2010 Comprehensive Plan.[39]

Hazouri faced another problem with regard to solid waste management: its expense. His successful recycling program introduced in the fall of 1988 cost more than anticipated because of weak markets for recycled materials. The outcome of the proposed southeast landfill was as yet undetermined, but its estimated cost had risen from $10 to $60 million dollars. Closing, then reopening and expanding existing landfills was also expensive. In July 1989 Hazouri sought funds to expand recycling as well as to meet other increased costs of solid waste disposal. In his proposed budget that October, the mayor requested a $10 monthly or $120 annual garbage fee from all single-family households. Businesses, apartment complexes, and condominiums would be assessed increased tipping fees at landfills. Provision would be made to pay the garbage fees for elderly and low-income renters and homeowners. Other cities in Florida had a similar tax.[40]

Unfortunately, the new fee was added to the budget without adequate explanation to city council. Their negative response was not surprising. In addition, city officials did a poor job of communicating to voters the necessity for the new fee, which was perceived rightly as a new tax. Their angry protests attracted council's attention but were partially offset by business support for the tax. After much lobbying, and threats of severe budgetary cutbacks if the fee was not passed, city council reluctantly authorized the tax by a ten to nine margin. The issue, however, dragged on. In his 1990 budget, the mayor reduced the annual levy to $96, and council again passed it. Voter pressures continued into the 1991 mayoral campaign with polls showing continued opposition to the tax and the way Hazouri introduced it. It played a part in Hazouri's defeat for reelection in May.[41]

Challenges to Minority Set-Asides and Affirmative Action

While the environment provided the mayor with his greatest opportunities for success and failure, race relations remained an ongoing challenge to make local government work fairly for the city's African American minority. Like his predecessors, the mayor was committed to equal opportunities for all residents. "In our Jacksonville," he said in his inaugural address and again in his first budget message, "there will be no place for racism, sexism or ageism. In our government, intolerance will never be tolerated."[42]

In his first week in office, Hazouri announced plans to review the city's minority set-aside program. Its goal of setting aside 10 percent of city contracts for minority contractors had never been met. Since its passage in 1984 by the Godbold administration, never more than 4 percent of total contracts had gone to minorities, with African Americans getting a little more than 1 percent.[43]

Another problem was that some, though not all, white businessmen were "violating the spirit and intent of the law." A disproportionate share of set-aside contracts were going to what critics called "false fronts," or "shell" companies where half-ownership might be minority or female but management remained with white males. Inge Willis Enterprise, Inc., an asphalt provider, was a case in point. When its founder, Inge Willis, was dying of cancer, he gave control of the company to his son but willed majority ownership to his widow, thus qualifying the firm to bid as a minority contractor. It did more minority set-aside work than any other company in Jacksonville. Investigative reporter Michael Romaner found that of 127 qualified minority contractors, 21, or almost 16 percent, were jointly owned by white men and white women (husbands and wives or sons and mothers). Yet they secured 34 percent of set-aside contracts, more than were obtained either by African Americans or by women alone. Often the occupational license was in the man's name as was the corporate presidency.[44]

The mayor appointed a special task force under mayoral aide Alton Yates, which recommended that minority contracts be limited to firms with at least 51 percent minority ownership. Minority owners would have to prove they actually controlled day-to-day operations, and they would have to have experience in the fields in which they bid. The task force also recommended a goal of 25 percent of contracts to be set aside for minorities, one-half for African Americans and one-half for women, to be implemented over three years. Despite opposition from the Florida chapter of the Association of General Contractors of America and C. H. Barco Contracting, Inc., city council passed the revisions in April 1988, a major victory for the mayor. It also authorized a study of minority contracting done with the city.[45]

Nine months later, with an increasing number of contracts going to minority businesses, the United States Supreme Court in *City of Richmond v. J. A. Crosson* reviewed the entire minority set-aside concept. The court ruled that racial preferences were unconstitutional in such programs unless authorities could prove they would remedy a pattern of previous discrimination. In response the city officials initially suspended the program, halting virtually all minority contracting with the city. Then in March 1989, the mayor, acting against the advice of his general counsel, reinstituted the program, assured that the disparity study in progress would justify its existence. The Association of General Contractors and Barco immediately challenged the decision in court. U.S. District Court judge John H. Moore II issued a temporary restraining order and subsequently an injunction overruling the mayor and closing down the program. The city appealed and the U.S. Circuit Court of Appeals overruled Moore, but the contractors returned to court and won again.[46]

Meanwhile, minority businesses suffered. Over the next year, minority contracts declined from $3.8 million to $750,000, mostly for janitorial or landscape work. The largest black construction company laid off half its workers. In another case, Marion Graham's Logistical Transportation Company, recently named Small Business of the Year by the Florida Department of Commerce, had successfully sold fuel oil to the city for two years at one cent a gallon over the wholesale price. Following the court injunction, instead of continuing the old contract in which both the wholesaler and Logistical did business, the wholesaler, Belcher Oil Company, squeezed out the smaller minority business, selling directly to the city.[47]

To verify past discrimination against minority businesses, the city contracted with D. J. Miller & Associates of Atlanta to examine conditions in Jacksonville. Its report in November 1989 verified the minority belief that past systematic discrimination had led to the extreme disparity between black and white businesses in the city.

The facts were there. From 1979 to 1989, the city awarded over $944 million in construction procurement, professional services, and construction contracts. Approximately $30 million, or 3 percent, went to minorities and women. Blacks received one-third of that, or about 1 percent. Even in the program's best year following passage of Hazouri's amendment to the set-aside ordinance, black participation never exceeded 2 percent. Most additional business went to women. By contrast, majority contractors secured 97 percent of city contracts. Clearly minorities were receiving only a fraction of the set-aside goals and a tiny portion of the city's business.[48]

The report examined the availability of black and female businesses to bid on city contracts and concluded that both "were significantly underutilized compared to their availability." Women fared slightly better than blacks.[49]

The consultants also looked at the historical record to find the pattern of racial discrimination required by the Supreme Court ruling. From slavery through segregation to the present, the white majority population dominated the black minority in virtually every aspect of city life in Jacksonville. (Even when blacks were a majority from the 1880s to the First World War, whites dominated.) In education, blacks first sued for school desegregation in 1960, six years after *Brown v. Board of Education.* Eleven years later, the federal courts finally forced a foot-dragging school board to comply. Still later, in 1985, the NAACP went back to court claiming segregation had increased since the 1971 ruling. In 1989, the federal circuit court of appeals agreed. In the area of criminal justice, the Supreme Court in 1972 struck down the city's vagrancy law enforced primarily against blacks, due to its vagueness and discriminatory effects. Two years later, the

Florida Advisory Committee to the U.S. Commission on Civil Rights criticized the sheriff's department for police harassment and discrimination. In the city's Department of Public Safety, firefighter Winston Nash brought suit against the city, claiming racial discrimination in his quest for promotion. Judge Moore in the U.S. District Court upheld the city, but the U.S. Court of Appeals once again overruled him in support of Nash. In the private sector, the courts found "substantial evidence" of "racial harassment" in the Southern Bell workplace. The record showed a pattern of discrimination even after the Supreme Court school desegregation decision of 1954 and the Civil Rights Acts of 1964, 1965, and 1968.[50]

Another line of inquiry by Miller & Associates examined economic barriers to African Americans. To begin, Jacksonville African Americans earned less than whites. In the Greater Jacksonville Metropolitan Area in 1979–80, black households on average earned 58 percent of the annual income of white households. They represented 19 percent of the metro population but earned only 8 percent of the total income of all households. At the lower end of the income scale, 53 percent of Jacksonville's welfare recipients were African American, two and one half times their proportion of the population. By whatever measurement, black income was substantially less than that of whites.[51]

So too was black wealth, which might be used to start a business. Over the years, due to the history of poverty and discrimination, African Americans had accumulated less wealth from inheritances, savings, or home ownership than had whites. Only 2,800 black households, or 3.3 percent of the population, received interest, dividends, or net rental income from property. That income equaled less than 2 percent of such income received by all Jacksonville households. Further, while more than half of Jacksonville's African American families owned homes, most lived in segregated neighborhoods where housing values were less than in the white suburbs and values appreciated at slower rates. The absence of wealth made securing loans, regardless of discrimination, more difficult.[52]

Another way for African Americans and others to enter business was to work one's way up from construction worker to self-employment and then to business owner. Again blacks fared less well than did women or white males. Barriers included exclusion from union-managed apprenticeship programs and state certification rules. In addition, very few black workers moved into supervisory ranks in white construction companies. Further, few larger white contractors were willing to hire black subcontractors. And there was limited access to outside funding. All of these barriers worked to keep African Americans out of the construction business. Still, by 1980 blacks had managed to establish 235 businesses in the various construction trades.[53]

Finally, Miller & Associates interviewed in depth a cross section of fifty-two business people—black, white, Asian, Hispanic, male, and female—in Jacksonville for their perceptions. Several themes emerged. Local banks discriminated in their issuance of credit. Minorities faced discriminatory apprenticeship, union, and licensing procedures. Shell companies took business away from legitimate minority firms. Frequently, blacks when employed were assigned the more dangerous, heavy, and menial work. City officials and prime contractors deterred, intimidated, and discouraged minorities by their rules, policies, and business practices. Suppliers jacked up prices to them. Overall, minority business respondents described an inner circle of white businessmen, "a good ole boy" network, keeping nonwhite businesses out of the marketplace. The business climate was so unfair and discriminatory practices so prevalent, they believed, that it became "commonplace for Blacks and others who want to go into business for themselves to have to leave Jacksonville in order to make a living."[54]

The report, released in November 1990, paved the way for the reinstatement of Jacksonville's minority set-aside program. The report also reflected the Hazouri administration's commitment to equal opportunities for minorities, as well as the limitations on its abilities to achieve that goal. The challenge of gaining minority access to government contracts would continue into the next administration.

Meanwhile, the mayor also sought to expand affirmative action in employment at city hall. By executive order in August 1987, Hazouri directed the Office of Equal Employment to remedy underutilization of minorities and women in city employment. The mayor authorized the director to make recommendations regarding employment, promotions, placement, and training toward meeting the goals of affirmative action passed by city council and the Tanzler administration in 1977.[55]

In each category of employment the goal for African Americans had been set at about 21 percent, or slightly less than their proportion of the city's population. For the less-skilled categories such as protective services or paraprofessional, clerical, or service maintenance employment, the goals were no problem. A disproportionate number of African Americans worked in these lower-paid jobs. But for administrative and professional categories, the goal of achieving full utilization of minorities challenged city hall. The Godbold administration never reached it. Neither did Mayor Hazouri, except with his immediate staff in the mayor's office. There he appointed ten African American administrators and professionals (six men and four women) out of a total of thirty-eight, for 26 percent. But across city government, the figures were less impressive. Among administrators, the number of African Americans increased during the first two years from sixteen to twenty, but as a percentage of total city employees, they declined from 7.9 percent to 7.6 percent. Black professionals increased from 113 to 137 during this period, up slightly from 9.7 percent to 10.8 percent, but far short of the goal of 21 percent.[56]

The affirmative action officer blamed the lack of progress in part on the continuing Rule of One policy that limited appointments and promotions to the individual with the combination of best test score and most seniority. Hazouri, like Godbold before him, saw the Rule of One as stifling management choice but was unable to change it during his tenure in office. There were other reasons, including the absence of sufficient minority applicants, limited searches, and at times a less than total commitment toward affirmative action goals on the part of some department heads.[57]

While Hazouri tried to increase minority hiring and legitimize minority set-aside policies, frustrations were building in the African American community. They exploded on the night of September 26, 1989, at a city council meeting in which three black members walked out and were forcibly returned to council chambers by sheriff's deputies. The three members—Dietra Micks, Denise Lee, and Warren Jones—had tried repeatedly without success to secure funding in the city budget for sewer and drainage relief in the aftermath of heavy rainstorms that flooded their north-side districts, resulting in two deaths. Their departure left city council without a quorum (four other council members had excused absences for the night). Council president Tillie Fowler recessed the meeting, ordered a lockdown of city hall to prevent the council members' departure, and issued warrants to force their return to the meeting. They were returned with council member Micks in handcuffs. Fowler's actions were legal but heavy-handed. City council was under a state mandate to vote that night on the city budget.[58]

The arrests triggered outrage in the African American community. At a news conference the following day, state senator Arnette Girardeau, supported by state representatives Betty Holzendorf and Corrine Brown, NAACP president Willye Dennis, and numerous black clergy, attacked the council president for her disrespect of the black council members. The following week, more than a thousand north-side residents marched on city hall protesting the arrests and what they considered a general city neglect of north-side schools, parks, streets, drainage, and other governmental services. Subsequently Hazouri met with a delegation of black ministers and agreed to consider a "shopping list" of projects for the north side. City council met on October 10 and approved a long-delayed Royal Terrace sewage project in Lee's district and funneled additional development dollars into a nearly depleted Northwest Quadrant Economic Development Trust Fund.[59]

But to ten-year council veteran Jones, these actions were mere Band-Aids. For years he had campaigned for infrastructure improvements on the north side. When federal dollars dried up in the early 1980s, he supported an increase in the local gasoline tax for that purpose. In the past three years, however, of six projects completed, four were in the more affluent south side and only one on the north side. City officials claimed that six projects had been identified on the north side but had been delayed by problems ranging from land acquisition to state and federal permits. Such explanations carried little weight. For Jones, south-side suburban projects got completed and north-side inner-city projects remained on the drawing boards.[60]

Drainage was just the tip of the iceberg. Twenty years after city-county consolidation, Jacksonville African Americans were still waiting for major road, park, and school projects to get done. In a series of stories about the north side (then referred to as the Northwest Quadrant because of the imprecise boundaries of Interstates 95 and 10), Florida Times-Union reporter David Hosansky investigated conditions in an area of Jacksonville inhabited by 112,000 residents, or one-sixth of the city's population. Two-thirds of that population were African American or other minorities; their earnings were two-thirds the median income of other city dwellers; their high school graduation rate was less than half the city rate; and the homocide rate was three times that of the entire city. Hosansky found an area with pockets of middle-income prosperity, but mostly there was blight caused by aging cinder block and clapboard houses, industrial and environmental wastes, inadequate parks and rundown schools, inferior municipal services, and too much crime. He also found in the early years of consolidation that while the city paved many streets and installed streetlights on the north side, it gave higher priority to providing multiple city services to the rapidly growing south side. The result had been an increasing deterioration of a major part of the city only partially offset by the efforts of a handful of local citizen associations struggling to maintain their neighborhoods.[61]

Hazouri was sympathetic to the problems of the north side (though he along with all five at-large council members lived on the suburban south side). He increased funding for north-side street projects in his 1991 budget, and he pledged to get the north side on a par with the rest of the city. But when asked whether the area deserved "disproportionate funding" to catch up with the rest of the city, the mayor demurred. Such an approach, he said, would be unrealistic. It could not be done at the expense of other areas of the city. In the past, of course, other areas had benefited at the expense of the north side. The walk-out by Micks, Lee, and Jones from city council reflected a frustration that had been building for many years.[62]

Frustrations with Downtown Development

If improving race relations remained an ongoing, often frustrating challenge, so too did the development of downtown. Hazouri faced a tough act following the accomplishments of his predecessor's "billion dollar" decade. Downtown Jacksonville in 1987 looked to be in the process of major transformation. There was the opening of the Jacksonville Landing, the Enterprise Center with its Omni Hotel, the bank and parking garage, and the Southern Bell tower. Construction had begun on the new American Heritage Life Building (later sold to the Humana Corporation) and would soon begin for a new Barnett Center (later Bank America). Construction also was underway for the 0.7-mile-long Automatic Skyway Express (ASE) mass transit people mover from the Prime Osborne Convention Center to Enterprise Center. Across the river the new Prudential Plaza, river walk, and duPont Center added their part. Clearly much had been accomplished during the Godbold years. In addition, Wilma Southeast, Inc., an Atlanta-based subsidiary of a Dutch conglomerate, offered to buy a five-block segment of waterfront property east of the then city hall to create a $500 million Renaissance Place, "a city within a city," that would house four office towers, retail complex, hotel, performing arts center, and marina. Observers compared the proposal to creating New York's Rockefeller Center.[63]

The new mayor praised this progress in his inaugural address and looked to the goal of creating "a city where people [would] live downtown, . . . a downtown that is alive 24 hours a day with business, theater, concerts and conventions, . . . a city safe by day and safe by night."[64]

Achieving these goals, however, proved elusive. The Hazouri administration proposed and supported multiple development projects over the next four years. The mayor wanted to bring first the Houston Oilers and then other National Football League teams to Jacksonville. He considered moving the Jacksonville zoo downtown and building an aquarium as a tourist attraction near the Gator Bowl. There was talk of moving city hall from the riverfront to Hemming Plaza (accomplished in a later administration), replacing the outdated civic auditorium with a modern arts and entertainment center (also accomplished in a later administration), locating the PGA Hall of Fame in Jacksonville, building hotels adjacent to the Prime Osborne Center to stimulate the convention trade, creating a downtown shopping mall, developing downtown housing, and completing Renaissance Place on the river. None of these projects broke ground during Hazouri's one term, in part because of the national recession beginning in late 1989 that shut down plans for the convention hotels and downtown housing.[65]

The city did build new jails (under court order), a city hall annex, and multistory parking garages. City officials persuaded Maxwell House not to leave town, and they secured council support for a $60 million overhaul of the Gator Bowl in anticipation of landing a professional football franchise. But offsetting these achievements were the closing of downtown's largest department store (May Cohens); closing of the shipyards, also downtown; bankruptcy of two south-bank hotels and a restaurant; sale and removal of Gulf Life Insurance Company from Jacksonville; and sale of Florida National Bank, a Jacksonville landmark, to First Union of Charlotte.[66]

A good example of the frustration for the Hazouri efforts downtown was Renaissance Place. Wilma Southeast offered $42 million for five blocks of prime real estate on the river that then included the jail, courthouse, a warehouse, and parking lots. In return, they wanted the north-bank river walk extended at a cost of $7 million from the Jacksonville Landing to Renaissance Place to create a pedestrian access. They wanted the city to build nearby parking lots. They also wanted an extension of the Automatic Skyway Express from Enterprise Center (the Omni Hotel) to the Gator Bowl with a stop at Renaissance Place, at a cost upward of $55 million.[67]

The biggest obstacle was funding the people mover. For segments already built or under construction, the federal government had provided one-half the cost, the state one-quarter, and the city the rest. City officials feared that if the city committed up front to expand the people mover, the feds would not support it, leaving the city to go it alone. Negotiations dragged on for two years. Finally, the best Hazouri could do was an offer committing the city to build the people mover *provided* (emphasis mine) the state and federal governments did their part. By then the national economy was slipping into recession and Wilma Southeast backed out.[68]

Should Hazouri have been bolder in his quest for Renaissance Place? Critics said yes, but supporters argued that his predecessors provided excessive enhancements for the Jacksonville Landing at taxpayer expense. Mitch Atalla, the mayor's chief administrative officer, supported partnering for downtown development but cautioned against subsidies, adding "We'll always work together in a public-private partnership . . . but you reach a point where you have to . . . weigh the alternatives of whether the public's good that's to come from the project is worth the taxpayers' money as a direct subsidy." Already city dollars were committed to new jails, solid waste disposal, expansion of park and recreational facilities, senior citizen centers, suburban libraries, public housing, more firefighters, and more police to fight crime, especially the crack cocaine epidemic that hit Jacksonville and other American cities in the mid to late 1980s. Hazouri saw downtown as important, but he did not give it the same high priority that Godbold did. He claimed to see a broader view where human services, the environment, public safety, parks and recreation, transportation, and neighborhoods of the entire consolidated Jacksonville ranked with the importance of downtown.[69]

The puzzle about the Hazouri years is why he was not reelected in 1991. Most incumbent mayors in Jacksonville since World War II had been reelected, and this mayor four years earlier had won a landslide victory. At the end of his first year, *Times-Union* reporter William A. Scott wrote that

Hazouri's "first year in office is being regarded almost universally as successful," based on his anti-odor and tax-for-tolls referendum campaigns. Jacksonville University political science professor Joan Carver added, "He provided strong leadership, taking hold quickly."[70]

A year later, Scott reported Hazouri's continued popularity in public opinion polls, but he also described the criticism that came from certain business leaders over the toll referendum, odor controls, and the failure to land the Wilma project or some comparable major downtown development. Not all business leaders, however, felt that way. Chamber of Commerce chairman Mark Hulsey met regularly with the mayor and called him "a populist who cares for people." William Hightower, president of the recently arrived AT&T Transtech, praised "his commitment to the economic development of the city." Professor Carver gave Hazouri credit for "tackling some tough issues" like trash and odors. A University of North Florida history professor described the mayor's efforts with regard to crime fighting, environment, transportation, downtown development, and race relations and concluded, "Much of the report card on the Hazouri administration remains to be written."[71]

By 1990, three years into Hazouri's mayoral administration, opinion seemed more sharply divided. A *Florida Times-Union* series on the most powerful people in Jacksonville ranked Hazouri number one, but only because of his office. In the story, reporter Paul van Osdol stressed the antagonism between certain business leaders and the mayor because of the latter's "fat cats" remarks during the tax-for-tolls referendum campaign. But the issue was larger than that one campaign. Whereas Hazouri's predecessor had forged a partnership with the business community based on consensus building, this mayor challenged the old guard. In reaction, they felt Hazouri was too combative and did not listen to them. Other business leaders disagreed. They liked his "independent thinking" challenging the "good ole boys" who had run the city for too long. The issue of Hazouri's style became a factor in the search for an opponent for the 1991 mayoral campaign.[72]

That fall, the old guard found their candidate to oppose Hazouri in 64-year-old Ed Austin, a popular, long-time state's attorney who thought he could do a better job than Hazouri of running the city. Austin also was unhappy with the mayor's attempts to capture the spotlight in the local war on drugs. That fall Hazouri hurt himself politically by pushing through city council the $96 garbage tax as part of the city's annual budget. A *Florida Times-Union* poll taken shortly afterward showed the mayor's favorable rating at only 23 percent, down from 52 percent in March 1989.[73]

A subsequent December poll of Democrats pairing Austin against Hazouri gave the challenger a 53 percent majority, more than twice the incumbent's 24 percent return. The remaining poll respondents were undecided. These numbers were significant in this still predominantly Democratic, albeit conservative, community, as the Republican party was not expected to field a candidate in the May general election. Thus at the beginning of 1991, with the primary in April, the challenger apparently had taken a decisive lead over the incumbent.[74]

Four months later, Austin narrowly won the primary and thus the mayoral election. Out of 104,619 ballots cast, the challenger won 50.86 percent, just 1,819 more votes than the incumbent. Hazouri had closed the gap in part by recanting on the garbage tax and promising to repeal it if reelected. He also ran an aggressive campaign championing his tax-for-tolls victory, anti-odor successes, and the substantial economic development during the years of his administration. In contrast, Austin's efforts appeared lackluster as he challenged fiscal mismanagement, criticized what he called "the solid waste crisis," and took credit for the city's fight on crime. At times as the momentum shifted toward the incumbent, the issues seemed subordinate to the images of a hard-charging, youthful Hazouri challenging the older, more cautious Austin. In the end, the 2,311 Republican voters who switched party allegiance and presumably voted for Austin in the Democratic primary may have provided the margin of victory.[75]

Yet also important was the question of Hazouri's declining popularity since 1987. If incumbents usually won elections, what happened to him? First, his introduction of the garbage tax, though later rescinded, provoked opposition among tax-conscious voters. He also lost some earlier business support with the anti-odor campaign and the tax-for-tolls referendum. Further, persistence on the southeast landfill prompted many environmentalists, including both the Sierra Club and the Florida League of Conservation Voters, to endorse Austin. Union support was split, and while he won heavily in the African American community, significant leaders like state representative Betty Holzendorf opposed him. So too did Jake Godbold, his predecessor, with many of his supporters. Mayors inevitably lose support over time by the policy decisions they make and by the way they respond to interest groups in the community. Successful mayors heal wounds after fights. Hazouri apparently would not or could not do that sufficiently, and he lost his governing majority as a result.[76]

He left office with some solid accomplishments for consolidated Jacksonville in the odor cleanup, abolition of bridge tolls, and construction of the long overdue jail. He also built libraries, senior citizen centers, and parks in the suburbs. Unresolved were the challenges of solid waste disposal and downtown development. Beyond his and perhaps anyone's control were the closing of the shipyards, sale and removal of Gulf Life Insurance Company to Nashville, sale of Florida National Bank, and the national recession that affected local revenues for downtown and across the city. Still, there were new bridges across the St. Johns River (the Acosta and Broward), major expansion of the airport, new Barnett Center and American Heritage Life buildings, and continued development across the consolidated city. Despite a recession at the beginning of the 1990s, Jacksonville during Hazouri's term continued to grow in population, business, and suburban sprawl. There was some progress downtown, in race relations and the environment, but major challenges remained. For Hazouri, his chance to shape the city's future ended when voters rejected his bid for a second term by the narrowest of margins.

CHAPTER 8

THE AUSTIN YEARS

If the previous two mayors, Jake Godbold and Tommy Hazouri, loved the political game, from its ceremonial ribbon cutting to its power brokering, the new Jacksonville mayor, Edward T. Austin, was more in the tradition of Hans Tanzler, the first person to occupy the top seat at city hall after consolidation. Tanzler came to the mayor's office in response to elite leadership calls to clean up what many people perceived to be a corrupt political system, combined with his own desire to set things right. Austin likewise responded to concerns about the city's leadership as well as his own belief that he could do a better job. Neither man was a career politician in the manner of Godbold or Hazouri. As a result, neither man played the political game as well, either. Yet each had a vision of Jacksonville becoming a better city as a result of his term of office.[1]

The 64-year-old, six-foot-four-inch Austin grew up in the Tidewater area of Virginia, played football, and graduated from Duke University, served as an officer in the 101st Airborne Division, earned a law degree from the University of Florida, and came to Jacksonville, where he was elected state's attorney for the Fourth Judicial District in 1969. A popular public official, he served four terms as the lead prosecutor for the area's criminal justice system before his election as mayor.[2]

Following his election in 1991, one of Austin's first decisions brought back to Jacksonville the very capable Alexander "Lex" Hester from Broward County to become his chief administrative officer (CAO) and handle the details of city governance. Hester had been Tanzler's very effective CAO for seven years. The new mayor established his agenda, focusing on developing the downtown, expanding the port, providing more services for children, solving the garbage crisis, and healing racial divisions. Underlying these major themes was a concern to build consensus and to bring the diverse and dispersed Jacksonville community together, spread as residents were over the city's 840 square miles.[3]

Within days of his inauguration Austin met with Tom Petway, insurance executive and chairman-elect of the Chamber of Commerce, to discuss building community consensus. He also recruited Warren Jones, city council's African American president, to take part in the discussion. Together they convened on July 30 a thirteen-member Jacksonville Insight steering committee from diverse constituencies across the city. Austin told the group that he saw consensus building as one of the most important things he could do in office. Jones reported that council members felt the same way. Petway voiced the Chamber's support. Over the succeeding weeks, the steering committee agreed to develop a community vision targeting issues beyond immediate day-to-day concerns, to recruit broad community participation to develop the vision, and to make decisions by a process of consensus.[4]

They chose Bill Nash, retired Prudential Insurance Company regional headquarters president, to chair the process and Carol Spaulding Minor, provost of Florida Community College at Jacksonville, to organize and implement the effort. Together Nash, Minor, and the steering committee recruited community volunteers to begin the vision-building dialogue. Newspaper ads with clip-out coupons resulted in almost 1,400 individuals volunteering and 800 attending the first session at the Prime Osborne Convention Center on February 2, 1992. Meeting in thirty-seven small groups, the volunteers learned about the city's history, discussed contemporary urban problems, and began to envision what the future of Jacksonville might become. They also selected representatives to become part of an ongoing stakeholder group to refine and prioritize the issues. Each city council member also selected a representative. These 101 stakeholders reflecting the racial, ethnic, gender, and geographical composition of the city spent the next four months developing a vision for the city.[5]

Their report, *The Jacksonville Vision,* presented to the mayor on June 4, 1992, identified ten themes. In order of priority, they were:[6]

- quality education for all citizens
- a safe, secure city

- a healthy environment
- planned economic growth
- an effective transportation system
- excellent community relations
- responsive, responsible government
- outstanding parks, recreation, and the arts
- thriving neighborhoods and downtown
- inclusive health and social services

While the vision perhaps appeared too vague to serve as a basis for developing direction for the city, the mayor pledged action toward achieving its goals. He had no direct authority with regard to the goal of "quality education for all citizens," which fell under the purview of the Duval County School Board. Nor was he responsible for "a safe and secure city," which was the elected sheriff's responsibility (though city government did fund law enforcement, unlike the schools). But he could influence the remaining goals.

The third goal, a healthy environment, had been a major community priority since consolidation. Mayor Tanzler cleaned up the St. Johns River; Mayor Godbold focused on solid waste disposal; and Mayor Hazouri campaigned to eliminate odors. None of the efforts were completed by the beginning of the Austin administration, and new threats, such as storm water runoff and the discovery of hazardous waste sites, kept presenting themselves.

Solving Solid Waste Disposal

The immediate problem facing the new mayor was the solid waste disposal crisis carried over from the Godbold and Hazouri administrations, resulting from the state veto of the proposed southeast landfill. Existing landfills were full or approaching capacity and new sites were needed. Even before taking office, Austin in partnership with city council president Eric Smith appointed a landfill advisory commission chaired by John Lanahan, former city council president and JTA board chair. It recommended what became the Trail Ridge landfill in southwestern Duval County on the border of largely rural Baker County. City council awarded a contract to Waste

Fig. 16. Edward L. Austin, mayor of Jacksonville, 1991–1995. By permission of the City of Jacksonville.

Management of North America, Inc., to build and operate the landfill. Neighboring Baker County initially opposed the new site as St. Johns County had done with the southeast landfill. The Baker County Commission, however, responded positively to a Jacksonville offer of $1.3 million plus technical assistance to close its existing landfill. Approval by the Florida Department of Environmental Regulation followed in November 1991, with ground breaking in January. By May 1992 the city had a new functioning landfill good for an estimated twenty years.[7]

The opening of the Trail Ridge landfill successfully ended a five-year saga of politics, economics, and waste disposal, largely to Mayor Austin's credit. Another factor in the saga was the reduced amount of waste to be dumped. It had decreased from 3,300 tons to 2,000 tons per day over the preceding five years. This 40 percent reduction in solid waste was due to the response of Jacksonville residents and businesses to the recycling program introduced in 1988 by Mayor Hazouri. The National Recycling Coalition named the city best in the nation for 1993. Not quite half of Jacksonville households participated in the program, which led Lucy Wallace of the local Sierra Club to note how much more waste could still be reclaimed.[8]

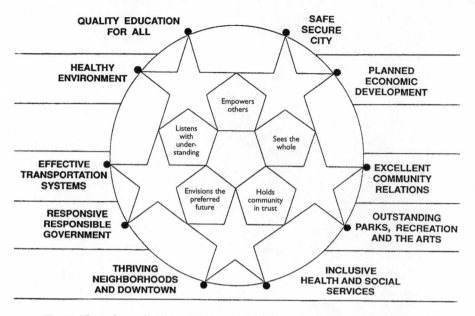

QUALITY EDUCATION FOR ALL

SAFE SECURE CITY

HEALTHY ENVIRONMENT

PLANNED ECONOMIC DEVELOPMENT

Empowers others

Listens with under- standing

Sees the whole

EFFECTIVE TRANSPORTATION SYSTEMS

EXCELLENT COMMUNITY RELATIONS

Envisions the preferred future

Holds community in trust

RESPONSIVE RESPONSIBLE GOVERNMENT

OUTSTANDING PARKS, RECREATION AND THE ARTS

THRIVING NEIGHBORHOODS AND DOWNTOWN

INCLUSIVE HEALTH AND SOCIAL SERVICES

Fig. 17. The Jacksonville Vision. Design by Ted Pappas, a symbolic representation of the priorities and recommendations of the Jacksonville Insight citizens committee.

Hazardous wastes, however, were another matter. Jacksonville had seven Superfund sites awaiting cleanup by the federal government. Work had begun at the notorious Hipps Road site, but it was slow and expensive. The Department of Defense alone earmarked $22 million to clean up hazardous wastes at Jacksonville's three navy bases. The federal Environmental Protection Agency estimated the cost of cleaning up dioxin in the rural community of Whitehouse at $20 million. A wood preserving company had treated lumber with chemicals and simply discharged the residue there from 1954 to 1988.[9]

Meanwhile, air pollution in the city appeared to have improved since the advent of consolidation. According to World Resources Institute, a private environmental group in Washington, Jacksonville at the end of 1993 had not violated federal ozone standards for more than five years, due in part to auto emission inspections introduced by the state and stricter regulation of polluting industries. A year later, the federal Environmental Protection Agency formally removed Jacksonville from the list of cities that violated clean air standards for ozone.[10]

Odor pollution controls introduced by the Hazouri administration also bore fruit during the Austin years. In January 1993, complaints about odors had fallen to a six-year low, particularly as a result of the closing of the Seminole Kraft paper mill in 1992. Not all odors were gone, but as Stafford Campbell, chair of the Greater Arlington Civic Council's environmental committee observed, "Both the severity and frequency of incidents [were] down," adding that though they had not totally disappeared, they were less annoying. The Arlington suburb had suffered disproportionately from the malodorous smells.[11]

Visual pollution controls, in the form of a sign ordinance to remove billboards, also enacted during the Hazouri years, achieved more limited success. Due to take effect in 1992, the law's implementation was delayed by Naegele Outdoor Advertising, the largest billboard company in Jacksonville. It challenged in the courts the right to deprive a business of what it considered to be private property without due compensation. Negotiations followed, and the city reached an agreement with Naegele to reduce but not totally eliminate the signs over a twenty-year period. By the end of the Austin era, 100 billboards had been removed. By 2014, Naegele promised to dismantle 711 out of a total of 1,037 signs, about two-thirds of the signs in the city. Most would be in residential neighborhoods. Signs on federal highways were excluded from the ordinance.[12]

A major challenge to the environmental conscience of Jacksonville came with the construction of AES Cedar Bay beginning in 1988. A coal-fired plant built to provide electricity for Florida Power & Light Company customers in south Florida, it also partnered with Seminole Kraft, promising to generate steam for the paper mill. Supporters of AES Cedar Bay, Inc., claimed the plant would provide jobs and reduce air pollution over Jacksonville and northeast Florida by enabling the neighboring paper mill to shut eight polluting smokestacks. Opponents, led by north-side resident Barbara Broward, saw continuing air pollution with 5,000 tons of discharge annually, more than one-half of which would be sulfuric acid, the primary source of acid rain. City council listened and agreed, passing unanimously a resolution to oppose the power plant. Despite the opposition, AES Cedar Bay secured a state permit until word leaked that fall about Seminole Kraft boilers not being completely shut down. Mayor Austin asked the state Department of Environmental Regulation to revoke

AES Cedar Bay's permit. DER reported "misrepresentation of fact" in the application and recommended suspension of construction until environmental issues were settled. The governor and his cabinet agreed.[13]

In response, AES Cedar Bay made concessions sufficient to win the support of the Jacksonville Chamber of Commerce (which previously had been split on the issues) and the state, but not of Broward and her environmental allies. They persisted until outside forces intervened. Reports of AES Cedar Bay employees falsifying data in Oklahoma and Maine led to the company's stock tumbling on Wall Street. Subsequently, AES Cedar Bay sold its Jacksonville property to U.S. Generating Company of Bethesda, Maryland. The new owners proposed further concessions to reduce airborne emissions and water requirements. They also proposed using low-sulfur coal and natural gas for Seminole Kraft's three boilers. Environmental consultants accepted the modifications and Broward agreed. We have "achieved most of our goals for reducing the project's impact upon the environment," she said. The Sierra Club representatives also agreed. Though not yet able to win battles on their own, environmentalists and neighborhood activists had developed sufficient influence to bring other players to the table and ultimately obtain favorable concessions.[14]

Jacksonville faced continuing environmental threats. The jewel of the city, the St. Johns River, had been substantially cleansed in the early years of consolidation, but many pollutants remained. On the eve of Mayor Austin taking office, *Florida Times-Union* reporter Beverly Keneagy began a monthly series of investigative reports, "A River in Decline." Where there were 48,600 septic tanks in the early 1970s, there now were nearly 90,000, which directly or indirectly drained into the river or its tributaries. Of 569 systems inspected over the preceding nine months, 99, or 17 percent, were failing. Fecal coliform, product of human or animal waste, was the largest water quality problem in the tributaries. In tests conducted in 1990, 47 percent of them failed to meet appropriate health standards. The city allocated $6 million to extend sewers and replace septic tanks beginning in 1987, taking care of seven neighborhoods, but an additional fifteen neighborhoods had been identified for similar upgrading at an added cost of $35 million. One spokesperson estimated $100 million would be needed to clean up all the septic tank spillage into the waterways.[15]

Another category of polluter was privately owned sewage treatment plants. Over the past twenty years, the number of privately owned plants discharging either treated sewage or industrial wastes into the waterways had increased from 125 to 184, and not all of the discharges were adequately treated. In 1990, one-half of the plants violated local regulations, and city officials had more enforcement cases than they could handle.[16]

The worst pollutant was storm water runoff. "When it rains," Keneagy wrote, "the water runs off into the [St. Johns] river and its tributaries. It takes with it oil and grease from roadways [and parking lots], pesticides and chemicals from green lawns and potato and cabbage farms, pet [and other animal] droppings and garbage." An estimated 80 percent of the pollutants in Jacksonville's waterways came from storm water, with the tributaries particularly incapable of flushing or diluting storm water and industrial wastes.[17]

Beginning in 1982, the state required retention ponds for storm water runoff in new developments, but a decade later only about one-half of Jacksonville's storm water runoff systems functioned properly, largely due to lack of proper maintenance. In older neighborhoods of the city, the absence of storm water controls resulted in flooding of streets, homes, and local businesses. The city developed a storm water master plan in partnership with the St. Johns Water Management District in 1993 with anticipated costs in excess of $100 million. To pay for it, Mayor Austin in October 1994 proposed a $30 per year residential storm water tax and made its passage a major goal for his remaining time in office. Other Florida cities, including Miami and Orlando, had already created storm water utilities. But the mayor was unable to persuade city council to act. Polls suggested voters opposed the new tax. Council members raised questions about its fairness to large and small homeowners, large and small businesses, and renters. They also worried about the citywide elections approaching in the spring of 1995. Passage had to await another mayor. Meanwhile, the state Department of Environmental Regulation for the first time in years rated the water quality of the southern portion of the St. Johns River from downtown to Clay County and St. Johns County as poor. The environment and the consolidated city were the losers.[18]

The main source of storm water pollution was development. The Department of Environmental Regulation had downgraded formerly pristine areas of Julington and Durbin Creeks in southern Duval County from good to fair water quality due to storm water, sewage, and other runoffs from the rapidly growing suburb of Mandarin. One-half of the original wetlands that once had helped to filter storm water in the area had disappeared over the preceding five years, destroyed by new housing and waterfront bulkheads. Carole deMort, a marine biologist from the University of North Florida, summed up the problem: "It's more cars, more people, [and] more runoff of fertilizers." These two creeks were among the best in the St. Johns River system.[19]

The worst areas on the river were opposite the Jacksonville naval air station (a Superfund site), downtown (site of shipping wharves until the 1960s), the still-operating shipyards just east of downtown, and the Talleyrand industrial area where for years industrial wastes, heavy metals, chemicals, creosote, and other toxins had spilled into the river. Immediate consequences of waterways pollution included the decline both of commercial and sport fishing and increasing reports of diseased fish with large gaping sores on their bodies, some even rotting alive, attributed to pesticides and PCBs in the river and its tributaries. Responding to the conditions, Congressman Charles Bennett and, later, Governor Lawton Chiles recommended adding the river to the National Estuary Program, opening doors to special federal funding for polluted waterways.[20]

Despite the efforts of the city's Bio-Environmental Services Division, the region's St. Johns Water Management District, state environmental regulators, and the federal Environmental Protection Agency, Jacksonville's environment remained fragile. The needs and desires of developers, home owners, and businesses continually threatened the land, air, and water of the region. Progress occurred but so did environmental deterioration. It was an ongoing struggle that would continue into the twenty-first century.

Rising Racial Tensions

Comparable struggles during the Austin administration came in the effort to improve community relations, another goal of the Jacksonville Vision. Most African Americans had not voted for the mayor, yet initially he attempted to show good faith with the appointment of a black deputy mayor, two black fire chiefs, three black department heads, and one black each to the boards of the Jacksonville Transportation Authority and Jacksonville Electric Authority. Almost all of the appointments met with criticism from black community leaders. Some questioned the qualifications of certain appointments. Others voiced concern that some appointees lived in predominantly white suburbs, not on the north side. Still others criticized appointments of African Americans who had not supported the mayor in his election campaign.[21]

Of greater importance were events in Jacksonville contributing to interracial tensions. Just prior to the new mayor entering office, a community advisory board at the *Florida Times-Union* warned that race relations in the city were becoming more polarized. In May 1991, the NAACP charged that the voluntary magnet program to desegregate the Duval County public schools was failing to achieve its goals. At Neptune Beach, police sought an acknowledged white supremacy leader suspected of slaying an African American veteran of Operation Desert Storm. Downtown, a sheriff's office investigation found that two police officers "had violated department regulations" in the handling of an African American who died following a scuffle at the city jail. A Duval County judge subsequently ruled the action "justifiable homicide." In June, police arrested an eighty-year-old white male in Springfield who suddenly began shooting at black neighbors. In suburban Arlington, a street brawl between whites and blacks led to stepped-up police patrols. On Halloween, two youths dressed as Ku Klux Klansmen burned a wooden cross in the yard of a black family recently moved into a white neighborhood. In school, interracial violence also appeared to be increasing.[22]

These events were but a prelude to the explosion resulting from the tape-recorded comments of Chief Circuit Judge John E. Santora Jr., published by the *Florida Times-Union* on Sunday, December 22, 1991. The 68-year-old judge grew up in the segregated Deep South. Born in Birmingham, Alabama, he moved to Jacksonville as a teenager, playing football at old Landon High School. He enlisted and became a navy fighter pilot during World War II. Subsequently he graduated from the University of Florida Law School and was elected first as a municipal judge and then circuit judge in 1972. In 1985 his judicial peers chose him to become the Fourth Circuit's chief of judges, a position he was reelected to repeatedly. Personally an often funny and sociable man, on the bench Santora was blunt and outspoken, competent but not distinguished. The Jacksonville Bar Association consistently ranked him in the bottom quartile of Duval County judges. In his early years on the bench, Santora gained the reputation for fairness toward African Americans in the courtroom, expecting police officers to press their cases against blacks as convincingly as they did against whites. He created a juvenile program where youths served as jurors in trials involving other youths. He named John Thomas, an African American, as head of one of these juries. He honestly believed race was not a factor in his courtroom. Yet like many white males of his generation, privately he held racist and sexist views. In the *Times-Union* interview, Santora expressed his opposition to interracial marriages, blamed crime in the public schools on desegregation, stereotyped welfare mothers as black and irresponsible, and believed society held blacks to lesser standards of behavior and achievement.[23]

Reactions to the publication of Santora's private views came quickly and with vehemence. A. Wellington Barlow, president of the D. W. Perkins Bar Association, a group of primarily black lawyers, reported his office was inundated with calls and comments. "The basic gist of public sentiment," he said, "is that regardless of what the chief judge says, no person with those racial views can sit on the bench and be fair." Rodney Gregory, board chairman of the Jacksonville Urban League, called the judge's remarks "inappropriate, insensitive and unprofessional." Willye Dennis, president of the Jacksonville branch of the NAACP, added, "It's a crying shame that a person holding the highest official position in the Duval County court makes such public remarks of a clearly racist nature, and then claims that his ability to judge others is untainted." Members of the predominantly black Interdenominational Ministers Alliance also criticized Santora's views, as did city council president Warren Jones. The Reverend Jesse Jackson, in town to watch his son play in the Gator Bowl, added his condemnation.[24]

Protest demonstrations followed at the Duval County Courthouse beginning on Christmas Eve. White Jacksonvillians also participated. The Board of Governors of the Jacksonville Bar Association called Santora's comments "inappropriate, insensitive and harmful to the entire judiciary system and to the community as a whole." Mayor Austin called the judge's remarks "inexcusable, thoughtless, unfortunate and distressing." Even the conservative *Times-Union* editorial board suggested Santora should step down as chief judge and allow the Judicial Qualification Commission to determine his overall record for fairness. Meanwhile, backers of the chief judge rallied with their own demonstrations of support.[25]

On Thursday, January 2, at a press conference in the mayor's office, with Austin at his side, Santora apologized. "I would never purposely say anything to hurt any group of people. Those remarks did hurt some of our citizens and for that I am truly sorry." Black community leaders responded by calling the apology not enough. The picketing of the courthouse continued, climaxing in a 4,000-person rally and march led by the Reverend Jackson the next day.[26]

The issue, however, was no longer just the intemperate remarks of a chief judge. In the week following the rally, the focus shifted to the larger reality of the great racial divide in Jacksonville. The Reverend Tom Diamond, perhaps tongue-in-cheek, "thanked" the judge for waking up the black community. Bishop Philip R. Cousin of the African Methodist Episcopal Church agreed. The Interfaith Council of Jacksonville sought to bridge the racial divide. More important were the actions of the executive committee of the Jacksonville Chamber of Commerce under the leadership of its chairman, Tom Petway. It first called for the judge's resignation from the circuit court. Then it recognized its responsibility "to begin healing the wounds suffered by our community—both black and white, Christian and Jew." Following meetings with both black and white leaders, it announced its support for a community summit "to focus on resolving the social and economic issues that now threaten to damage Jacksonville and its residents." Again the conservative *Times-Union* editorial board agreed.[27]

On January 9, Mayor Austin met with more than one hundred community leaders at the Prime Osborne Convention Center. Groups taking part included the NAACP, Urban League, Chamber of Commerce, United Way of Northeast Florida, Advocates for a Better Jacksonville, and the Interdenominational Ministers Alliance. Individual community leaders attending included the mayor, city council president, sheriff, state's attorney, and school superintendent. At the meeting the mayor announced the formation of Jacksonville Together, the Mayor's Council on Community Reconciliation.[28]

A series of public meetings followed over the next six weeks involving some five hundred volunteers. Their efforts, in large groups and small, led to forty-four recommendations directed to twenty-one community organizations seeking economic, social, religious, governmental, educational, criminal justice, media, and health and human services solutions for the inequities in the city. Major recommendations included:

- reinstatement of minority set-aside programs for government contracts;
- infrastructure improvements on the predominantly minority north side of the city;
- increased minority representation in all aspects of the criminal justice system;
- increased job training opportunities for minorities;
- commitment to increased minority hiring at entry and executive levels;
- full-service community education opportunities with special attention to parenting, drugs, and sex education;
- renewed talks between the school board and the NAACP;
- balanced news coverage in the media;
- neighborhood/community meetings to establish dialogue; and
- a series of citywide annual events to celebrate Jacksonville's multicultural diversity.[29]

Following the submission of the report to the mayor, Rev. B. Fred Woolsey, executive director of the National Conference of Christians and Jews and of the Interfaith Council, and one of five cochairs of Jacksonville Together, summed up his feelings in an essay in *Folio Weekly*. He saw the beginning of a community consensus on race relations resulting from the dialogue and its recommendations. A broad cross section of Jacksonville had asserted that "racism has no place in our community, [and] disparities must end." Jacksonville Together, he concluded, was a sign of the fundamental health of the city in its response to the Santora incident.[30]

Implementation of the task force recommendations moved slowly. In midsummer the mayor assigned oversight responsibility to the Jacksonville Community Relations Commission (JCRC) under the leadership of its executive director, Vivian Jackson, another of the five cochairs of Jacksonville Together. At year's end the JCRC requested status reports from the twenty-one agencies assigned to implement the forty-four recommendations. Fourteen of them responded, reporting limited progress. Jackson saw few new initiatives, mainly reports of ongoing programs. The Duval County School Board had expanded multicultural awareness training for teachers and students; the Chamber of Commerce had taken steps to provide greater access for minority businesses; and the sheriff's department, in focusing on at-risk children, had introduced half a dozen community programs with partners including the Police Athletic League, Urban

League, Abyssinia Baptist Church, Daniel Memorial, and Jacksonville Chapter of Black Psychologists. Health care agencies had increased their efforts to provide medical and psychological services for poorer blacks with the creation of the Northwest Quadrant Community Health Care Center, Inc., the first full-service public health clinic in the area. Reactions were mixed. Bryan Davis from the state's attorney's office sensed some progress. So did Deputy Mayor Ronnie Ferguson. Yet city council president Jones added, "We still have a long way to go in educating the majority community about the plight of the minority community. . . . We're no longer dealing with overt forms [of racism] but covert forms, and those are the most difficult to address." A year later, the JCRC reported further progress in cultural diversity training, job opportunities, especially in city contracts, and governmental services to lower-income families. Mayor Austin acknowledged that racial problems continued to hinder improved community relations as well as economic development.[31]

Probably the biggest obstacle to improved race relations in the minds of many African Americans came from the mayor's reaction to the proposed new minority set-aside ordinance resulting from one of the recommendations of Jacksonville Together. Shortly after Austin accepted the recommendation in February 1992, city council president Jones moved to implement it. The city's original set-aside program had been nullified by the Supreme Court decision in *The City of Richmond v. J.A. Crosson* in 1989. Subsequently, Atlanta consultants had conducted a disparity study reporting a past history of local discrimination, which met the criteria of the U.S. Supreme Court. Jones's bill, entitled the Equal Business Opportunity Program, also sought to meet the criteria and level the playing field for African Americans and women. Other minorities were not included at this time. Jones shepherded his bill through committees, and city council passed it unanimously on June 23.[32]

A week later Mayor Austin vetoed the bill and the African American community once more rose in protest. Austin claimed the bill established quotas, which it did to the extent that 10 percent of contracts might be allocated to minorities if voluntary goals were not achieved. The mayor vehemently opposed the quota, which was a fall-back position if the goals failed. He preferred linking majority contractors with minority contractors and providing incentives to the former to include the latter in their bids. That way minority firms, weakened by the absence of legislation over

the past three years, could build their businesses and eventually bid com-
petitively on their own. Though on the surface a trickle-down approach to
minority contracts, Austin's plan had merit. Austin, however, lost credibility when, in a television interview, he compared existing set-aside plans to
a "welfare type system," clearly a negative stereotype in the eyes of the African American community.[33]

Next, Jones tried to pass the bill over the mayor's veto but failed to secure the necessary two-thirds majority. Austin offered as a substitute his
plan to incorporate incentives to majority contractors, but Jones refused to
support it. Deadlocked, Jones managed to persuade council to pass a resolution to force implementation of the old set-aside law dating from the
1980s. It too had quotas, but the Austin administration began to implement it. No one was satisfied.[34]

In July the Florida Advisory Committee to the U.S. Commission on
Civil Rights came to Jacksonville and heard the anger of outraged African
Americans. Bryan Davis, chief assistant state's attorney (and later circuit
court judge), testified as a Jacksonville native that he had "never experienced a period in which I believe racial tensions are as high as they are
now." Deputy Mayor Ronnie Ferguson agreed. "We are in a city," he said,
"that has felt this rise in racial tension over the past five years." The JHRC's
Vivian Jackson reported 1,051 complaints about employment discrimination filed in her office in the past year. Willye Dennis, president of the Jacksonville branch of the NAACP, stated that her office had received 2,562
complaints relating to discrimination in jobs, age, sex, housing, and police
brutality. Rev. John Allen Newman, pastor of Mount Calvary Baptist
Church, and another cochair of Jacksonville Together, spoke passionately
about Jacksonville as "the most racist city in the United States of America
. . . a powder keg waiting to explode." These hearings took place three
months after the April 1992 Los Angeles riots following the acquittal of the
police officers accused of beating Rodney King, and doubtless reflected
some of the anger resulting from those events.[35]

Parallel to the frustrations over the mayor's veto came reports about
Jacksonville's public housing program housing mostly poor African
Americans. A federal audit released in May 1992 ranked the city's program
in the bottom 10 percent of the nation's 249 housing agencies and as "one
of the worst" in the country. More than 600 apartments (22 percent of the
housing stock) stood vacant, with waiting lists numbering more than

3,000 applicants. Boarded-up apartments were plundered of their plumbing and electrical fixtures. Occupied housing had broken heating units,
damaged walls, chipped lead-based paint, electrical hazards, leaky roofs,
and vermin infestations. Grounds were poorly maintained. The complexes
looked like slums. Mayor Austin, upon touring one complex, called it "a
disgrace." His newly appointed chief of staff, John Delaney, acknowledged
that the city was "a slum lord."[36]

The problems dated from the early 1970s after the old Duval Housing
Authority had been disbanded in favor of a city Department of Housing
and Urban Development. Local and federal audits repeatedly pointed to
inadequate records, wasted resources, and overall mismanagement during
prior administrations. Inadequate funding combined with politicians who
filled positions at HUD on a patronage basis with little regard for qualifications added to the mess. The Austin administration's response became one
of persuading city council to disband the current system and create a new
Jacksonville Housing Authority under a blue-ribbon board of directors
who appointed the capable Ronnie Ferguson as executive director. The creation of the Jacksonville Housing Authority became one of the most
significant accomplishments of the Austin administration as the agency
changed from being one of the worst housing programs in the nation to
one of the best.[37]

Meanwhile, the set-aside issue simmered at city hall and in the African
American community. In October, Austin, by executive order, announced
the implementation of his minority business plan of working through majority contractors. In response city council prepared to pass Jones's bill
again despite the threat of another mayoral veto. Council member Matt
Carlucci proposed a compromise to combine the mayor's and the council's
bills. Both Austin and Jones agreed to accept the compromise. Austin
would give priority to his plan, but he would also use the set-aside goals.
Thus an increasingly bitter, six-month fight over how best to provide African Americans and women with greater access ended with both sides able
to claim victory. Hard feelings, however, remained in the black community.[38]

Evidence of these feelings surfaced in a Jacksonville University poll that
very week that showed the mayor's approval rating at only 29.5 percent.
His disapproval rate was 50 percent, with two-thirds of African Americans
responding negatively. Fifty-three percent of the respondents were some-

what or very negative about the city government's handling of race relations. A Jacksonville Community Council, Inc., survey reported that fall that two-thirds of a sampling of residents saw racism as a problem across the city. For African Americans, the proportion was 75 percent. The consolidated city still had a long way to go.[39]

Downtown's River City Renaissance and the Coming of the Jaguars

The consolidated city also had a long way to go in revitalizing its downtown despite the progress of previous administrations. Shortly after his inauguration, Mayor Austin directed the Downtown Development Authority (DDA) to begin creating a Downtown Master Plan based on the Jacksonville Vision report and a white paper developed by the Central Jacksonville Improvement Board of the Chamber of Commerce.[40]

The white paper analyzed the downtown scene. During the twenty-four years since consolidation, there had been substantial physical growth and development, including half a dozen new skyscrapers, the Jacksonville Landing, Omni Hotel, Prime Osborne Convention Center, south-bank river walk, Metropolitan Park, and the beginning of an elevated mass transit system. Yet downtown's 3.38-square-mile urban core was, the report said, "spiraling toward disaster," marked by a high (20 percent) office vacancy rate and "severe under-utilization and near abandonment of older buildings." Though 60,000 people worked downtown, five major department stores had left the area, as well as a number of other major businesses. Restaurants and entertainment facilities were virtually nonexistent except at the Landing. "Much of downtown," said the report, "is deserted in the evenings and on weekends." While the metropolitan area had thrived since consolidation, and from a distance the riverfront skyline looked prosperous, on the streets "plywood has become the window treatment of choice, the streets hold few shoppers even at Christmas and those people who do venture downtown after dark move quickly and warily from their cars to the Florida Theatre, Landing or Civic Auditorium."[41]

Other American cities had experienced suburban migration and downtown deterioration. Some, like Portland, Boston, and Orlando, had countered the trend with some success. Others had not. The white paper asked whether downtown Jacksonville was worth saving. It concluded that the health of downtown had a real and significant impact for all Jackson-villians. For example, a healthy urban core provided property tax revenues far beyond its costs. In 1991 downtown Jacksonville comprised less than one-half of 1 percent of the city's land area but provided 13.5 percent of its ad valorem tax revenues. It provided 15 percent of its school funds without a school even being located there. One office tower was assessed at $78.8 million, more than six times the largest similar-sized suburban land parcel. Not only did downtown support the suburbs with its tax revenues, further decay of downtown would cost suburban taxpayers in reduced assessed values and returns.[42]

In contrast, a revitalized downtown could attract new businesses to the urban core. It would reduce urban sprawl and the high cost to taxpayers of paying for the additional infrastructure and services required by that sprawl. A revitalized downtown also could provide more jobs, particularly for the city's minority population living nearby. It could encourage mass transit. Further it could become the center for culture, entertainment, and increased convention business.[43]

To turn around downtown, the white paper recommended a practical master plan that would lead to increased security, develop new cultural fa-cilities, create a governmental complex around Hemming Park, develop mass transit, build housing, and increase the visual enhancement or attrac-tiveness of the urban core. The last named included greater cleanliness and maintenance of streets, sidewalks, and vacant lots, plus public art, more effective landscape ordinances, downtown parks, pedestrian-friendly retail shops, and improved gateways to downtown, particular from the north and west. These recommendations closely paralleled the goals of Jackson-ville Insight in its vision for a thriving downtown.[44]

In conclusion, the white paper noted that the *Wall Street Journal* had called Jacksonville "one of the rising stars of the New South, [with] its clus-ter of steel and glass skyscrapers that dominate downtown along with its trendy waterfront shopping plaza." The white paper added, however, that "unless Jacksonville's civic and business leaders recognize and address the consequences of neglect, . . . this area will be lost as a community resource. The result will be not only a significantly increased economic burden, but the loss of the historical and emotional heart of the city."[45]

In response to the mayor's September directive, the Downtown Devel-opment Authority solicited voluntary help from local architects and city planners. Under the leadership of Jack Diamond, president of KBJ Architects, an ad hoc committee developed a mission and guidelines for downtown. The mission stated, "Jacksonville's downtown will provide an environment which is highly livable, safe and economically viable for all. It will also serve as the entertainment/economic center for the region and it will emphasize public use of the St. Johns River." In November, the DDA and Diamond, as chair of the ad hoc committee, presented to the mayor their initial conceptual report for his review and that of the Insight committee.[46]

By January 1993, Diamond had prepared for the DDA a master plan for downtown that, a month later, became part of the mayor's $230 million "River City Renaissance." It included six broad areas of concern: environment, children, health and social services, economic development, neighborhoods and downtown, and parks, recreation, and the arts. The downtown thrust was significant. The River City Renaissance proposed for the east side of downtown major renovations of the Gator Bowl (later renamed Alltel Stadium), Veterans Memorial Coliseum, Wolfson Baseball Park, and Metropolitan Park. It included money for a homeless center modeled after Orlando's Coalition Campus to serve Jacksonville's 2,000–3,000 homeless people, and funds for upgrading the Florida Theatre. At the center of the urban core, Renaissance proposed renovating the historic but unoccupied St. James Building at Hemming Plaza into a new city hall. The city would build a new main library and reconstruct the obsolescent civic auditorium into a state-of-the-art multicultural performing arts center. On the western edge of downtown, Renaissance proposed renovating the decayed but historic LaVilla neighborhood into a countywide recreational complex with an attractive entryway from the city's two interstate highways. Except for the LaVilla recreational complex, which took a different form, all of these projects got underway in varying stages of development over the succeeding decade. For Diamond, the River City Renaissance provided the greatest good for the greatest number of Jacksonvillians because, he said, "downtown is the only place we come together as a community."[47]

Not all Jacksonville residents approved of the focus on downtown development. During the year in which volunteers did their work, the local media reported stories critical of the emphasis on downtown. Several major downtown businesses expressed their views by moving to the suburbs. The most significant losses were IBM and American Heritage Life Insurance Company. Both moved because of bottom-line issues. Either the city would not subsidize their staying downtown (IBM) or rental costs were cheaper elsewhere (American Heritage Life). Market forces were hard to beat. Leading suburban developers also spoke against prioritizing downtown development. Herb Peyton, president of Gate Petroleum, urged the mayor not to give preferential treatment to downtown, while Bryant Skinner of Bryant Skinner Company (a suburban developer) argued that the suburbs, not downtown, attracted new businesses to Jacksonville. Skinner's son, Charlie, a vice president in the firm, observed that the move to "edge cities" had become a megatrend ongoing since World War II because of cost, accessibility, and safety for private developers. Neighborhood advocates agreed. They felt their needs should have priority over downtown because people lived in the neighborhoods. Other community leaders, like the venerable Ira Koger, founder of suburban office parks, believed cities needed both their downtown and their suburbs. Both should be developed as attractive locations for new and expanding businesses. Public opinion, however, appeared unconvinced. A poll taken early in 1994 showed a sampling of Jacksonville voters evenly split over the Renaissance plan, 47 percent for and 45 percent against. Of six priority issues for the city, downtown ranked last. Clearly advocates of the River City Renaissance had not formed a citywide consensus on downtown development. In consolidated Jacksonville, the challenge of balancing downtown with suburban development and the neighborhoods would continue beyond the Austin administration.[48]

Despite the lack of consensus, the mayor moved forward with the River City Renaissance. Criticism accompanied almost every step of the way. On the west side of downtown, urban renewal of the fifty-block, dilapidated LaVilla neighborhood brought protests from residents and others concerned about the destruction of the area's African American heritage. Once the center of black business and popular culture, as well as for European immigrants at the beginning of the twentieth century, LaVilla had deteriorated since the 1960s. The movie theaters were gone, most businesses had closed, and the formerly segregated Brewster Hospital had moved north to Springfield. Much of the housing looked ragged, with unpainted exteriors, broken steps and railings, cracked window panes, overgrown lawns and shrubs, and accumulations of litter and trash. Still, there was the old Stanton High School building, the leading secondary school for African Americans during the segregation era; an impressive five-story Masonic

Temple, once home to lawyers, doctors, and pharmacists as well as fraternal members; Clara White Mission, monument to a prominent black philanthropist; the ruins of the old Ritz Theater; and residents.[49]

City planners believed most of the dilapidated buildings needed to be razed but saw possibilities for an African American cultural heritage district on the northern fringe. On the southern fringe, hotels, restaurants, and shops could locate adjacent to the Prime Osborne Convention Center. In the center, planners spoke about a regional recreational park. Residents protested against the destruction of historic buildings but were largely ignored. So, too, were suggestions for renewal. The city assisted residents in moving to other areas of the city and then leveled their housing. Plans for affordable housing to replace the old stock never bore fruit. Several small businesses relocated to LaVilla and/or expanded there. An African American district began to develop with the construction of the Jacksonville Urban League offices and the reconstruction of the Ritz Theater. City officials also endorsed the building of a magnet middle school for the arts. The park vision disappeared. Meanwhile, roads leading to and from I-95 were repaved and bordered by new sidewalks, lighting, and palm trees. Jack Diamond had his attractive western entrance to downtown. Still, by the end of the Austin administration, renewal remained in its early stages and much of the area remained vacant. As one reporter wrote, "Walk or drive LaVilla and the emptiness has an air of expectancy. Change hangs like a dust cloud behind every truck bounding through LaVilla."[50]

During these same years, other parts of the River City Renaissance moved forward, including the construction or renovation of the historic St. James Building to become the new city hall facing Hemming Park; the Florida Times-Union Performing Arts Center, a public-private funding match replacing the old civic auditorium; and the I. M. Sulzbacher Homeless Shelter named for a long-time civic benefactor and head of the homeless coalition. Other renovations included the coliseum, Wolfson Baseball Park, old city hall, courthouse, and Museum of Science and History.[51]

Perhaps most criticized among the downtown projects (not part of the mayor's Renaissance Plan) was the Automatic Skyway Express (ASE), also known as the people mover. It dated from downtown plans of the early 1970s, when consultants recognized that the urban core had expanded beyond pedestrian distances and required some sort of rapid transit to move people from one point to the next. They discarded proposals for adding

Fig. 18. Urban renewal in LaVilla, against a backdrop of downtown Jacksonville. By permission of the *Florida Times-Union.*

street-level rapid transit, such as buses or street cars, due to already existing traffic congestion, and recommended elevated transit as the alternative. Consultants planned for a north-south and east-west axis. During the Godbold administration the mayor and city council decided the first leg would extend seven-tenths of a mile, from downtown to the newly renovated Prime Osborne Convention Center on the western fringe. When completed in 1989, few people rode it. The Jacksonville Transportation Authority had projected 10,000 daily riders, but two years later fewer than 1,000 each day chose the people mover. The shortfall was attributed to too many parking lots downtown, the economy then in recession, and the fact that only the first leg of the system had been completed. Efforts during the Hazouri administration to expand the ASE eastward to the Gator Bowl collapsed without federal funding guarantees. The Chamber's white paper on downtown development in 1992 revived the effort and gained Austin's support. It proposed building a 1.8-mile north-south axis from the community college on the northern fringe of the core city to and across the river to the south bank and San Marco. Advocates argued that when finished, it would become part of a larger system of light rail and bus lines linking to the suburbs and essential for downtown revitalization.[52]

The expense of the people mover with its construction cost overruns and the paucity of riders appalled many folks. Federal transportation authorities also opposed it but were overruled by Congress under the leadership of the Florida delegation. In 1993, the Washington-based Citizens against Government Waste included the Automated Skyway Express in its "Pig Book" under the label of pork barrel spending. ABC News's Sam Donaldson on national television called it "a mass transit system desperately seeking riders." Perhaps most outspoken but not alone was economist and community gadfly Marvin Edwards. In op-ed pieces in the *Florida Times-Union* and *Folio Weekly*, the city's alternative newspaper, Edwards attacked the people mover as a "$25 million swindle" and "Skyway to nowhere." He estimated its eventual 2.5-mile length would cost $250 million, or $1 million per mile. Still, construction of the line from the community college across the river continued with federal dollars until its completion in 1998. Whether the people mover ridership ever would justify its cost remained in doubt into the twenty-first century.[53]

Edwards also thought the River City Renaissance was a financial boondoggle benefiting special interests in downtown development. He believed the money would be better spent elsewhere. Yet, as the handsome performing arts center opened and city government moved to the newly renovated, historic St. James Building, downtown renewal gained support. Under the next mayor, voters even chose to raise their sales tax rate by a half penny to do more of the same in the Better Jacksonville Plan.[54]

The willingness of normally conservative Jacksonville voters to tax themselves for a new coliseum, baseball park, library, courthouse, and other public improvements in subsequent years can be explained in part by the acquisition of the Jacksonville Jaguars National Football League franchise on November 30, 1993, without doubt the most exciting event of the decade. The city had been seeking a franchise since 1979 when then mayor Jake Godbold invited Baltimore Colts owner Robert Irsay to Jacksonville before he moved his team to Indianapolis. In 1987, Mayor Tommy Hazouri brought K. S. "Bud" Adams of the Houston Oilers to town before that team moved to Tennessee. St. Louis Cardinals and Atlanta Falcons owners also talked briefly about locating in Jacksonville. Meanwhile, the city had franchises in the short-lived World Football League and the United States Football League, which fans supported with enthusiasm. Thus, in 1989, when the NFL announced a proposed expansion of two teams, local investors, led initially by Tom Petway but later including multimillionaire shoe magnate J. Wayne Weaver, formed Touchdown Jacksonville, Inc., to secure the franchise.[55]

Outsiders saw little chance of success because of the competition of Baltimore, St. Louis, and Memphis, the first two proven major league cities. Next to Green Bay, Jacksonville would be the smallest market in the league. Yet league executives saw the potential from past and present franchise efforts, as well as the local enthusiasm for major league football. They also saw the population growth in the Southeast when they awarded a team to Charlotte, North Carolina, in October. Meanwhile, Baltimore and St. Louis had problems finalizing their plans. This combination of reasons led to the decision for Jacksonville. Local fans exploded in celebration at the Jacksonville Landing, in city hall, on the streets, and across the city from downtown to the beach communities. The excitement ranked not far behind celebrations for the Armistice ending World War I and V-J Day ending World War II. Mayor Austin captured the enthusiasm at the Landing when he exclaimed, "There's been no greater day in Jacksonville's history!"[56]

The enthusiasm for the Jaguars continued, but criticism of the Austin administration resurfaced during the negotiations to rebuild the Gator Bowl to NFL standards. Costs escalated. What began as a $49 million renovation for the Jacksonville Renaissance increased to $121 million, though state grants, ticket surcharges, and an increase in the hotel/motel bed tax covered most of the cost. Another issue became the Jaguars' benefits from the lease with the city. Jacksonville promised to pay virtually all of the stadium's maintenance and repairs over the next thirty years, including utilities, game day personnel (police, ticket takers, ushers, etc.), renovations, and upgrades, while the Jaguars kept the receipts from ticket sales, concessions, parking fees, and advertising. A *Florida Times-Union* study suggested that no NFL team had better lease terms than the Jaguars. The city's chief negotiator, John Delaney, disagreed. He claimed the deal benefited both parties. Jaguar rent, ticket surcharges, and the like funded the bonds sold to pay the greater expense of the new stadium and cost the taxpayer nothing. Jacksonville paid game day costs, but less than in many other cities. Meanwhile, the return in self-esteem for the city was tremen-

Fig. 19. River City Renaissance. *Jacksonville Action Line,* fall 1994.

dous. Team president David Seldin claimed one could not compare costs with other teams because costs depended upon circumstances at the time of negotiation. In the Jaguars' case, the cost of entry into the NFL had escalated in recent years and the team paid $140 million just for the franchise. Meanwhile Mayor Austin claimed the city negotiated a fair deal with the Jaguars, with compromises on both sides. Critics remained unhappy with the arrangements, but the fans seemed not to care. Season tickets sold rapidly, and the first games in the fall of 1995 were virtually sold out in the newly renamed Alltel Stadium. If the Jacksonville Landing was Mayor Godbold's signature accomplishment, the Jaguars' arrival belonged to Ed Austin.[57]

The popularity of the Jaguars coming to Jacksonville boded well for Austin's reelection as mayor in 1995. Yet less than three months later, in February 1994, he announced that one term was enough. The 67-year-old incumbent simply did not want to be mayor any more. With thirty years of public service, he wanted to spend more time with his wife and family. He did not need the job.[58]

His surprise decision opened the doors for a bevy of candidates, including former mayors Hazouri and Godbold. Both had left substantial positive and negative impressions upon the electorate, and Republicans sought out Austin's chief of staff, John Delaney, to contest the race. A hard-fought primary eliminated Hazouri, and the runoff defeated Godbold. On July 1, 1995, the newcomer, 37-year-old Delaney, began what became two terms as mayor of consolidated Jacksonville. Elected with him (actually before him in the first primary), Sheriff Nat Glover became the first African American to serve in that office in the city's history.[59]

Meanwhile, Austin finished his term in office. Besides the Jaguars, the Renaissance Plan played a major role in once again jump-starting downtown development in the tradition of Jake Godbold and Haydon Burns. Austin's environmental efforts built on the achievements of Hans Tanzler and Tommy Hazouri. In race relations, the mayor won fewer friends. Yet the Minority Business Program did provide substantially more business opportunities for African Americans and women, and the creation of the Jacksonville Housing Authority started a much needed cleanup of the city's public housing serving lower-income, mostly black residents. His creation of the Children's Commission and six Citizens Planning Advisory Commissions to provide for neighborhood input bore fruit in the succeeding administration. He also ran a frugal administration, introducing more efficient management techniques, cutting city jobs by attrition, and limiting expenses.[60]

Given Austin's record, it became a puzzle why his public opinion polls rarely recorded the support of more than 30 percent of the voters during his term of office. He admitted that at times the results discouraged him. Part of the problem lay in his political skills, or perhaps lack of them. A person of integrity, he had a hard time compromising fixed ideas in order to achieve specific goals. At times he appeared inflexible. He frankly acknowledged limited public relations skills. Austin did not do well selling himself, his programs, or the city—all necessary attributes in winning favor with the voters. In the end, the mayor's one term showed considerable progress for the consolidated city, though there remained much to be done in fighting crime, developing the port, providing services to children, controlling growth, and building bridges between the races. Austin left office relieved, relatively unappreciated, and quickly forgotten in the shadow of his younger, personable, energetic, and eloquent protégé, Delaney. Austin's achievements probably deserved better.[61]

CHAPTER 9

Consolidated Jacksonville

The Austin administration celebrated twenty-five years of consolidated government in 1993, bringing back to city hall many of the men and women who had worked for what Richard Martin called "the Silent Revolution." Almost from its beginning, observers gave positive grades to this shift to city-county governance. After one year, Mayor Hans Tanzler praised centralized data processing, purchasing, and legal services for their economy and efficiency. Street paving, demolition of substandard housing, new swimming pools, and the hiring of minorities in white-collar jobs at city hall reflected efforts to include the African American community. Polls showed two-thirds of the citizenry supported the decision to consolidate. The All-America City award received from the National Municipal League in 1969 provided another recognition of the successful consolidation.[1]

Other participants praised the effort. Sheriff Dale Carson implemented the consolidation of city police and county sheriff's deputies into one department. The one agency provided uniform law enforcement across the county, received increased financial support from city hall, made better use of manpower and facilities for crime prevention and traffic control, and introduced comprehensive planning to meet current and future law enforcement needs. Money saved in eliminating duplication of services paid for upgrading and adding law enforcement officers to increase protection across the expanded city's 840 square miles.[2]

For Fire Chief John Waters, the merger replaced largely volunteer firefighters in Duval County with paid professionals and substantially enlarged the firefighting capacity in the county. It enabled the department to modernize equipment, expand services at the airport and port, create a separate Emergency Medical Rescue Service that achieved national recognition, and reduce fire insurance premiums for home owners and businesses throughout the consolidated city.[3]

The independent authorities responsible for Jacksonville's expressways, port, and electric power production expressed less enthusiasm for consolidation. All of them initially dragged their feet on merging their purchasing and other services into central governmental agencies. All also saw their unique manpower needs merged into generic citywide civil service classifications. School superintendent Cecil Hardesty agreed. The elected Duval County School Board had to submit its annual budget to city council for approval, permit its teachers and other employees to receive civil service classification, and accept delays in the purchases of goods and services because of an additional layer of bureaucracy in the city's central purchasing department.[4]

Five years after consolidation, the National Association of Counties convened a national conference on consolidation at Jacksonville University to assess changes not only in Jacksonville but also in the consolidated cities of Baton Rouge, Nashville, and Indianapolis. For all of these recently consolidated governments, speakers generally agreed that public services had been expanded and economies achieved. Consolidation meant providing urban services to suburban areas that heretofore had lacked them, and upgrading them in the central cities. In addition, Lex Hester, Jacksonville's chief administrative officer, noted the greater level of professionalism characterizing these services compared to preconsolidation days.[5]

Voters supported consolidation, often believing greater efficiencies in government would lead to reduced taxation. Jacksonville's finance director, Royce Lyles, partially disagreed. It was true that tax rates were lower in the early years, but the demand for new services for policing, firefighting, and waste disposal required new funding. It came from service charges on water and sewers, federal grants for urban renewal, increased property assessments, and an enlarged taxable base as new businesses opened and new homes were built. No one could determine whether consolidated government cost more or less than its predecessor because the comparisons were between apples and oranges. If services had been maintained at their old levels, costs would have decreased. But salary adjustments, new technology, and expanded services made cost comparisons impossible. The success of consolidation, Lyles and others concluded, lay not in lower taxes,

Fig. 20. Lewis Alexander "Lex" Hester, Jacksonville's chief administrative officer under three mayors. By permission of the City of Jacksonville.

which often were marginal for home owners, but in a better served citizenry. Even then tax revenues never met all of the city's needs.[6]

In an article in the *Urban Review* that year, journalist Park Beeler praised Jacksonville's five years of consolidation for reducing the crime rate, fostering economic development with close to full employment locally, reducing air and water pollution, improving health care, particularly in the area of emergency services, achieving reaccreditation of the county's high schools, and inspiring a broader "bold new spirit" in the cultural revitalization of the Jacksonville Symphony Orchestra.[7]

In 1973, Joan Carver, a Jacksonville University political scientist, published a more thorough analysis of Jacksonville's consolidation. In attempting to assess its consequences, she focused on three issues:[8]

• the structure and process of decision making before and after consolidation to determine changing patterns of influence;

- major sources of support for consolidated government to determine the accessibility by different citizen groups to the system; and
- policies of the consolidated government to determine whether shifts in service priorities had occurred and who benefited compared to earlier days.

First, consolidation "sharply altered" the decision- making structure of government. Preconsolidation governments in both city and county were largely fragmented, with power dispersed among a large number of boards and commissions. The new government largely, though not completely, centralized the making of decisions. There remained an autonomously elected sheriff, civil service board, and school board, along with independent authorities for transportation, power, and the port. The old system was highly politicized in a pejorative sense; officeholders reciprocated favors at the expense of the larger community's concerns for schools, public safety, and the environment. The new system saw the mayor exerting strong leadership and setting community priorities, appointing professionals to administrative posts, and working closely with both black and white community leaders heretofore largely detached from local government. Carver concluded, "Personal considerations had been reduced in favor of professional consideration in decision-making." While socioeconomic elites still had a strong voice in the new government, efforts had been made to include the black community in the political system and make government to a degree sensitive to their needs.[9]

In the second area of the new system's responsiveness to various citizen groups in the city, Carver interviewed a diverse group of community leaders and examined election returns. White community leaders reported a very high degree of support for consolidation. Less enthusiastic African American leaders recognized "much greater accessibility" than in the past. In the mayoral election of 1971, Hans Tanzler defeated Haydon Burns, the preconsolidation segregationist mayor of Jacksonville, in a race that many observers saw as a test of consolidation. Tanzler won overwhelmingly in both the more affluent white suburbs and in the predominantly black inner-city precincts. Burns fared best among lower-income, working-class whites, a substantial group without much visible influence at city hall.[10]

The third area focused on who benefited from policy decisions of the new system. Carver saw consolidated government moving forward most decisively in programs and services broadly benefiting the entire community. Postconsolidation mayors acted decisively on water and sewer construction, urban renewal, and downtown development. These achievements provoked little controversy as the entire community benefited. Funding came mostly from user fees, state grants, and federal dollars.[11]

Policy decisions in planning and regulation made less progress. Preconsolidation Jacksonville had no comprehensive land use plan or zoning regulation. By 1973, a planning board had begun working on guidelines for growth and development but had not yet developed a citywide plan. Meanwhile, the new government moved quickly to establish a zoning code. But zoning remained controversial as property owners fought efforts to regulate private use of their land. Effective regulation of growth and development existed primarily when federal or state authorities pressured the city in behalf of environmental regulation or affirmative action.[12]

A third policy issue lay in the redistribution of resources by government to less affluent areas of the community. Here consolidated government achieved relatively little. Tax cuts benefited large taxpayers disproportionately. Carver estimated that for more than 80 percent of homes valued under $15,000, in the five years after consolidation, each mill of tax cut provided less than $10 per year of tax relief. Meanwhile water, sewer, and electric rates for large users declined as consumption increased. In terms of city expenditures, the largest proportion of the old city and new city revenues went for law enforcement, public safety, and public works impacting the entire city. Human services funding increased but accounted for a relatively small part of the budget.[13]

Overall indicators of taxing and spending could be seen in Jacksonville having one of the lowest tax burdens for a city its size in the United States. The city spent less for recreation, parkland, libraries, and police officers than the national average. Despite these limitations Carver concluded that consolidation had produced major positive changes in Jacksonville's governance. It confronted tough issues, responded to countywide needs, introduced professionalism in governmental services, and fostered a positive can-do spirit across the community. At the same time, while minorities and poor people benefited from consolidation, affluent white Jacksonville residents gained disproportionately, a situation common to most cities. Whether consolidated government could respond equitably to all segments of Jacksonville's neighborhoods and peoples remained to be seen.[14]

Consolidation and Race Relations

Four years later, in 1977, at the First Conference on Jacksonville History organized at the University of North Florida, Professor Carver expanded her analysis to look at consolidation's impact specifically upon the African American community. Overall, she felt that "its general thrust had been favorable to the interests of blacks," with some reservations.[15]

On the one hand, black participation throughout government had increased due to the election of district representatives to city council and the commitment of top city officials to appoint blacks to positions of responsibility. Blacks were making white officials aware of black needs. Further, the willingness of the consolidated government to accept federal dollars provided resources to expand public health and public housing programs in the black community. On the other hand, consolidated government had little interest in legislating equal job or housing opportunities. Further, the city's low-tax, low-spend policies meant fewer social services in the minority community, where they were greatly needed. It also meant slower infrastructure improvements in the older, inner city. Still, Carver saw consolidation providing an important intangible result in molding the city into one community in which blacks and whites could work together in ways quite different from most of the preconsolidation era.[16]

Jacksonville's African Americans, who comprised one-quarter of the population, did not see equity or equal opportunity as a consequence of consolidated government. Twenty-five years later, many blacks still looked for its benefits. As part of the consolidation observances in October 1993, the University of North Florida Humanities Council hosted a symposium, "Race Relations in Jacksonville since Consolidation." African Americans comprised eight of the eleven participants. They spoke from their personal experiences. Rev. Charles B. Dailey, pastor of Oakland Baptist Church for thirty-four years, began by reminiscing about his participation and arrests in the integration demonstrations of the 1960s. Over the years his church had served the community, building housing in its inner-city east Jacksonville neighborhood. Dailey believed consolidation had not fulfilled its promises of public services; school desegregation had undermined neighborhoods; and greater animosity existed among young people in 1993 than twenty-five years earlier.[17]

In contrast, Harold Gibson, administrative aide to both Mayors Tanzler and Austin, saw progress during the Tanzler years in minority hiring at city hall and in street paving, street lighting, and playgrounds in African American neighborhoods. State senator Betty Holzendorf disagreed. She had served as affirmative action officer for both Mayors Tanzler and Godbold before seeking elective office in Tallahassee. She believed consolidation hurt the Jacksonville community, "not just the black community but this entire community," because racial segregation continued to separate Jacksonville residents. Part of the promise of consolidation came in meeting new acquaintances and friends from the majority race. We learned, she said, that not everybody was racist. But consolidation did not end segregation. It was systemic and institutionalized, "and as a matter of fact, [consolidation] made the problem worse."[18]

Wendell Holmes, the first African American elected to a school board in Florida, and eventually the chair of the Duval County School Board, saw desegregation under consolidation mismanaged by both the courts and the schools. Black students endured more busing from their neighborhoods than did white students. Black students, he believed, also experienced a disproportionate number of suspensions and expulsions from school because too many white teachers could not or would not teach them. State representative Willye Dennis agreed that consolidated government did not serve African American youngsters well in the public schools. As president of the local NAACP branch, she reopened the federal desegregation suit in 1990 to force the school board to renegotiate more equitable terms.[19]

Alton Yates, a mayoral aide or administrator for most of the twenty-five years of consolidation, saw the biggest problem in police-black community relations but remained optimistic about progress achieved and progress yet to come. Police chief Jerome Spates agreed. Police-community relations had been bad, but in recent years under Sheriff Jim McMillan minority recruitment had improved substantially. Spates saw a current need for more minority officers in middle management and a removal of the glass ceiling for qualified blacks.[20]

Perhaps the most articulate panelist was Rev. John Henry Newman from Mount Calvary Baptist Church, cochair for Jacksonville Together, Mayor Austin's task force on reconciliation formed after the Judge Santora incident. Newman, a relative newcomer to the city, had arrived from Philadelphia in 1982. Thirty years after the civil rights movement and twenty-five years into consolidation, he believed a societal denial of racism continued to exist in the city. It was an attitude that lay beneath the surface in many Jacksonville whites. Pastor Newman expressed particular concern about the failure of organized religion to provide leadership in this area.[21]

The eight African American leaders clearly did not speak for the entire Jacksonville community. Yet their views were not unique. That year a Jacksonville Community Council, Inc. (JCCI) quality of life survey reported that two-thirds of Jacksonville respondents in a telephone survey believed that racism was a community problem, a figure that had more than doubled over the preceding decade. A year earlier, in 1992, a biracial JCCI study of young black males found persistent racism and limited opportunities for minority youth employment. Plus it found "suspicion and fear surrounding all [sic] young black males because of negative stereotyping and the behavior of a minority." A decade later, in the new century, another JCCI study on improving race relations reported significant differences between blacks and whites in their perceptions about fairness in employment, housing, police-community relations, health care, and education. Data supported these perceptions, showing African Americans doing less well in school, household income, incarceration rates, and health care.[22]

A University of North Florida study published in 1999 showed comparative median household incomes for blacks and whites had barely changed since consolidation. African Americans earned 53.6 percent of white income in 1970 and 56.5 percent in 1990. While the black poverty rate had declined over the twenty years from 35 to 25 percent, white poverty declined proportionately more (from 9 to 5 percent). Meanwhile black unemployment during these years remained generally twice that of whites, and households headed by black women had increased by 80 percent. Clearly regional and national economic factors played important roles in these numbers, but it was also the case that consolidation did little to close the gaps.[23]

Comparing Jacksonville's experience in race relations with other cities that did not consolidate their city and county governments is difficult because of many other variables. Clearly the consolidated charter allocating district city council seats to minority voters led to Jacksonville having black representation in local government before Tampa with its at-large system of elections. Whether lack of representation prior to the 1980s hurt

Tampa's blacks more than Jacksonville's African Americans is moot. Tampa's mayor Sandra Freedman appointed her city's first black police chief two years before Jacksonville elected its first black sheriff. Minorities in both cities did not prosper comparable to whites during these years. Wages, access to affordable housing, social services, and police-community relations in both cities reflected systems of discrimination. In addition, school desegregation in Duval and Hillsborough Counties put the primary burden of busing on minority children. Tampa's African Americans fought against these conditions by forming a Coalition of African American Organizations, but with limited results.[24]

In south Florida, Miami-Dade developed a federated form of city-county government in the 1950s that reduced some overlapping services but did not necessarily improve police–black community relations. Miami suffered the state's most violent riot in 1980, following the acquittal on a technicality of four Dade County police officers accused of chasing, beating, and killing an unarmed African American insurance agent, Arthur McDuffie, following a motorcycle chase on December 17, 1979. The riot followed the acquittal four months later. It raged for four days, cost eighteen lives, and resulted in more than $100 million in property damages. It climaxed a series of abusive incidents by police during these years. Whether a consolidated police force might have had better training and showed greater restraint is moot. Clearly the Duval County sheriff's department also abused minorities. Alton Yates reported that blacks told him, "I would much rather take my chances with the criminal element than call the police to my neighborhood."[25]

Across the South during these years, the lack of consolidation in cities like Atlanta, Richmond, Birmingham, and New Orleans led to black majority populations and the election of black mayors. They in turn appointed minorities to leadership posts and funneled substantial city dollars to minority contractors. Equally important, they negotiated with the predominantly white business community from positions of political power. In contrast, consolidated Jacksonville with its 27 percent African American population elected four out of nineteen district council members but filled only one citywide electoral slot. Their influence at the bargaining table with the white political and economic power structure remained substantially less than in a black majority city, which Jacksonville would have become without consolidation.[26]

Table 1. Jacksonville and Jacksonville's Minority Populations, 1950–2000

Year	Jacksonville	African American	Native American	Hispanic	Asian
1950	204,517	72,518 (35.5 percent)	n/a	n/a	n/a
1960	201,030	82,744 (41.2 percent)	n/a	n/a	n/a
1970	528,865	118,158 (22.3 percent)	n/a	n/a	n/a
1980	571,003	140,561 (24.6 percent)	1,259	13,366	5,921
1990	672,971	163,902 (24.3 percent)	1,904	22,479	12,940
2000	778,879	216,800 (27.8 percent)	2,598	31,946	21,940

Source: U.S. Department of Commerce, Bureau of Census, *1970 Census of Population: Characteristics of Population*, vol. 1, Florida, part 2, sec. 1 (Washington, D.C., 1973), tables 16, 23, 97; U.S. Department of Commerce, Bureau of Census, *Census Tracts, Jacksonville, Florida, Standard Metropolitan Statistical Area*, "General Characteristics of Persons: 1980" (Washington, D.C., 1983), tables P-1–P-6; U.S. Department of Commerce, Bureau of Census, *1990 Census of Population: General Population and Housing, Jacksonville, Florida* (Washington, D.C., 1993), tables 1–5; University of Florida Bureau of Economic and Business Research, Warrington College of Business Administration, *Florida Statistical Abstract, 2001* (Gainesville, 2001), table 1.

Note: Based on 1970 census data, the preconsolidated city that year would have been 47.3 percent African American.

Still, progress in race relations had taken place in consolidated Jacksonville from the 1960s to the 1990s. Minority employment at city hall, the sheriff's office, and the school board and in the private sector increased substantially. Black high school and college graduates more than doubled during the consolidation years, perhaps due in part to school desegregation and the opening of the University of North Florida. African American professionals who once left Jacksonville and other southern cities upon completing their education began to return in the 1970s. Other blacks from outside the region also moved there. Governmental services to African American neighborhoods improved over the years, though they did not measure up to the rest of the city. The needs of the growing suburbs competed for limited tax dollars, and city flooding after storms, limited housing inspections, lax garbage collection, and uneven street paving continued in the inner city. The social and economic discrimination that Jacksonville's minority residents experienced characterized most American cities during these years.[27]

Also important, whites' attitudes about race relations began to change. While Rev. Newman's charge of systemic and perhaps subconscious racial attitudes rang true, consolidated Jacksonville also saw evidence of positive efforts by whites in schools and colleges to build better lives for all students. The election of an African American sheriff over two white opponents in 1995 included substantial white support. Further indications of a changing community atmosphere included the multiracial volunteer efforts in JCCI studies, creation of multiracial study circles under the sponsorship of the Jacksonville Human Rights Commission, and media and corporate efforts to encourage diversity.

In Jacksonville, as across the region, race relations remained a major problem twenty-five years after consolidation both in attitudes and practices. Combining city and county governments in 1968 was no panacea in this critical area of community life. The history of inequality existed in the very social and spatial fabric of the modern city, and consolidation did little to change it. Still, virtually all participants acknowledged that progress had taken place under the four mayors leading consolidated government. There just remained many more steps to take.[28]

Consolidation and the Environment

In contrast to its limited impact upon race relations, consolidated government made a major difference in the urban, rural, and wetlands environment of the new 840-square-mile Jacksonville. Initially the new government's efforts lay in confronting serious problems in the deterioration of the city's water, air, and land quality. The 1960s saw significant environmental legislation passed on the federal level with states, including Florida, following suit. Jacksonville, however, lagged behind.[29]

A 1962 Chamber of Commerce report (see ch. 1) reflected the preconsolidation city's and Duval County's apparent lack of concern with air pollution and the worsening condition of the St. Johns River system. In 1967, the state board of health threatened to block further development along the river and ordered the city to clean up the river. Jacksonville also had a statewide reputation for its malodorous air. Further, the county's flat terrain, with its woods, fields, marshes, swamps, and tidal estuaries, was pockmarked with piles of trash and garbage. The head of the local health department described flying over rural areas of Duval County in the late 1960s and seeing "one huge dump."[30]

The newly consolidated city government confronted the challenge to clean up the mess. The Tanzler administration spent most of its eleven years doing just that. It spent $400 million on cleaning up the river. Still, pollution by chicken processing plants, restaurants, apartment complexes, and other businesses continued along its tributaries. Over time, consolidated government's Environmental Protection Board compelled most of these violators to manage their wastes or close. The Tanzler administration also closed unauthorized dumps and established sanitary landfills for the city's solid wastes. Again, violations in dumping continued, but at a much reduced rate. Most significantly, consolidated government had the capacity to clean up the entire 840 square miles, something that preconsolidated Jacksonville could not have done.

By the late 1970s, when the Godbold administration took office, protecting the environment had gained popular support in Jacksonville, if not fully at city hall. The local television documentary, "The Smell of Money," exposing odor conditions caused primarily by the city's paper mills and chemical plants, prompted the mayor to begin efforts to eliminate them. The filling and closing of landfills led to studies as to where new landfills could be located, or whether the city should build an incinerator. The Hazouri administration fumbled the landfill siting but made major progress combating odors with legislation forcing polluters to clean up their discharges. Hazouri also initiated the recycling of solid wastes. The Austin administration finally resolved the landfill problem but faced other challenges, including the dumping of hazardous wastes. Chemicals and other contaminants dumped into old landfills, military waste disposal sites, open fields, and ravines on Jacksonville's poorer west and north sides had leached into the soil and nearby wells, causing sickness and deaths. Governmental officials identified more than two hundred active and inactive dumps and landfills. Limited federal Superfund dollars made the cleanup a slow and expensive process not yet completed by the end of the century.[31]

Across the nation during these years, Americans developed new attitudes toward their environment. With greater affluence and leisure time, they spent more of their lives out-of-doors hiking, hunting, fishing, and camping. They became aware of endangered species like the bald eagle. Further, the move of Americans to suburbia led to a desire for a more attractive environment of cleaner air, lawns, trees, gardens, and parks. Also important, they became aware of ecological disasters like Alaskan oil spills, Love Canal hazardous waste disposal sites, and pesticides like DDT progressing through the food chain, affecting the health and welfare of individuals. This lifestyle and desire for improved quality of life, along with books like Rachel Carson's *Silent Spring* and events like Earth Day, begun in 1970, helped to awaken Americans to the importance of protecting the environment. Jacksonville residents may have begun their efforts later, but they too wanted to pursue a better lifestyle in their northeast Florida environment. Increasingly they wanted cleaner air, clean water, and a clear landscape and to enjoy their beaches, rivers, parks, and marshes. Their changing attitudes led consolidated government to become proactive in acquiring Hanna Park by the ocean, constructing walkways downtown on the St. Johns River, recycling refuse, and establishing the Preservation Project to permanently withdraw land from commercial development.[32]

Despite the commitment to protect its natural attractions, the city faced continuing threats to its environment. First Jacksonville's population grew from roughly 560,000 men, women, and children at the time of consolidation to almost 780,000 by the end of the century. These 220,000 newcomers settled in homes, apartments, and trailer parks throughout the county, but mainly south and east of the St. Johns River. To accommodate their presence, the city built streets, power, water, and sewer lines, fire stations, schools, and libraries. Developers cleared the land of trees, built single-family, low-density homes, installed sewers and septic tanks, drained wetlands, and bulkheaded waterfront properties. They also built apartment complexes, strip malls, office parks, and shopping malls, paved parking lots, and turned previously attractive thoroughfares into sign-ridden, traffic-congested, commercial arteries. The developers did not create these conditions alone. Residents wanted housing and automobile access to nearby stores. Enterprising businessmen wanted to sell their goods and services. But as the population grew, their efforts resulted in the deterioration of the rural and suburban environment within the consolidated city.

Among the consequences, storm water runoff carried pesticides, fertilizers, and other chemicals from lawns, driveways, streets, and parking lots into the St. Johns River system. Environmentalists protested the indiscriminate cutting down of trees, filling of marshes, and raising of commercial signs. At city hall and in the state legislature, they secured laws to regulate these actions. Special interest opponents challenged their efforts, delaying enforcement. The state passed growth management legislation in the 1970s that set guidelines. In 1985, the state authorized local governments to require construction of public infrastructure (roads, sewers, water lines, etc.) to be concurrent with private development. These efforts improved standards among developers, but the pressures remained. Forces of population growth and new construction continued to threaten the quality of life in the city. After thirty years of consolidation, Jacksonville had improved the quality of its natural environment, but preservation of that quality depended upon an alert citizenry and a watchful city government, susceptible to the pressures of special interests.[33]

Compared with other cities, Jacksonville's consolidated government had advantages. In Pinellas County, Florida, twenty-four separate municipalities had to coordinate their efforts to clean up the environmental disaster of polluting Boca Ciega Bay in the 1950s. St. Petersburg and Pinellas also experienced rapid population growth with consequent water shortages, air pollution, absence of landfills for solid waste disposal, and gradual deterioration of Tampa Bay. As in Jacksonville in northeast Florida, they needed the assistance of the state and regional water management districts to protect the fragile local environment.[34]

Other cities across the country had their particular struggles to combat pollution and protect their unique natural environments. In Jacksonville, nature played a particularly important role because of the river system, ocean, and wetlands. They helped to shape the very character of the consolidated city. As a result residents turned to local government to protect and enhance this particular feature. Government's response rested upon the character and quality of its leaders. Often pressured in conflicting directions, they increasingly responded in an environmentally sensitive way.[35]

Consolidation and Downtown Development

Consolidated government had greater challenges combating the deterioration of the city's urban core. Across the nation, Americans had begun moving away from downtown following the advent of the streetcar. Automobiles accelerated the process. The move to suburbia that began in the nineteenth and early-twentieth centuries accelerated in the 1920s and became a major threat to downtown after World War II. As suburban neighborhoods spread outward from the urban core, retailers opened branches of downtown stores and other businesses to be nearer to residents. Over time, strips of stores led to malls, which led to office parks and then to entertainment centers of motels, restaurants, and cinemas. Meanwhile, downtown hotels, restaurants, theaters, and department stores closed. "Downtown" as the retail and commercial center in many, if not most, cities across the nation disappeared in postwar America. Jacksonville was no exception.[36]

City governments fought this sprawl. Right after World War II, community leaders in Pittsburgh, New Orleans, New York, and other cities began to revitalize their urban cores. In Jacksonville, Mayor Haydon Burns recruited new businesses (Sears Roebuck, Atlantic Coast Line Railroad, Prudential Insurance Company) and built the civic auditorium, city hall, coliseum, and baseball park. Subsequently, in the tougher economic decade of the 1970s, when Cleveland and New York approached bankruptcy, Jacksonville's Mayor Tanzler survived fiscally but could not implement his downtown plan for urban renewal. Then economic prosperity in the 1980s provided fresh opportunities for downtown development in Baltimore, Boston, and beyond. In Jacksonville, the Godbold administration oversaw construction of the south-bank river walk, Metropolitan Park, Jacksonville Landing, and Prime Osborne Convention Center. The economy slowed again at the end of the decade as did new construction during the Hazouri years. The 1990s saw it revive, and Mayor Austin launched his River City Renaissance for downtown. It would continue under his successor into the twenty-first century.[37]

The off-again, on-again efforts to revitalize downtown met with only partial success. Historian Jon Teaford has described the trials of northern city mayors during these years. Matching successes in Pittsburgh's Golden Triangle were Detroit's failed mass transit people mover system and Renaissance Center. Baltimore built its Inner Harbor showcase but saw its downtown department stores close. In addition, crime, poverty, and homelessness increasingly shaped images of the inner city. Again, Jacksonville had many of these same problems.[38]

Where downtown Jacksonville was the center for shopping, entertainment, and hospitality into the 1960s, three decades later Southpoint, Regency, The Avenues, Orange Park, and the Beaches offered alternative, sometimes more attractive sites for residents and visitors to the city. Downtown remained the center for government, finance, and sports. It offered Alltel Stadium (after the arrival of the Jaguars), Times-Union Center for the Performing Arts, Florida Theatre, and Ritz Theater, with promises of more to come in the new century in new housing, museums, library, and civic arena. Still, many vacant lots remained, buildings were boarded up, and streets were empty on weeknights and weekends. Increased occupancy at the Sulzbacher and other homeless shelters combined with the presence of the mammoth new jail also characterized downtown.[39]

Consolidation's role in downtown's struggle to survive and flourish brought mixed results. While most of the suburban commercial and residential growth came within the 840-square-mile city with property taxes being paid to the city, these tax dollars had to be spread over both downtown and the suburbs. Inner-city residents and businesses complained that suburban areas received a disproportionate share of tax dollars for infrastructure and services. Yet neighborhood residents had needs, most of them valid, and many unfulfilled. Tax revenues simply did not suffice to fund both downtown development and suburban growth. Whether separate governments for city and county could have done better is unanswerable. Preconsolidation Jacksonville and Duval County clearly had not served their constituents well.[40]

The Tampa–Hillsborough County Comparison

A comparison with Jacksonville's experience might be seen in Tampa, Florida, during these same years. This Gulf Coast city, though smaller than Jacksonville, had many similarities. Both had ports, military bases, substantial minority populations, and governmental corruption. Both began the era with a severely deteriorating downtown. In 1950, Jacksonville's downtown lacked modern office buildings. Its riverfront wharves and warehouses, according to one observer, "approached advanced decay." Public buildings were old and overcrowded, and hotels and restaurants badly needed upgrading. Tampa fared little better. Its "riverfront was a clutter of squat, unimpressive concrete and wooden wharves and ware-

Table 2. Population Trends, Jacksonville–Duval County and Tampa–Hillsborough County

Year	Jacksonville	Duval County	MSA[a]	Tampa	Hillsborough County	MSA
1940	173,000	210,143	210,143	108,391	180,148	272,000
1950	204,517	304,029	304,029	124,681	249,894	409,143
1960	201,030	455,411	455,411	274,970	397,788	772,453
1970	528,865	528,865	621,827	277,753	490,265	1,012,594
1980	571,003	571,003	722,252	271,523	646,939	1,613,600
1990	672,971	672,971	906,727	280,015	834,054	2,067,959
2000	778,879	778,879	1,100,491	303,447	998,948	2,395,997

Source: Kerstein 2001, 17; Local Government Study Commission, 1966, 22; U.S. Department of Commerce, Bureau of Census, *1970 Census of Population: Characteristics of Population*, vol. 1, Florida, part 2, sec. 1 (Washington, D.C., 1973), tables 16, 23, 97; U.S. Department of Commerce, Bureau of Census, *Census Tracts, Jacksonville, Florida, Standard Metropolitan Statistical Area*, "General Characteristics of Persons: 1980" (Washington, D.C., 1983), tables P-1–P-6; U.S. Department of Commerce, Bureau of Census, *1990 Census of Population: General Population and Housing, Jacksonville, Florida* (Washington, D.C., 1993), tables 1–5; University of Florida Bureau of Economic and Business Research, Warrington College of Business Administration, *Florida Statistical Abstract, 2001* (Gainesville, 2001), table 1.

Note: Jacksonville–Duval Metropolitan Statistical Area (MSA) included portions of Clay and St. Johns County beginning in 1970. Tampa–Hillsborough MSA included St. Petersburg, Pinellas County, and Clearwater, with Pasco County added in 1973 and Hernando County added in 1981. Kerstein 2001, 17; Bureau of Economic and Business Research, Warrington College of Business, University of Florida 2001, 7, 18.

a. Metropolitan Statistical Area—the city plus surrounding counties as defined by the census bureau.

houses." It lacked new hotels. No skyscrapers, the signature of contemporary urban development, interrupted the skyline. "An observer could not have been overly impressed with the present condition or future prospects of either community."[41]

Yet beginning in that decade, both cities began to transform their image. They built expressways to facilitate traffic into and through their urban cores. They successfully recruited national corporations, offering low taxes and low wages as incentives. Over time both cities created a Downtown Development Authority to plan urban core growth, built new airports, constructed convention centers, and built or substantially renovated performing arts centers.[42]

But the two cities also differed. Tampa–Hillsborough County voters chose not to consolidate city-county governments in 1967, 1970, and 1971, while Jacksonville–Duval County voters chose to consolidate in 1967. Further, Tampa's new international airport drew more airlines and flights, in part due to a larger metropolitan area that included Clearwater and St. Petersburg. The city's successful recruiting of a National Football League team in 1974, twenty years before Jacksonville, also reflected in part the larger metropolitan population base. Also, Tampa's geographical location in midstate provided easier access to markets from Miami to Pensacola than did Jacksonville's location in the northeast corner.[43]

But there was something more. In the 1950s, Tampa's business leaders began a partnership with city government to push for economic growth. They secured special legislation in Tallahassee to annex suburban areas in 1953 to double the population and increase the tax base. They adopted nonpartisan elections beginning in 1955 in an attempt to reduce corrupt influences. They obtained authorization to establish the University of South Florida, a decade before the University of North Florida in Jacksonville. They persuaded state legislators to pass a local bill enabling the city to apply for federal urban renewal funds in 1958 at a time when preconsolidation Jacksonville shunned such opportunities. Then, instead of planning riverfront renewal piecemeal, as Mayor Burns did along the St. Johns River, Tampa officials planned comprehensive bay front development. The Chamber of Commerce also sparked efforts to develop Tampa Industrial Park near the university, which drew both Schlitz and Anheuser-Busch to brew beer. Jacksonville also recruited Anheuser-Busch, but Tampa had Busch Gardens, which became one of the top tourist attractions in the state.[44]

The decade of the 1950s saw a strong progrowth effort begun by a coalition of Tampa business and governmental leaders that kick-started the city to regional prominence. Jacksonville also undertook progrowth measures, but its efforts to annex the suburbs failed. Jacksonville's leaders made no attempt to secure federal dollars for urban renewal or downtown development or to make a state university a priority on the local agenda. Also important, Jacksonville had its own unique problems that it appeared unable to resolve. It failed to recognize the scope of the pollution in the St. Johns

River system, as well as its odor problems. It also neglected its public schools to the point of disaccreditation.

Whereas Tampa began a broad-based "urban renaissance" in the 1950s, Jacksonville had a narrower focus until its business-government coalition formed a decade later to begin the effort for city-county consolidation. By then Tampa had a head start, securing an NFL team, building a hockey arena and baseball stadium for major league teams, and hosting three Super Bowls by the end of the century. Clearly the Tampa–Clearwater–St. Petersburg metropolitan area's population of twice that of Jacksonville's metropolitan area made a difference in securing these franchises. Still, in each case Tampa's progrowth leadership coalition initiated these singular achievements. None of these franchises necessarily made Tampa qualitatively a better city than its northern rival, nor did they ensure a better quality of life in residential neighborhoods. But clearly they put Tampa in the national spotlight in the last third of the twentieth century in ways that Jacksonville had yet to achieve, even with its consolidation.

Another way of comparing Tampa–Hillsborough County with consolidated Jacksonville–Duval County is to look at the experience of Hillsborough County during these years. How did it fare separate from its core city compared with Jacksonville–Duval County? In the 1950s and 1960s, Hillsborough and Duval Counties had similar experiences. Both were largely rural with suburban development spreading outward from the city. Both practiced essentially laissez faire government with few water, sewer, and other services provided, and even fewer restrictions on growth. After Duval County voters chose consolidation and Hillsborough County voters chose not to consolidate, progrowth policies continued in the consolidated city and in Hillsborough County into the 1980s.[45]

A corruption scandal led to the arrest and conviction of three of five Hillsborough County commissioners in 1983. Governor Bob Graham appointed replacements, leading to a majority who still supported growth, but it was, as one commissioner called it, "healthy growth," with provisions for adequate roads, water, sewers, parks, and fire protection. Over the next two years, the new county commissioners increased gasoline taxes and water and sewer rates and levied impact fees on new construction. They also strengthened planning efforts to review zoning requests, tightened subdivision regulations, adopted a landscape ordinance, and passed legislation to protect wetlands. A new county charter expanded the commission to seven members in 1985, and "healthy growth" continued. In 1986, the board of county commissioners approved a major bond issue to build new water systems, waste water treatment plants, sewer lines, and jail facilities.[46]

Passage of the state Growth Management Act in 1985 and the development of the I-75 corridor east of Tampa produced major conflicts in Hillsborough County over guidelines about who would pay for growth. The passage of a substantial increase in impact fees over builder association opposition in 1989 reflected the continuing effort to regulate development. County voters supported these decisions in the 1990 elections, resulting in a majority of four members continuing growth management policies. One of the new commissioners even belonged to the Sierra Club. Yet the county commissioners did not oppose growth. They continued to build roads, provide services, and support the development of the new ice hockey arena and major league baseball stadium. They also expanded human services with the passage in 1992 of the Hillsborough County Health Care Plan funded by a half-cent sales tax, to improve access to health care for working poor people ineligible for Medicaid. County commissioners expanded minority hiring and the minority business enterprise program. In effect, Hillsborough County raised taxes (including impact fees), provided new health care services, and expanded environmental protection programs while continuing to support managed growth. Consolidated Jacksonville could not match this record of accomplishment by the end of the century.[47]

Consolidation in the National Context

For Jacksonville, consolidation proved to be the right move. In 1993, David Rusk reflected upon the nature of American urban growth at the end of the twentieth century in his book, *Cities without Suburbs*. He had served as mayor of Albuquerque, New Mexico, state legislator, U.S. Department of Labor program development director, Woodrow Wilson Center fellow, and international consultant on urban and metropolitan areas. Rusk saw that cities across the country that had expanded through annexation, consolidation, or regional governments were using their resources more effectively to govern themselves than were cities surrounded by noncooperating suburbs. For Nashville, city-county consolidation had led to a revitalization of downtown. In Indianapolis, it led to better services, an expanding tax base, improved bond rating, and a greater sense of community. In contrast, while the metropolitan areas of Detroit, Cleveland, and Milwaukee grew and prospered, their central cities lost population, experienced increased racial segregation, and confronted a declining tax base to meet increasing social service needs. Rusk concluded that metro government of some form was essential for healthy cities. It could be a regional model as in Portland, Oregon, or Minneapolis–St. Paul, annexation as in Albuquerque or Phoenix, or city-county consolidation as in Jacksonville and most recently Louisville, Kentucky. Only these forms had the capacity to balance area infrastructure needs, provide economic opportunity, preserve the environment, or enable minorities to achieve their potential.[48]

Yet as Amy Bridges has shown in her study of the southwestern cities of Austin, Dallas, San Antonio, Albuquerque, Phoenix, San Diego, and San Jose, annexation alone was not enough. All of these cities grew rapidly by land area and population as a result of annexation in the years following World War II. As well, all neglected their Hispanic, African American, and Native American minorities. All emphasized growth on the expanding edge of their cities at the expense of older neighborhoods, downtown, and natural environment. Not until the 1970s did a loose coalition of neighborhoods, minorities, and environmentalists begin to challenge progrowth, business-dominated government. With assistance from the federal courts, they replaced citywide election of city councils with district representation, which resulted in greater voter participation, more conflict and negotiation between various interests groups, less orderly but more controlled growth, and more services to neighborhoods and minorities. Introducing district council representation was no panacea for the challenges of metropolitan governance, yet it clearly provided a voice for city dwellers heretofore ignored.[49]

Both the annexation examples and Jacksonville's experience with consolidation suggest that a city's control over a large metropolitan area provided a foundation or structure for governance but no guarantees about the outcomes. Providing adequate services with roads, water, sewers, schools, libraries, parks, police, and firefighting areawide proved expensive. Creating racially and economically inclusive neighborhoods along with respecting and protecting the natural environment challenged city leadership further. Downtown, with its office towers, courthouse, city hall,

Table 3. Jacksonville's Population and Its Proportion of the Metropolitan Area, 1950–2000

Year	Jacksonville	Jacksonville metro population	Percent of total population
1950[a]	204,517	304,029	67
1960	201,030	455,411	44
1970[b]	528,865	621,827	85
1980	571,003	737,541	77
1990	672,971	906,727	74
2000	778,879	1,100,049	71

Source: U.S. Department of Commerce, Bureau of Census, *1970 Census of Population: Characteristics of Population*, vol. 1, Florida, part 2, sec. 1 (Washington, D.C., 1973), tables 16, 23, 97; U.S. Department of Commerce, Bureau of Census, *Census Tracts, Jacksonville, Florida, Standard Metropolitan Statistical Area*, "General Characteristics of Persons: 1980" (Washington, D.C., 1983), tables P-1–P-6; U.S. Department of Commerce, Bureau of Census, *1990 Census of Population: General Population and Housing, Jacksonville, Florida* (Washington, D.C., 1993), tables 1–5; University of Florida Bureau of Economic and Business Research, Warrington College of Business Administration, *Florida Statistical Abstract, 2001* (Gainesville, 2001), table 1.

Notes

a. The 1950 and 1960 populations are preconsolidation.

b. Beginning in 1970, the surrounding counties of Nassau, Baker, Clay, and St. Johns became part of the metropolitan area.

apartments, and condominiums, hotels, convention centers, churches, theaters, stadiums, and other amenities, became the symbolic center by which each city became known beyond its boundaries. To achieve this urban quality of life required metropolitan governments with wise leadership and an engaged citizenry willing to pay the cost.

Almost from the beginning of Jacksonville's consolidation, Hans Tanzler warned about inadequate levels of local, state, and federal funding to do all that needed to be done. Early on, he bit the bullet and raised water and sewer rates to pay for cleaning up the St. Johns River. Mayor Godbold also recognized the need to more adequately fund city government. Mayor Hazouri persuaded Jacksonville voters to increase their sales tax by a half penny to eliminate tolls. Voters passed Mayor John Delaney's Better Jacksonville plan at the end of the century at the cost of another half cent added to the sales tax. Still, creating equity and providing equal opportunity for all residents remained challenges. Creating a viable downtown and healthy neighborhoods remained ongoing goals. Protecting the environment required continuing strong leadership supported by an engaged citizenry. Jacksonville's comparatively low tax rates slowed the pace.

As the twentieth century ended, however, Jacksonville had distinct advantages over many American cities because of consolidation. In northeast Florida, with almost three-quarters of the region's population, it remained the dominant player in the metropolitan area along Florida's First Coast. While economic growth along with suburban sprawl had begun to expand beyond the consolidated city's boundaries into the surrounding counties, it had not and, for the foreseeable future, would not overshadow the central city. Clearly expanding growth required increasing regional cooperation to combat land, air, and water pollution to maintain a healthy environment. Transportation planning and growth management also required regional efforts. These were the frontier for twenty-first-century metropolitan governance.

Meanwhile, within the consolidated city, economic and population growth resulted in new tax revenues supporting city services. Continued population growth in the consolidated city also meant more people engaged in civic efforts to improve further the quality of community life. Assuming wise leadership and taxpayer support, consolidated Jacksonville's prospects for the twenty-first century hold substantial promise to serve well all of its residents, environment, neighborhoods, and downtown.

NOTES

Abbreviations Used in the Notes

FTU   *Florida Times-Union*
JBJ   *Jacksonville Business Journal*
JCCI   Jacksonville Community Council, Inc.
JJ   *Jacksonville Journal*
JM   *Jacksonville Magazine*
MP   Mayors' Papers
PC   *Pittsburgh Courier*

Preface

1. The fifth mayor since consolidation, John Delaney, occupied the office during the writing of this book, succeeded by John Peyton in July 2003.

Chapter 1. Jacksonville before Consolidation

1. JM (fall 1963): 38; Sercombe, 9–13.

2. Gerry Wilson interview by author; FTU, 23 November 1987.

3. *Jacksonville Workbook for Community Development.*

4. Ibid., 4. A later generation saw the parking lots as an eyesore. Subsequently, the Jacksonville Landing, Richard P. Daniel State Office Building, and a new city hall were built on or adjacent to the lots.

5. Ibid., 3–10; Bill Beaufort interview by author.

6. Beaufort interview. One source asked how Burns on a $15,000 mayoral salary could own homes in Jacksonville, Fort Lauderdale, and the North Carolina mountains. One answer lay in the personal use of political contributions and campaign funds left over after election victories. Laws then did not regulate their use. Marvin Edwards reported that Burns acknowledged the existence of petty larceny at city hall among commission and city council members. *Folio Weekly,* 16 July 2002.

7. FTU, 23 November 1987; Colburn and Scher 1980, 122, 143, 276, 279, 282, 284, 285, 291, 294, 295. Burns's loss in the 1966 primaries to Miami mayor Robert High led to the election of Claude Kirk, the first Republican governor of the twentieth century.

8. Quoted in Dennis 1988, 42–43.

9. JM (fall 1963): 10, 11, 33, 44; Watts 1964, 29–31; Heaney 1965, 17–20, 29–34.

10. FTU, 14 September 1992.

11. Cummer Gallery of Art, undated, untitled pamphlet; *History,* Jacksonville Art Museum 1993, pamphlet; Museum of Science and History of Jacksonville, undated, untitled pamphlet.

12. *Papers,* Jacksonville Historical Society 1960, 57–62; R. Gentry 1991; Schafer 1982, 1, 10–12.

13. Sollee n.d., 80–102; Marian Chambers interview by author.

14. Larson 1964, 19–23. Larson was the state treasurer and insurance commissioner.

15. Jacksonville Area Chamber of Commerce 1962, 10–14.

16. School Bootstrap Committee 1963; George Peabody College of Teachers 1965; Rosenbaum and Kammerer 1974, 42–43.

17. School Bootstrap Committee 1963, 13–18; George Peabody 1965, 47–52, 55–56, 98–99, chap. 7.

18. School Bootstrap Committee 1963, 18–21; George Peabody 1965, chaps. 2, 4, 5.

19. Citizens Committee for Better Education in Duval County 1965; Nathaniel S. Washington interview by author. Washington described the efforts of many dedicated African American teachers, coaches, and administrators.

20. School Bootstrap Committee 1963, 24–31; George Peabody 1965, chap. 5.

21. George Peabody 1965, 201–8, 226–28.

22. Ibid., 46–48, 286–89.

23. School Bootstrap Committee 1963, 1, 5–6; George Peabody 1965, 295.

24. George Peabody 1965, 305.

25. Ibid., 307–8.

26. Ibid., 313–17.

27. School Bootstrap Committee 1963, 37–38; George Peabody 1965, 319.

28. George Peabody 1965, 9.

29. Ibid., 10–22; James R. Rinaman Jr. interview by author; Rosenbaum and Kammerer 1974, 44.

30. George Peabody 1965, 11–19.

31. *Jacksonville Workbook* 1962, 21.

32. Ibid., 23.

33. FTU, 6 December 1974.

34. Bio-Environmental Services Division 1975, 1.

35. Wilson T. Sowder, M.D., to Ray L. Wilson, 15 August 1966, in *Florida Health Notes* 59, no. 1., app. A, 57–60.

36. Ibid., 22–24; FTU, 6 December 1964; Local Government Study Commission of Duval County 1966, 124.

37. Health Planning Council of the Jacksonville Area 1971, M-2.

38. Harding 1967, 3–5; Bio-Environmental Services 1975, 41–42; Community Planning Council of the Jacksonville Area 1973, vol. 3 B, sec. 1, 2.

39. JJ, 30 June 1964; Harding 1967, 21–22, 37–40; City Health Department of Jacksonville, Florida, 1963.

40. Bio-Environmental Services 1975, 74.

41. Ibid., 74–75; E. R. Smith speech, 11 February 1970, scrapbook no. 2, Jacksonville Health Department Archives.

42. Melosi 1981, 219; JJ, 27 June 1961.

43. Landon 1964, 8.

44. Ibid.

45. Quillie L. Jones and Bob Ingram interview by author; Janet Johnson interview by author.

46. Ingram interview; Johnson interview; Lloyd Pearson interview by author; Alton Yates interview by author (1991).

47. Yates interview; Jones interview; Ingram interview; Pearson interview.

48. PC, 26 March, 23 April, 24 September 1960.

49. Perry 1963, 113.

50. Alton Yates interview by author (2000); Annette Girardeau interview by author (2003); Bartley 2000, 101–2; *Folio Weekly*, 15 August 2000. Stetson Kennedy, a longtime civil rights activist, was in Jacksonville at the time. Upon hearing of the riot on the radio, he rushed to the scene. He had participated as one of the few whites in the sit-ins. His article documents the KKK's instigation of the riot.

51. Bartley 2000, 115–16; Jones interview; Yates interview (2000); Pearson interview; PC, 3 September, 10 September 1960; JJ, 27 August 1960; FTU, 28 August 1960; Walch 1990, 73–74; Perry 1963, 115.

52. PC, 10, 24 September 1960; FTU, 29 August 1960.

53. FTU, 29 August 1960; PC, 10 September 1960.

54. Perry 1963, 118–19; JJ, 29 August 1960.

55. Bartley 2000, 103.

56. PC, 17 December 1960, 21 January 1961.

57. PC, 27 March 1961; 27 May 1963.

58. PC, 3 June 1961; Stetson Kennedy interview by author.

59. PC, 21 June, 15 July, 30 August 1961.

60. O'Riordan 1990.

61. O'Riordan 1990, 8; PC, 13 January 1962.

62. PC, 1 September 1962; O'Riordan 1990, 9.

63. PC, 29 February, 5 December 1964; FTU, 13 March 1964.

64. O'Riordan 1990, 11; FTU, 29 August 1964.

65. O'Riordan 1990, 15; PC, 19 December 1964. Wendell Holmes, the NAACP, the Interdenominational Ministers Alliance, and Citizens Committee for Better Education in Duval County continued to protest school segregation. In early 1966, the Citizens Committee sponsored another school boycott and appealed for federal assistance from the Department of Health, Education, and Welfare. Federal officials came to Jacksonville in March. They advised school officials to expedite desegregation under new guidelines that threatened the withdrawal of federal funds for lack of compliance. The school board responded by closing small, dilapidated, rural black schools and ceased busing students from the Beaches and Baldwin past all-white schools to schools in town. But the overall effect remained one of token integration: less than 5

percent of the total black population attended desegregated schools. JJ, 29 January, 4, 5, 7 March 1966; FTU, 9, 12 March 1966.

66. PC, 2 February 1963; Walch 1990, 74.

67. *New York Times,* 25 and 26 March 1964; PC, 3 August 1963.

68. FTU, 18, 20 March 1964; JJ, 19, 20 March 1964; Southern Regional Council 1964, 1, 2.

69. FTU, 22, 23 March 1964.

70. FTU, 23 March 1964.

71. JJ, 23 March 1964.

72. FTU, 24 March 1964; *New York Times,* 24 March 1964.

73. FTU, 24 March 1964; Bartley 2000, 109–11. Chappell's killer was eventually tried for manslaughter in front of an all-white jury, was convicted, and served two years in jail.

74. JJ, 24 March 1964; FTU, 25 March 1964; *New York Times,* 25 March 1964; Southern Regional Council 1964, 3, 4.

75. JJ, 24, 25 March 1964; *New York Times,* 25 March 1964; PC, 4 April 1964.

76. *Time,* 3 April 1964, 28; *Newsweek,* 6 April 1964, 21–22; *U.S. News and World Report,* 6 April 1964, 35–36.

77. Southern Regional Council 1964, 6–8.

78. FTU, 26 March 1964; JJ, 26 March 1964; Maness 2000, 128–40.

79. Maness 2000, 141–45; Subcommittee of the Jacksonville Community Relations Committee 1964.

80. Subcommittee of the Jacksonville Community Relations Committee 1964.

81. William H. Maness interview by author; Subcommittee 1964, parts 6 and 7; JJ, 18 April 1964; FTU, 18, 22, 26, 30 April, 31 December 1964; Maness 2000, 128–81.

82. Perry 1963.

83. Ibid., 145; Hallam 1988, 49–105. The quote is on page 52.

84. Perry 1963, 146.

85. Ibid., 147–50.

86. Ibid., 150–57.

87. Ibid., 157–60.

Chapter 2. Consolidation

1. Martin 1968, 49–54.

2. Local Government Study Commission 1966, 10.

3. Damon Miller 1968, 18, 26–29.

4. Ibid., 26–29; Local Government Study Commission 1966, 9–10.

5. Damon Miller 1968, 22–26; Martin 1968, 77–78.

6. *Miami Herald,* 29 May 1966; Damon Miller 1968, 22–26; Rosenbaum and Kammerer 1974, 46; George Peabody 1965, 13–14.

7. Damon Miller 1968, 41–43; Martin 1968, 42–47. In contrast, Tampa state legislators managed to annex suburban areas without a referendum. Kerstein 2001, 108–12.

8. Martin 1968, 46; Walch 1990, 100.

9. Martin 1968, 54–57.

10. Local Government Study Commission 1966, 172–73.

11. Martin 1968, 59.

12. Ibid., 61.

13. Damon Miller 1968, 59.

14. Local Government Study Commission 1966, 173; Martin 1968, 63.

15. Martin 1968, 62.

16. Ibid., 64–72; Damon Miller 1968, 61–68; Local Government Study Commission 1966.

17. Martin 1968, 76–79. Grove's quote is on 76.

18. FTU, 28 May 1966.

19. Martin 1968, 80–81; FTU, 1 July 1966.

20. Martin 1968, 82–83; FTU, 23 July 1966. Subsequently, charges against Lowe and Mattox were quashed because the defendants were not first read their rights before testifying to the grand jury, under *Miranda v. Arizona.* FTU, 11 January 1968. Robinson suffered a heart attack in the months after the indictments and died before ever going to trial. FTU, 10 March 1970.

21. Martin 1968, 83–84; FTU, 13 August 1966.

22. Martin 1968, 83; FTU, 24, 31 August 1966. Subsequently, Thomas pleaded no contest and received a prison sentence. FTU, 8 November 1967.

23. Martin 1968, 84–87; FTU, 10 September, 2, 3 November 1966. Hollister and Cannon were acquitted while Sharp and Smith were convicted. FTU, 7 December 1967, 27 January, 9 February 1968, 6 April 1969.

24. Kallina 1993, 60–64, ably describes the efforts of Governor Claude Kirk, Haydon Burns's successor in Tallahassee, to crack down on government corruption across the state.

25. JJ, 4 November 1966.

26. Damon Miller 1968, 76–80; Martin 1968, 106–7.

27. Damon Miller 1968, 80–83; Martin 1968, 108–9.

28. Damon Miller 1968, 83; Martin 1968, 122.

29. Damon Miller 1968, 84.

30. Damon Miller 1968, 85–89.

31. Ibid.

32. Martin 1968, 130–40. Martin was on the scene in Tallahassee reporting for the *Florida Times-Union* and gives a particularly dramatic account of events.

33. JM (summer 1966): 18–20.

34. *Los Angeles Times,* 24 July 1966; Pearson to Ritter, 24 June 1966, MP; Ritter to W. Ashley Verlander, 4 May 1967, MP.

35. Press release, GJEO, 2 September 1966, MP; Mayor-Commissioner to James E. Workman, 15 February 1967, MP; Department of Housing and Urban Development *News* (HUD-No. RH 66–768), 13 December 1966, MP.

36. *Daytona Beach News Journal,* 30 January 1966; Ritter to Verlander, 4 May 1967, MP.

37. Citizens Advisory Committee on Water Pollution Control 1966; Minutes of the Jacksonville–Duval Area Planning Board, 26 May 1966, MP.

38. Ritter, Speech to the Engineering Professional Club, 30 September 1966, MP.

39. FTU, 23 April 1967.

40. FTU, 21 June 1967.

41. Another factor was the weather on runoff election day. Rainstorms on the north side of the city may have prevented some of Ritter's African American supporters from getting to the polls. Wilson interview by author.

42. Walch 1990, 34–51, 96–107. Tanzler is quoted, 106.

43. Ibid., 56–73, 86–94, 107–17. Other newcomers to city council included Jake Godbold, who later served as mayor from 1979 to 1987.

44. Ibid., 99–100; FTU, 21 June 1967.

45. Damon Miller 1968, 92–93; Martin 1968, 151, 208–11.

46. Damon Miller 1968, 93–94; Martin 1968, 211–13.

47. Martin 1968, 151–52, 156, 167, 169–70; Damon Miller 1968, 94–96.

48. Damon Miller 1968, 98–101; Martin 1968, 165–67.

49. Martin 1968, 160.

50. Local Government Study Commission 1966, 6–7; Martin 1993, 218, 220–21.

51. Martin 1993, 153.

52. Ibid., 154–57.

53. Damon Miller 1968, 108–9.

54. Ibid., 106–8.

55. Crooks 1991, 46–47; Martin 1968, 171–75.

56. Damon Miller 1968, 114–18; Martin 1968, 224–25.

57. Martin 1968, 227; Walch 1990, 100; Hardy Fletcher interview by author.

58. Bartley 2000, 144–52; Meeting Summary of "Beyond the Talk: Improving Race Relations in Northeast Florida," 6 November 2002, author's possession; Jacksonville Community Council, Inc. 2002, 3.

59. Sloan and French 1971, 32.

60. Rosenbaum and Kammerer 1974, 65–69.

61. Ibid., 36–41.

62. Ibid., 41–49.

63. Ibid., 69–70.

64. Research and Policy Committee, Committee for Economic Development 1976; Lotz 1976; Sofen 1966, 257–259.

65. Robert E. McArthur 1976; John M. DeGrove 1976; Hawkins 1966. See also Doyle 1985, chap. 7.

66. Carver 1973, 214–20.

67. Martin 1993, 240–41.

68. Ibid., 234–72, describes the transition year.

Chapter 3. A Bold New City

1. Leander Shaw, Wendell Holmes, Rev. Charles Dailey, John D. Montgomery and Nathan H. Wilson to Tanzler, 12 July 1967, MP. Attorney Shaw later became a justice

of the Florida Supreme Court. Wendell Holmes was a mortician, elected to the Duval County School Board and later its chairman. Rev. Dailey was pastor of the prestigious Oakland Baptist Church and president of the black Ministerial Alliance. Montgomery and Wilson were white lawyers and community leaders. JJ, 20 August 1967; FTU, 30 July 1967. Key players assisting Tanzler in reaching out to the African American community were Clanzel Brown and Bob Ingram from the Jacksonville Urban League and Mack Freeman, Bob McGinty, and Gordon Bunch of the Greater Jacksonville Economic Opportunity (GJEO) antipoverty program. Following the mayor's visit to Vernell's Diner at Florida Avenue and Pippin Street, GJEO neighborhood organizer Mack Freeman said, "We have to give this man credit for facing us big black Africans in the deepest part of our jungle. We should give him a standing ovation." And, added the reporter, George Harmon, they did. JJ, 20 August 1967.

2. JM (fall 1967).

3. Ibid.

4. Ibid.

5. Minutes of the Mayor's Advisory Panel on Employment, 6 November 1967, Jobs for Jacksonville file, MP; JM (summer 1968): 33–37.

6. Mayor's speech (no title), Jobs for Jacksonville file, MP.

7. Ordinance GG-16, passed unanimously by city council 8 August 1967 and signed by the mayor 9 August 1967, MP.

8. The twenty commission members included representatives from the Urban League, Greater Jacksonville Economic Opportunity, Florida State Employment Service, and League of Women Voters, plus three clergy, a doctor, a dentist, an architect, two attorneys, a realtor, two union representatives, an undertaker, a restaurant owner, a general contractor, and two corporate executives. At least six, perhaps seven members were African Americans, including Clanzel Brown, who was executive director of the Jacksonville Urban League, Rev. C. B. Dailey from Oakland Baptist Church, funeral director Wendell P. Holmes, restaurant owner Andrew Perkins, Rev. J. C. Sams, pastor of Second Baptist Church and president of the National Baptist Convention of America, and Landon Williams, president of the International Longshoremen's Association, Local no. 1408, AFL-CIO. Three members were women. First Annual Report, Community Relations Commission, City of Jacksonville, 30 September 1968, MP; Press Release, Mayor's Office, 30 October 1967, MP; Remarks of Nathan H. Wilson, 30 October 1967, MP; Minutes of the Community Relations Commission Organizational Meeting, 26 January 1968, Community Relations Commission file, MP; JJ, 26 January 1968; FTU, 27 January 1968.

9. Press Release, Mayor's Office, 29 February 1968, MP; text, WJXT *Midday Show*, 24 May 1968, MP; Program, Open House and Dedication, Emmett Reed Center, 28 September 1969, MP.

10. JJ, 6, 8, 9 April 1968.

11. Ibid., 10, 13 April 1968.

12. "Progress 1968," Fall, Community Relations folder, MP.

13. Ralph H. Baker Jr., director, Division of Waste Water, Florida State Board of Health, to Mayor and City Commission, City of Jacksonville, 28 November 1967, MP;

E. E. Bentley, city engineer, to Florida Air and Water Pollution Control Commission, 20 February 1968, Water Pollution file, MP.

14. Minutes of Meetings of the Mayor's Advisory Committee on Pollution, 27 June, 17 July 1968, MP; Tanzler to members of Consolidated City Council, 2 July 1968, MP.

15. Mildred Adams, "The Censored Chapter of 'The Jacksonville Story,'" attached to a letter from James T. Townsend, M.D., to Tanzler, 10 October 1967, MP; Jacksonville League of Women Voters, "The City Electric Generation Stations, a Community Air Pollution Problem," statement presented to the Jacksonville Electric Authority, 13 June 1968, MP; Jacksonville League of Women Voters, "Statement regarding Automotive Pollution Control," 20 May 1968, MP; Ordinance 68–16–40, passed by city council 22 October 1968 and signed by Mayor Tanzler 25 October 1968, MP.

16. [Lex Hester?], "Consolidation Transition," typescript, MP; Martin 1993, 244–60.

17. "Consolidation Transition," 2–3.

18. Martin 1993, 273, 275.

19. In his budget report to city council in July 1969, Mayor Tanzler identified urban renewal as the number two goal of his administration after the elimination of water pollution. Tanzler, Report to the Council on the 1969–70 Budget of the Consolidated City of Jacksonville, 22 July 1969, MP; Tanzler, Address to Duval County legislative delegation, 20 February 1969, MP; "Community Redevelopment: Jacksonville," 20 February 1969, MP.

20. "Community Redevelopment," 17–21.

21. Ibid., 5–8; Tanzler to Congressman Charles E. Bennett, 2 October 1969, MP.

22. "Mayor Hans G. Tanzler, Jr. Speaking Before the City Council," 7 July 1969, typescript, MP.

23. Unlike an earlier renewal program in the 1960s resulting in the expansion of University Hospital at the expense of the substantial African American community in the Sugar Hill neighborhood, the new proposal included residents like Vera Davis in its Project Area Committee to help shape the direction of both demolition and new construction. Vera Davis telephone interview by author. Also JM (winter 1970/71): 12–18, 43–44.

24. JM (winter 1970/71): 12–18; FTU, 6 December 1970.

25. JJ, 22 February, 19 August 1971; Official [Press] Release, Mayor's Office, 1 November 1971, 16 August 1972, MP.

26. Minutes of the HUD Advisory Board Meeting, 19 January 1971; Official Release, Mayor's Office, 31 May 1972, MP; FTU, 30 June 1971.

27. Minutes of the HUD Advisory Board Meeting, 19 January 1971, MP; Official Release, Mayor's Office, 31 May 1972, MP.

28. Downtown Development Council, Bulletin, 22 March 1968, MP; FTU, 23 February 1969; William K. Jackson to Downtown Development Council, 9 May 1969, MP; Downtown Development Council, Report to the Membership, June, July, October 1969, MP.

29. RTKL 1971, v.

30. Ibid., 10–14, 17–64, 68–72.

31. FTU, 17 September 1970; JM (winter 1971): 7–8, 25; JJ, 22 June 1971; *Bold View Annual Report* 1972?, 15–20, MP.

32. Thomas J. Rouzie Jr., P.E., "Water Pollution Control in the Consolidated City of Jacksonville," presentation to the U.S. Senate Subcommittee Hearing on Air and Water Pollution in Jacksonville, Florida, 23 June 1969, MP.

33. WJXT News Special Report, 13 April, 1 May 1970, MP; FTU, 9, 10 October 1969.

34. Community Planning Council 1973, 3–4.

35. Water and Sewer Division, Public Works Department, "Management Improvement Team Report," attached to letter, Tanzler to Lynwood Roberts, president, and members of City Council, 20 March 1972, MP.

36. Community Planning Council 1973, 6–7.

37. Ibid., 4–5; Bio-Environmental Services 1975, 2–3.

38. Official Release, Mayor's Office, 13 March 1973, MP; *Bold View Annual Report* 1976–77, 1978, 3, MP; U.S. Environmental Protection Agency 1978, 1–10, MP.

39. Air Pollution Control Board Public Hearing, 14 September 1970, MP; Robert J. Stroh, chief, Bio-Environmental Services Division, to Morton A. Kessler, 1 April 1971, MP; Minutes of Air Pollution Control Board Regular Meeting, 21 June, 16 August, 15 November 1971, MP; Air Pollution Control Board Public Hearing, 19 November 1971, MP.

40. Community Planning Council 1973, 1–5; "Air Pollution Problems," attached to letter, William A. Ingram, director, Office of Intergovernmental Affairs, to Members of Mayor's Grants Review Committee, 31 May 1973, MP; Bio-Environmental Services 1975, 55–71; Bio-Environmental Services, *Big Scope* 1977, July/August/September, 5, MP.

41. Jacksonville Area Planning Board 1978a, vol. 2, 1–5, MP.

42. Hamilton S. Oven, Testimony before the Air Pollution Control Board Regular Meeting, 16 November 1970, MP.

43. Air Pollution Control Board Public Hearing, 29 November 1971, MP.

44. R.P.T. Young to Tanzler, 2 February 1972, MP.

45. Bio-Environmental Services 1975, 74–75.

46. Reynolds, Smith, and Hills 1971; Williams S. Hutchinson Jr., deputy director of public works, to Dan Scarborough, 19 February 1974, MP; Community Planning Council 1973, B.5.2; Jacksonville Area Planning Board 1978b, 15, 23–34.

47. FTU, 8 October 1969; Tanzler, "Intergovernmental Cooperation in Metropolitan Transportation," paper delivered at Florida State University, 25 September 1970, MP; Jacksonville Coach Company (author's name illegible) to Lynwood Roberts, president, city council, 26 July 1971, MP.

48. Rinaman to Tanzler, 21 June 1971, MP; Minutes of Jacksonville Expressway Authority Conference, 12 July 1971; FTU, 22 July 1971, 14 January 1972; Tanzler to Members of the Jacksonville Expressway Authority, 21 July 1971; JJ, 13 January 1972. Following the takeover, bus ridership increased in the first six months by 300,000 passengers. "The Harvest Year" [budget message], 10 July 1973, MP.

49. Official Release, Mayor's Office, 9 July 1970, MP; Tanzler, Budget Presentation, 28 July 1970, MP; Budget Message, 27 July 1971, MP; "The Harvest Year," 10 July 1973, MP.

50. *Harper's Magazine* 1971, July, 20–24; Fischer 1975, chap. 7.

Chapter 4. Race Matters

1. Community Relations Commission 1969, MP.

2. Community Relations Commission 1970, 1–11, MP.

3. Tanzler to Nathan Wilson, chairman, Community Relations Commission, 4 November 1969, MP; Girardeau to Tanzler, 3 November 1969, MP; Community Relations Commission 1970, MP.

4. Community Relations Commission 1970, 25, MP.

5. Ibid., 41–44.

6. Ibid., 44–45.

7. Ibid., 49–54.

8. Ibid., 55–59.

9. Ibid., Sec. 2, 1–29.

10. Ibid.

11. Ibid., 55–59.

12. Jerome Glover, Community Relations Commission 1971, 1–4, 6–13, 14–17, MP.

13. Department of Housing and Urban Development 1969; Press Release, Mayor's Office, 10 February 1969, 2 July, 14 October 1971, MP; Nathan H. Wilson to Jack Chambers, 10 April 1969, MP; Tanzler to Jacksonville Housing Authority, 23 January 1970, MP; FTU, 24 March 1970. The quotation is from Tanzler's letter to the Housing Authority.

14. Nathan H. Wilson to Chairmen and Members of the Employment Committee, Community Relations Commission, Civil Service Board, and City Council, 28 July 1970, MP.

15. H. Jerome Miron, director, Community Relations Commission, to Tanzler, 29 June 1970, MP.

16. "Evaluation Report from the Consultants on Search Procedures for Firemen, City of Jacksonville, Florida, to the Mayor's Committee on the Selection Program for Appointment to the Uniformed Service of the Fire Division, City of Jacksonville, April 19, 1971," MP.

17. FTU, 19 June 1971.

18. *Florida Star,* 19 June 1971; John C. Nelson, "Civil Disorder June 16, 1971," MP.

19. FTU, 17, 18, 19 June 1971; JJ, 18 June 1971.

20. FTU, 18, 20 June 1971.

21. Community Relations Commission 1971, 2, MP. The arrested woman was released that evening with an apology.

22. Ibid., 3.

23. FTU, 25 June 1971.

24. Girardeau to Askew, 30 September 1971, MP. Accompanying the letter in the

MP was a two-inch packet of affidavits, reports, and summaries of events of the previous summer, hereafter referred to as the Askew packet.

25. Notarized affidavit of Eugene Soloman, 25 June 1971, supported by a notarized affidavit from Edith Soloman, 25 June 1971, and a letter from Mrs. Leila M. Laney, 27 June 1971, Askew packet. Mrs. Laney's letter also lists eight witnesses to the event.

26. Affidavit of Gloria Jean Leroy, September 1971, Askew packet.

27. City of Jacksonville Community Relations Commission 1971, Askew packet. The report was supported in the Black Community Coalition's request to Gov. Askew by five affidavits from prisoners. Mayor Tanzler called for the Community Relations Commission investigation and voiced "shock" at the report, securing promises from Sheriff Dale Carson that such indiscriminate overcrowding would not occur again. Transcript of WJXT television taped interview, 19 August 1971; JJ, 26 August 1971. Earlier, prison farm police chief F. W. Murray was asked by reporters how he selected the prisoners to be punished. He replied, "I recognized some of them that were doing most of the hollering and threats. The others you go in and your young men are predominantly the ones that are giving you the trouble. So you pull your young ones out ... the older people, you left." Transcript of WJXT television interview, 13 August 1971, MP.

28. Sworn statement of Mary Mitchell, 25 August 1971, Askew packet; sworn statement of Randy Frazier (Perry's friend), 25 August 1971, Askew packet.

29. Statement of Andrew Perkins, no date, Askew packet; statement of A. E. Girardeau, no date, who was called by Mrs. Perkins to go to the jail and get her husband's release, Askew packet.

30. Sworn statements of Bernice Stokes (the mother) and Bernard Stokes, no date, Askew packet. Each statement lists five other witnesses to the event.

31. Statement of Isiah Johnnie Jones, no date. Jones's pastor subsequently wrote to the sheriff protesting the treatment of "one of the most respected men of our community." Rudolph W. McKissick to Office of Sheriff Dale Carson, 6 September 1971, Askew packet.

32. Statements of Billy Dan Reeves and Mrs. Frankie Mae Adams, with witnesses listed, no date, Askew packet.

33. Affidavit of John H. Farmer, 16 September 1971, Askew packet.

34. Affidavit copy, unsigned and undated, Askew packet.

35. "Preface" and "Overall Summary" to the Askew packet, submitted by the Black Community Coalition, 30 September 1971, MP.

36. The *Jacksonville Journal* story of 7 September 1971 was based on the police report. Affidavits from Valinda Lampkins, Annette Lampkins, Johnell Lewis, Thomas Lampkins, Reginald Payne, and Luther Jackson in the Askew packet told a very different story. After hearing the Lampkinses' testimony, Arnette Girardeau believed that the officers who arrested Lampkins should be charged with aggravated assault.

37. JJ, 8, 13, 16, 19, 28 September 1971.

38. Report of the Grand Jury in the Circuit Court, Fourth Judicial Circuit of Florida, in and for Duval County, Fall Term, 1971, dated 14 April 1972, MP.

39. FTU, 17 January 1972.

40. FTU, 17 November 1971, 22 January 1972.

41. Rodney Hurst, paper presented to the Conference on Race Relations, MP; FTU, 17 November 1971.

42. Minutes of Meeting, Conference on Race Relations, 20 December 1971, MP.

43. FTU, 18 March 1972; Minutes of the Employment Committee, Council of Leadership for Community Advancement, 29 March 1972; Minutes of Meeting, Council of Leadership for Community Advancement, 21 April 1972, MP.

44. "Task Force on Housing," attachment to Minutes of Meeting, Conference on Race Relations, 20 December 1971, MP.

45. Minutes of Meeting, Conference on Race Relations, 20 December 1971, MP.

46. Ibid.

47. Jacksonville Council on Citizen Involvement 1977, 15–19, MP.

48. Community Planning Council 1974a, 9–13, MP. For comparisons to early-twentieth-century Jacksonville, see Crooks 1991, 34.

49. Community Planning Council 1974b, 11; Community Planning Council 1975, 4–17; Northeast Florida Manpower Consortium Evaluation Report, Summer Employment Program for Economically Disadvantaged Youth, October 1975; Kevin M. O'Melia to George Harmon, 17 September 1975, MP.

50. Community Planning Council 1974b, 2, 65–67; FTU, 29 May 1976; Jeanna D. Tully, director, Office of Revenue Sharing, to Tanzler, 14 March 1977, MP; Tanzler to Bernadine Denning, director, Office of Revenue Sharing, 8 April 1977, MP.

51. Jacksonville Community Relations Commission 1974, 13, MP; Community Planning Council 1974b, 65–67.

52. Community Planning Council 1974b, 2, 67.

53. Community Planning Council 1974a, 14–16; Office of Mayor and Office of Intergovernmental Affairs, "Housing in Jacksonville, Florida: Opportunities and Problems," Jacksonville, 1976, 59–60, MP.

54. "Housing in Jacksonville, Florida," 70–71, 149–50, MP.

55. Eric Hall to Jerris Leonard, administrator, Law Enforcement Assistance Administration, 17 January 1972, MP.

56. Florida Advisory Committee to the United States Commission on Civil Rights 1975, 10, 16–17, 20, 23, 27–29, 41, 47.

57. Ibid., 47.

58. Ibid., 51–56.

59. Jacksonville Urban League 1979, 2, 7–8, 12–13, 23.

60. Ibid., President's Message.

Chapter 5. Economic Obstacles and Community Initiatives

1. Carroll 1990, chap. 8; Goldfield and Brownell 1990, chap. 12; Teaford 1990, chap. 6; New York Times, 30 January 2000.

2. "Current Data Jacksonville Electric Authority," 24 August 1971, MP; Northcutt Ely, Preliminary Memorandum re Impact of Executive Order no. 11615 on the Jacksonville Electric Authority, 27 August 1971, MP; Remarks by Hamilton S. Oven Jr., before the Florida Pollution Control Board, 2 September 1971, MP.

3. Statement of Hans G. Tanzler Jr., Mayor of Jacksonville, Florida, "Public Hearing–Project Independence," 23 September 1974, MP.

4. Executive Orders nos. 47–A and 50, 8 and 9 November 1973, MP; FTU, 9 January 1974.

5. Tanzler, "Public Hearing–Project Independence," 5, MP.

6. Mayor's Budget Message, 16 July 1974, MP.

7. "The Mayor Talks to Taxpayer," *Bold View Annual Report* 1973–74, vol. 7, no. 1, 3, MP; Tanzler, Budget Message, 22 July 1975, MP; *Bold View Annual Report* 1973–74, vol. 7, no. 1, MP; *Bold View Annual Report* 1974–75, vol. 8, no. 1, MP.

8. R. C. Peace, managing director, JPA, to William B. Mills, chairman, JPA, 29 September 1971, MP; *Wall Street Journal*, 24 May 1972.

9. *Wall Street Journal*, 24 May 1972.

10. Report Number 72–5: Projected Economic Impact of Westinghouse-Tenneco Facility on Jacksonville, 25 April 1972, MP.

11. *Wall Street Journal*, 24 May 1972.

12. Devereux 1976, 41–42.

13. Ibid., 44; Routa to Joe Kuperberg, director, Board of Trustees of the Internal Improvement Trust Fund, 28 April 1972, Carlucci Papers, Box 7, Folder 69.

14. Devereux 1976, 43; Christianson to Routa, 7 April 1972, Carlucci Papers.

15. Devereux 1976, 42–46; *St. Petersburg Times*, 8 June 1975; *Wall Street Journal*, 24 May 1972.

16. *St. Petersburg Times*, 8 June 1975.

17. "Analysis of the Commentary on Draft Contract of the Offshore Nuclear Power Proposal," 29 August 1975, MP.

18. Ibid., 7, 9, 11, 15, 26.

19. FTU, 30 August 1974; Harry L. Shorstein et al., "Legal Feasibility Report on Offshore Nuclear Power Plants Project of the Jacksonville Electric Authority," 28 June 1974, MP.

20. Devereux 1976, 47.

21. Ibid.

22. *St. Petersburg Times*, 8 June 1975. Political scientist Clarence Stone has written extensively about corporate regime politics in urban development. He observes that one of the most powerful shapers of economic development policies is the business interests that both influence and benefit from them. The old boy network in Jacksonville clearly was an example of Stone's corporate regime politics. Stone 1987, especially chaps. 1 and 10.

23. JM (November/December 1980), 42–43; JM (November/December 1981), 66–67.

24. 1977 Budget Message, MP; City of Jacksonville, Florida, Annual Budget 1978.

25. FTU, 15 December 1974.

26. Ellis 1974.

27. Ibid.

28. Presentation by Philip Hammer, 15 January 1976, MP.

29. Ibid., 3.

30. Ibid., 7–8.

31. Ibid., 14.

32. Ibid., 14–21.

33. Ibid., 21–23.

34. Ibid., 24–30.

35. Ibid., 31.

36. *Bold View Annual Report* 1976–77, vol. 10, no. 1; *Bold View Annual Report* 1977–78, vol. 11, no. 1. Despite the two-term limitation on mayors under the consolidation charter, Tanzler served two-plus terms. His first election took place prior to consolidation in May 1967. His reelection in May 1971 was four years after his first election but did not include a full four-year term under consolidation, which took effect in October 1968. The city's general counsel and the state attorney general agreed that Tanzler was eligible to run for two full terms under the consolidation charter, which validated his candidacy and further reelection in May 1975. Rinaman to Tanzler, 30 November 1971, MP.

37. Ibid.

38. FTU, 12 September 1980.

39. Warren n.d., 12–23, 34–37.

40. FTU, 11 December 1974.

Chapter 6. The Godbold Years

1. FTU, 7 May 1978, 4 February 1979.

2. FTU, 4 February, 2 May, 23 May 1979, 8 November 1990; Leon Green interview by author.

3. FTU, 24 July, 28 December 1979; JJ, 29 January 1979.

4. FTU, 24 June 1979. Note the Godbold syntax in the quote.

5. JJ, 18 April 1979; FTU, 26 July 1979; City of Jacksonville 1971–95, 1982.

6. JJ, 29 January, 16 February 1979, 7 August 1980; FTU, 26 February 1979, 7 November 1980.

7. FTU, 7 July 1980, 11 January, 30 December 1981; JJ, 2, 10 July, 20 August 1980, 30 December 1981.

8. FTU, 11 July, 23, 30 September, 4 November 1980, 23, 25, 27 February, 23, 26 June, 28 October 1981, 6, 25 July 1982.

9. FTU, 28 December 1979, 5 July 1980, 7 May, 25 July, 12 October 1981, 10 January 1982; JJ, 31 January 1980.

10. FTU, 8 September, 12 October 1979, 16 October 1980, 24 May 1983; *Chattanooga Free Press*, 23 January 1986.

11. FTU, 18, 19 July 1979, 13 October 1980, 17, 22 November 1981.

12. JJ, 20 February 1979, 4 August 1982; FTU, 6, 14 January, 16 September 1981; Green interview by author. Godbold also showed the courage to propose tax increases to fund city government more adequately. City of Jacksonville 1971–95, 1980.

13. Downtown Development Authority, *Jacksonville on the Move*, [1980?], color brochure, MP; JJ, 24 November 1982.

14. Jacksonville Area Chamber of Commerce 1979, "Focus," 11 July; Albert Ernest,

untitled talk at Job Opportunities through Economic Development conference, Jacksonville, Florida, 3 September 1980, MP.

15. Jacksonville Downtown Development Authority, [1980], *Downtown,* newsletter, MP; FTU, 6 July 1986; Patterson 1993, 12–15.

16. FTU, 18 April 1982.

17. Charles M. Thompson to Godbold and Joe Forshee, 2 June 1982, with enclosures containing resolutions of the Downtown Development Authority, Downtown Jacksonville Merchants Association, the American Institute of Architects, Jacksonville chapter, and Jacksonville Historical Landmarks Commission, MP; FTU, 18 April 1982; JJ, 21 June 1982.

18. Thompson to Godbold and Forshee, 2 June 1982, MP.

19. Backers supporting the terminal site included the Charter Corporation, Florida Title Group, Reynolds, Smith, and Hills, Wesley Paxson, W. W. Gay, and Martin Stein, FTU, 23 June 1982; JJ, 28 April 1982; *The Metropolis,* 23 June 1982.

20. JJ, 7 July 1982; FTU 6, 8, 25 July 1982, 30 June 1985; Patterson 1993, 9–11. By 1985, six department stores had closed downtown: Sears, Penney's, Ivey, Rosenbloom, Furchgotts, and Levy Wolfe. May Cohens soon followed. FTU, 30 June 1985.

21. FTU, 14 April, 1 August 1982, 18 July 1985; Patterson 1993, 16–18.

22. FTU, 26 May, 6 July, 18 August, 2, 18 October 1983; *USA Today,* 13 June 1983; JJ, 23 August 1983, 5 November 1986; *New York Times,* 18 October 1983; City of Jacksonville 1971–95, 1987.

23. FTU, 21 August, 30 December 1984, 27 November 1985. Water and sewer trunk lines built by the city to serve Mayo led to rapid residential development and sprawl in the surrounding area, an unintentional consequence of the original development.

24. FTU, 20 October, 14 November 1983.

25. JJ, 10, 11 May 1984.

26. JCCI 1984, 2–5.

27. Ibid.

28. Ibid., 7–9; JJ, 10 May 1984; Jacksonville Planning Department 1985, A-1 to A-5.

29. JCCI 1984, 18; FTU, 13 July 1984, 25 March 1985.

30. FTU, 5 June 1985.

31. JJ, 23 April 1986; *Builder News,* June 1986; FTU, 21 August 1986.

32. WJXT-TV 1984.

33. Ibid.

34. Press release, "City of Jacksonville, A Major Metropolitan In-Depth Odor Study," 14 January 1980, 1–2, MP.

35. Ibid., 2–3.

36. FTU, 25 July 1981, May 26 1984.

37. WJXT-TV 1984.

38. FTU, 18 October 1984.

39. FTU, 18 November 1984; JJ, 28 November 1984; *Bio-Scope* 1987, May, MP.

40. JJ, 27 February 1981.

41. JJ, 28 September 1982.

42. FTU, 15 February 1983, 11 December 1984.

43. Bio-Environmental Services 1978, 39; Environmental Protection Board 1985, 81; Environmental Protection Board Minute Book, 13 July 1987, MP.

44. FTU, 31 May 1984, 25 July 1986; JJ, 31 May 1984.

45. FTU, 27 May 1986.

46. FTU, 15 September 1986; JJ, 28 January 1987.

47. Environmental Protection Board 1986. See also Environmental Protection Board Minute Book, 9 February 1987, on need to establish a septic tank superfund; 18 November 1986, on the Asian tiger mosquito threat; 5 November 1986, on nonpoint surface water runoff; 8 June 1987, on ulcerated fish. Jacksonville Environmental Protection Board Archives. Also, FTU, 2 June 1986, 16 March 1987.

48. Farmer to Godbold, 16 February 1982, MP; FTU, 28 April 1984. The four-year gains saw technicians increase from 15.7 to 16.9 percent, professionals from 11.7 to 13.1 percent, and administrators from 7.7 to 14.5 percent.

49. Jacksonville Community Relations Commission, n.d.; Jacksonville Community Relations Commission 1984, MP; FTU, 28 April, 26 May 1984.

50. Victoria W. Lewis, chairman, Civil Service Board, to Godbold, 18 February 1986, MP; FTU, 14 February 1986; Richard Danford interview by author.

51. Holzendorf to Godbold, 26 February 1979, MP; Walch 1993, 3; and FTU, 17 June, 2 July 1985.

52. Ordinance 83–1200–647; FTU, 11 January, 3 February 1984, 12 August 1987; JCCI 1985, 8.

53. JCCI 1985, 8; FTU, 22 September 1985, 12 August 1987.

54. JCCI 1985, 10; FTU, 21 February 1985, 22 January 1986; Jacksonville Urban League 1985, 7.

55. Ronnie A. Ferguson to Godbold, 18 September 1985, MP.

56. Jacksonville Urban League 1981, tables 2, 4, 5.

57. Ibid.

58. Ibid.

59. Ibid.

60. FTU, 30 September 1983; City of Jacksonville 1984.

61. FTU, 23, 25 October, 22 November 1983.

62. City of Jacksonville 1984.

63. Ibid., 6–12.

64. FTU, 11 January, 11 February 1984; JJ, 8, 9 March 1984.

65. City of Jacksonville Mayor's Office of Equal Employment 1988; Crooks 1989, 9–10.

66. Jacksonville Urban League 1989, 1.

67. Jacksonville Urban League 1988, 6–14.

68. Ibid., 30–35.

69. FTU, 12 April, 6 July 1983; JJ, 25 May 1983.

70. *Miami Herald*, 16 July 1984; *Tampa Tribune*, 3 May 1984; *New York Times*, 16 October 1983; *Chattanooga News-Free Press*, 23 January 1986; *Atlanta Constitution*, 21 June 1987.

71. *Miami Herald,* 24 May 1987.

72. JJ, 9 April 1985, 3 February 1987; FTU, 7, 8 December 1986, 26 January 1987.

73. FTU, 8, 12, 13 February, 31 March 1985, 14 January 1990.

74. FTU, 7 August 1985, 11, 27 September, 7, 31 October 1987, 10, 14 January 1990.

75. JJ, 21 February 1987; FTU, 26 February 1987; Mike Tolbert interview by author.

76. FTU, 4 February 2001.

Chapter 7. The Hazouri Years

1. FTU, 19 April, 24 May 1987.

2. FTU, 4 October 1985, 10 March 1987; *Financial News & Daily Record,* 18 August 1986.

3. FTU, 15 April, 6 May 1987; JJ, 27 May 1987. In the second primary, Hazouri's Lebanese heritage became an issue when Lewis told a reporter that many voters would not support a candidate of Arab descent. A subsequent endorsement of Lewis as a good Christian by his pastor, Rev. Homer Lindsay Jr., of First Baptist Church, may have hurt more than it helped as Hazouri's second primary vote total increased by 18,054 compared to Lewis's 5,830. Hazouri, also a Christian, was a member of Mandarin Presbyterian Church. FTU, 19, 26 April 1987.

4. City of Jacksonville 1971–95, 1988, 17–24.

5. FTU, 10 February 1988; *Miami Herald,* 27 March 1988.

6. FTU, 3 October 1987, 30 May 1988; *Florida Trend* 1988, April, 38–42; *Tampa Tribune,* 20 October 1988; W. Gentry 1987, 13. See also Mehta and Manning 1988; and Minutes of Environmental Protection Board Regular Meeting, 14 December 1987, for a summary of the Water Services Division study that concluded that "90 percent of odor constituents . . . at the Buckman Wastewater Treatment Plan . . . [came] from the SCM Glidco factory."

7. *Florida Trend* 1988, April, 38–42.

8. FTU, 3 August 1987; William Gentry interview by author.

9. FTU, 3 October 1987; W. Gentry 1987, 13.

10. FTU, 31 January 1988.

11. FTU, 13 December 1987, 31 January 1988; JBJ, 11 January 1988; *Miami Herald,* 27 March 1988.

12. FTU, 10 February, 26 March, 30 May 1988; Gentry interview by author.

13. FTU, 15 June 1988, 6 February 1990.

14. FTU, 4, 11 November 1988, 17 August 1990.

15. FTU, 30 April, 14 May, 31 August, 12 October, 1988, 1 June 1989.

16. FTU, 30, 31 January, 16 November 1990.

17. FTU, 12 April 1989, 31 January 1990.

18. FTU, 26 December 1989, 10 January 1990, 1 April 1991. Other odor polluters cited by the city included two local landfills, Jacksonville Electric Authority, two sewage treatment plants, St. Vincent's Hospital, and Nutri-Turf, a sod farm owned by Anheuser-Busch. JBJ, 29 June 1990.

19. FTU, 17 January, 6 March 1988, 6 August 1989.

20. FTU, 13 January 1988; JBJ, 8 February 1988.

21. FTU, 24 January, 26 February, 5 March 1988.

22. FTU, 20 February, 7 March 1988.

23. FTU, 16 February, 6 March 1988.

24. FTU, 3 March 1988.

25. FTU, 13 March 1988; JBJ, 14 March 1988; *Tampa Tribune*, 27 March 1988.

26. FTU, 12 August, 6 September 1989; JBJ, 4 September 1989.

27. FTU, 8 November 1987, 25 January 1988, 8, 11 June, 27 October 1989.

28. JCCI 1985; FTU, 11 August 1988, 26 April, 6 June, 10 October 1989, 12 February 1990; *Folio Weekly*, 23 May 1989.

29. FTU, 12 October, 16 December 1988, 25 June, 11 July 1989, 2 March, 5 July 1990; JBJ, 24 April 1989; JM 1990, February; Environmental Protection Board 1979–92, 1989, 1990, 1991.

30. Environmental Protection Board 1979–92, 1986, 31–32; Flood Engineers-Architects-Planners 1983; Camp, Dresser, and McKee 1986.

31. Minutes of the Environmental Protection Board Regular Meeting, 13 February 1989; FTU, 21 January 1989; Steve Crosby interview by author.

32. FTU, 28 October 1988, 2 February 1989; Reynolds, Smith, and Hills 1989, 4–16.

33. T. R. Hainline Jr. interview by author; FTU, 22, 23 February 1989.

34. FTU, 7, 8 March 1989.

35. FTU, 17 October 1989.

36. FTU, 12 November 1989, 23 January, 14 February, 21 November 1990, 13 February 1991. T. R. Hainline Jr. claimed the cabinet decision was motivated more by political considerations than environmental; busloads of opponents traveled to Tallahassee for the hearing and probably influenced the results. Hainline interview.

37. FTU, 13 October, 16 December 1988, 6 January 1989, 11 April, 8 May 1990, 9 May 1992.

38. FTU, 21 September, 22 December 1988, 29 January, 26 February 1989; Stephenson 1997, 175.

39. FTU, 14 January, 17 March, 11 April, 21 May, 27 June 1989; *Folio Weekly*, 16 May 1989; Minutes of the Environmental Protection Board Regular Meeting, 19 April 1989; Crosby interview. Nationally, while initially seen as a simple, popular solution, incineration never achieved more than 15 to 17 percent of solid waste disposal due to high construction costs and concern about environmental pollution. Melosi 2001, 78–9.

40. City of Jacksonville 1971–95, 1989, 22–23; FTU, 12 July, 26 September 1989.

41. FTU, 13 July, 2 August, 4, 12, 17 December 1989, 26 September 1990, 6 February 1991.

42. FTU, 2 July 1987; Hazouri 1987, Inaugural Address, author's files; City of Jacksonville 1971–95, 1987.

43. D. J. Miller 1990, 65.

44. FTU, 8 July, 9 August 1987.

45. Alton Yates to Hazouri, 27 August 1987, author's files; FTU, 12 August 1987, 19 April 1988.

46. Press Release, Office of the Mayor, "Statement by Mayor Tommy Hazouri regarding reaffirmation of the minority set-aside ordinance," 22 March 1989, author's files; FTU, 24 January, 16, 23, 30 March, 7, 21 April, 5 May 1989, 1 June 1990; *Florida Star*, 10–16 March 1989.

47. FTU, 9 June 1989, 29 January 1990.

48. D. J. Miller 1990, 40–42, 65. These figures exclude contracts in the Jacksonville Electric Authority's set-aside program (less than 1 percent to blacks), school board contracts (again less than 1 percent to blacks), and Jacksonville Port Authority contracts (again less than 1 percent to blacks). Miller 1990, 44–6.

49. Ibid., 112.

50. Ibid., 132–35.

51. Ibid., 144–46.

52. Ibid., 146–55.

53. Ibid., 158–62.

54. Ibid., 203–4.

55. Executive Order no. 87–109 1987, Delegation of Authority and Approval of Personnel Actions Involving Employee Status Records, Mayor's Office, 31 August.

56. Skitch T. Holland, director, Office of Equal Employment, to Hazouri, 22 January 1988, author's files; City of Jacksonville Mayor's Office of Equal Employment 1990, 2–6, 9, 34, 86–87.

57. Richard Danford Jr. to Hazouri, 24 February 1989; City of Jacksonville Mayor's Office of Equal Employment 1988.

58. FTU, 27 September, 6, 7 October 1989; Jacksonville Community Relations Commission 1989. The latter failed to assess what happened at the meeting but did provide testimony of the participants in the minutes of special meetings of the commission.

59. FTU, 28 September, 3, 4, 11 October 1989. The black-owned *Florida Star* reported 2,000 marchers, 7–14 October 1989.

60. FTU, 1 October 1989.

61. FTU, 12, 13, 14, 15 August 1990.

62. FTU, 14 August 1990.

63. Downtown Development Authority 1987; FTU, 18 July 1987.

64. Tommy Hazouri 1987, Inaugural Address, 1 July, author's files.

65. *Sports Illustrated* 1987, 2 November; FTU, 30 April, 4, 10 May, 17 April, 15 December 1988, 3 January, 12 April, 6 June, 9, 17 August 1989, 26 January, 4 May, 7 August, 24 October, 31 December 1990, 12 January 1991.

66. FTU, 28 July 1987, 5 March, 10 November 1989, 8, 9 February, 28 June, 6 August 1990, 13 February 1991.

67. FTU, 26 March 1988.

68. FTU, 3 March, 11 May, 8 June 1989, 2 June 1990.

69. Patterson 1993, 17–24; FTU, 2 July 1989; *Jacksonville Today* 1989, March, 25–28; Tommy Hazouri interview by author. Hazouri's four annual budget messages to city council provide a good indication of his concerns for all of the consolidated city.

70. FTU, 3 July 1988.

71. FTU, 6 March, 2, 12 July 1989. Pursuant to an agreement between the mayor's office and the University of North Florida, the author spent one day a week at city hall as "historian in residence" with the Hazouri administration, from September 1987 through June 1991, networking and attending meetings.

72. FTU, 29 July 1990.

73. FTU, 20 October 1990.

74. FTU, 13 December 1990.

75. FTU, 10, 11 April 1991.

76. FTU, 30 September 1990, 6, 7, 10, 11 April 1991; Alton Yates interview (2002); Mitchell Atalla interview by author; Mike Tolbert interview by author.

Chapter 8. The Austin Years

1. In an interview after he left office, Austin remembered thinking he had served as state's attorney long enough, was looking for a new challenge, and thought he could do a better job as mayor than his predecessor. Ed Austin interview by author (2002).

2. FTU, 22 July 1990.

3. FTU, 30 June, 2 July 1991; Jacksonville Chamber of Commerce 1991, June; Austin interview (2002).

4. Notes of meeting, Jacksonville Insight, Tuesday, 30 July 1991; Meeting summaries, Jacksonville Insight, 30 July, 3, 15 October, 26 November, 17 December 1991; FTU, 3 August 1991. The author attended the meetings and saved the notes and summaries prepared by staff.

5. FTU, 1 November, 1 December 1991, 2 February, 23 February 1992.

6. FTU, 5 June 1992; *Jacksonville Vision,* Florida Community College, Jacksonville, 1992, 12 pages. The author drafted the document at the direction of and with the approval of the stakeholders.

7. FTU, 19 April, 11 June, 2 November 1991, 28 January, 9 May 1992.

8. JBJ, 15–21 1994; FTU, 13 November 1991, 16 October 1993.

9. *Folio Weekly,* 12 October 1993; FTU, 11 May 1993, 4 July 1995; JBJ, 15–21 April 1994.

10. FTU, 19 January, 29 December 1994.

11. FTU, 13 September 1992.

12. FTU, 23 March, 3 December 1995.

13. FTU, 11, 26 June, 10 September, 21 October, 7 December 1991, 4 March, 6 May 1992; *Folio Weekly,* 10 September 1991.

14. FTU, 7, 8, 27 May, 10, 17, 24, 25 June, 25 August 1992, 13, 18 April 1993.

15. FTU, 2 June, 19 September 1991.

16. FTU, 2 June 1991.

17. FTU, 2 June, 11 August 1991.

18. FTU, 22 May 1994, 8 February, 20 May 1995; JBJ, 21–27 April 1995.

19. FTU, 7 July 1991.

20. FTU, 2 June, 26 September 1991, 2 February, 1 April 1992.

21. FTU, 21 October 1991; *Florida Star*, 26 October–1 November 1991.

22. FTU, 17, 21, 26 May, 11, 12, 25, 31 July, 1 September, 29 October 1991; *Florida Star*, 1–7, 15–21, 22–28 June 1991.

23. FTU, 22 December 1991, 4, 12 January 1992.

24. FTU, 24, 30 December 1991.

25. FTU, 25, 27, 28, 31 December 1991, 6, 12 January 1992.

26. FTU, 3, 5 January 1992. The Florida Supreme Court removed Santora as chief judge by a unanimous vote following the failure of his peers on the circuit court to remove him. FTU, 18 January 1992. The Florida Judiciary Qualifications Commission subsequently formally reprimanded Santora but did not remove him from office. FTU, 12 May 1992. Santora retired from the circuit court at the end of 1992.

27. FTU, 4, 5 1992. Reporter Karen Mathis reported that while welcoming the Chamber's initiative, several African American community leaders questioned whether the city's pursuit of a National Football League team and the city's overall concern for its image in recruiting new businesses influenced its decision. Over the next two weeks twenty-eight of the Chamber's 5,300 members resigned in protest of its call for Santora's resignation. FTU, 18 January 1992.

28. FTU, 10 January 1992.

29. The *Florida Times-Union* (14 February 1991) identified all forty-four Jacksonville Together recommendations. A more detailed description of the recommendations is found in Mayor's Council on Community Reconciliation 1992, author's files. The author participated in the series of public meetings leading to the development of the recommendations, cochairing the task force on education.

30. *Folio Weekly*, 24 March 1992.

31. FTU, 30 July 1992, 3 January 1992, 21 December 1994; Vivian C. Jackson to JCRC Commissioners, 2 December 1992, author's files.

32. FTU, 10 February, 24 June 1992.

33. Austin to Warren Jones, 14 July 1992, author's files; FTU, 17 April, 15 July 1992; *Florida Star*, 18–24 July 1992; *Jacksonville Advocate*, 13–19 April 1992.

34. FTU, 16, 29 July, 10 September 1992.

35. Florida Advisory Committee 1996, 22–28.

36. FTU, 28, 30 May, 11, 13,17, 22, 25 June 1992.

37. FTU, 28 June 1992; Austin interview (2002).

38. FTU, 7, 8, 11, 13, 28, 29 October 1992.

39. FTU, 23, 26 October 1992; JCCI 1992, 67.

40. Jacksonville Downtown Development Authority 1992, 4.

41. Jacksonville Chamber of Commerce 1992, 1–4; FTU, 19 March 1992.

42. Jacksonville Chamber of Commerce 1992, 5–6.

43. Ibid., 9–11.

44. Ibid., 11–16.

45. Ibid., 16.

46. Jacksonville Downtown Development Authority 1992, 4.

47. Jacksonville 1993; Jacksonville 1994. The Renaissance plan also included:
- children's programs for immunization, preschool education, after-school services, drug treatment, family preservation services, and intensive community-based services for troubled youth;
- a health and social service initiative to include a new and larger outpatient clinic at University (now Shands) Medical Center, plus the homeless center;
- additional economic development to include the Gateway Shopping Mall in the predominantly African American north side and expansion of the Jacksonville port;
- a town center at Atlantic and Neptune Beach;
- input from neighborhood associations on priority needs for infrastructure, parks, and playgrounds;
- a new southeast regional library and a substantially enlarged Regency Square library;
- purchase of environmentally endangered lands and expansion of water and sewer systems; and
- major renovation of the Jacksonville Zoo.

These ambitious plans were estimated to cost $570 million to be funded through new bonds, a small increase in the water bill, refinancing of maturing bonds, and state and federal grants. See also FTU, 6 March 1994.

48. FTU, 19 March, 5 April, 13 November 1992, 6 March 1994; JBJ, 17–23 April 1992; *Folio Weekly*, 22 September 1992.

49. FTU, 27 July, 13 October 1995, 25 April, 15 September 1996.

50. JBJ, 22–28 April 1994; FTU, 16 May 1994, 1 January, 30 March, 2 May 1995, 16 July, 16 September 1996; *Folio Weekly*, 27 June 1995.

51. Jacksonville Public Information Office, *Action Line*, spring 1995.

52. FTU, 2 June, 30 July, 4 August 1991, 19 March 1992, 24 February, 4 March 1995; Jacksonville Transportation Authority 1993.

53. FTU, 31 January 23, 28 March, 22 May 1993, 24 October 1998; JBJ, 20–26 January, 3–9 November 1995; *Folio Weekly*, 24 October 1995.

54. *Folio Weekly*, 12 December 1995.

55. FTU, 2 December 1993.

56. FTU, 1, 2 December 1993.

57. FTU, 7, 24, 25 July 1994; John Delaney interview by author.

58. FTU, 5 December 1993, 25 February 1994; Austin interview (2002).

59. FTU, 30 April 1994, 13 May 1994, 12 April 1995, 10 May 1995.

60. FTU, 14 August 1994, 1 July 1995.

61. FTU, 25 February 1994, 1 July 1995.

Chapter 9. Consolidated Jacksonville

1. *Florida Trend* 1969, December, 41–45.

2. *FBI Law Enforcement Journal* 1970, October, 11–15.

3. *Fire Journal* 1970, May.

4. *Florida Trend* 1969, December, 41–45.

5. National Association of Counties 1973, 5–18.

6. Ibid., 39–48. Whatever successes consolidation had, it "produced no measurable impact upon the taxing and spending policies" of consolidated Jacksonville different from those of Tampa or Hillsborough County. Benton and Gamble 1984, March, 190–98.

7. *Urban Review* 1973, 57–61.

8. Carver 1973, 213–14.

9. Ibid., 214–20.

10. Ibid., 220–25.

11. Ibid., 225–27.

12. Ibid., 227–32.

13. Ibid., 232–43.

14. Ibid., 243–45. Fifteen years later at Jacksonville's twentieth-anniversary celebration, Mayor Tommy Hazouri praised the city's low tax rate compared with Orlando, Tampa, and Miami, crediting consolidation for its success. JJ, 28 September 1988.

15. Carver 1977, 41.

16. Ibid., 41–43.

17. University of North Florida Humanities Council 1993, 4–7. The symposium, funded in part by the Florida Humanities Council, was conceived and designed by the author and directed by UNF history professor Carolyn Williams.

18. Ibid., 7–11 and 15–21. Gibson had been a supporter of consolidation at its passage in 1967 but twenty years later felt it was a mistake. Blacks were worse off, he said, because of the "terrible neglect of the black community." JJ, 28 September 1988.

19. University of North Florida Humanities Council 1993, 21–30.

20. Ibid., 30–37.

21. Ibid., 39–44.

22. JCCI 1995, 67; JCCI 1992, 1; and JCCI 2002.

23. Will and Owens 1999, 55–57, charts 4–6.

24. Catlin 1989, 142–60; Kerstein 2001, 165–72, 210–14, 235–51.

25. Dunn 1997, 267–316; University of North Florida Humanities Council 1993, 33. Further complicating race relations in Miami, of course, was the growing number of Cubans and other Latinos who rose to political and economic power during these years, experiences that Jacksonville did not have. Portes and Stepick 1993, chap. 8.

26. Goldfield 1997, 172.

27. Bullard 1989, 161–173.

28. Under the consolidation city charter, the Jacksonville sheriff and school board members were separately elected, and the mayor virtually had no control over race relations within the sheriff's department or public schools.

29. Hays 1998, 345.

30. Fortunately the quantity and quality of the city's potable water supply from the

Florida aquifer was not a critical concern during these years. JCCI 1991. As noted in chap. 3, the city met EPA standards on air pollution for auto and industrial emissions, but odors were not covered.

31. *Folio Weekly*, 12 October 1993.

32. Hays 1987, 22–29, 527–531, 541.

33. DeGrove and Miness 1992, 1–4, 7–31; JCCI 2001.

34. Stephenson 1997, 134–48.

35. Accounts of of other cities' environmental experiences are described in Hurly 1997; C. Miller 2001; Kerstein 2001, 254–60; Teaford 1990, 83–92, 310–11.

36. Fogelson 2001.

37. Teaford 1990.

38. Ibid., 287–307.

39. Sources for Jacksonville's development cited here and throughout this chapter may be found in earlier chapters and in the book index.

40. In the southwestern cities of San Diego, Phoenix, and Albuquerque, which had expanded by annexation, similar conflicts existed between developers on the edge and downtown business interests. Bridges 1997, 159.

41. Rosenbaum and Kammerer 1974, 35.

42. Kerstein 2001, 151, 157–58, 172–74, 177–79, and 196–205. Jacksonville built its new airport in 1967, Tampa in 1971. Jacksonville constructed its convention center in 1983, Tampa in 1990. Tampa built its performing arts center in 1987, Jacksonville renovated its center in 1995.

43. Ibid., 177–79, 180–82.

44. Ibid., 103, 108–12, 132–38, 151–53. Initially Tampa tried to annex suburban areas by referendum, but it failed to obtain a majority suburban vote. Its state legislators then secured special legislation in Tallahassee to annex without a referendum. Tampa's urban renewal funds totaled $52 million by the time Jacksonville consolidated.

45. Ibid., 153–54, 182–87.

46. Ibid., 214–18.

47. Ibid., 253–62.

48. Rusk 1993, 121–27. See also Orum 1995, chap. 12; Dreier, Mollenkopf, and Swanstrom 2001, chap. 6. A dissenting view to expanding centralized governmental power by either consolidation or annexation can be found in Bish 1971, chaps. 4, 5. Bish argues that decentralization can better serve voters in smaller communities and that these communities can negotiate cooperation on services that overlap jurisdictions.

49. Bridges 1997, chaps. 7 and 8.

Bibliography

Archives and Collections

Carlucci, Joseph. Papers. Carpenter Library, University of North Florida.

Godbold, Jake. Scrapbooks. In Godbold's possession.

Grimes, Robert. Papers. Carpenter Library, University of North Florida.

Hazouri, Thomas. Scrapbooks. Carpenter Library, University of North Florida.

Jacksonville Environmental Protection Board. Archives.

Jacksonville Health Department. Archives.

Jacksonville Historical Society. Papers.

Jacksonville Human Rights Commission (formerly Jacksonville Community Relations Commission). Archives.

Mayors' Papers. Letters, memoranda, minutes, petitions, press releases, reports, and speeches from the administrations of Mayors Burns, Ritter, Tanzler, and Godbold. City Hall Annex, Jacksonville.

McGehee, Charles White. Papers. In author's possession.

Tanzler, Hans, Jr. Scrapbooks. In Tanzler's possession.

Interviews

Atalla, Mitchell. 1991. Interview by author. Tape recording. Jacksonville, August 29.

Austin, Edward T. 1992. Interview by author. Tape recording. Jacksonville, May 11.

———. 2002. Interview by author. Tape recording. Jacksonville, September 12.

Beaufort, William. 1992. Interview by author. Tape recording. Jacksonville, January 28.

Bowers, Richard. 1991. Interview by author. Tape recording. Jacksonville, September 27.

Carver, Joan, and Jay Carver. 1991. Interview by author. Tape recording. Jacksonville, November 15.

Chambers, Marion. 1991. Interview by author. Tape recording. Jacksonville, October 22.

Crosby, Steve. 1990. Telephone interview by author. Jacksonville, March 29.

Danford, Richard, Jr. 1999. Interview by author. Tape recording. Jacksonville, March 10.

Davis, Vera. 1999. Telephone interview by author. Jacksonville, February 18.

Delaney, John. 2002. Interview by author. Tape recording. Jacksonville, September 12.
Fletcher, Dorothy, and Hardy Fletcher. 1991. Interview by author. Tape recording. Jacksonville, October 2.
Gentry, William. 2001. Interview by author. Tape recording. Jacksonville, September 19.
Green, Leon. 1990. Interview by author. Jacksonville, November 8.
Hainline, T. R., Jr. 2001. Interview by author. Tape recording. Jacksonville, December 6.
Hazouri, Thomas. 2002. Interview by author. Tape recording. Jacksonville, August 28.
Hester, Lewis Alexander "Lex." 1998. Interview by author. Jacksonville, January 21.
Ingram, Robert. 1991. Interview by author. Tape recording. Jacksonville, November 4.
Johnson, Janet. 1992. Interview by author. Tape recording. Jacksonville, March 10.
Jones, Quillie. 1991. Interview by author. Tape recording. Jacksonville, November 4.
Kennedy, Stetson. 1991. Interview by author. Tape recording. Jacksonville, October 4.
Maness, William H. 1992. Interview by author. Jacksonville, January 25.
Martin, Edgar, and Ann Turner. 1991. Interview by author. Tape recording. Jacksonville, November 22.
Milano, Barbara. 1991. Interview by author. Tape recording. Jacksonville, October 2.
Pearson, Lloyd. 1991. Interview by author. Tape recording. Jacksonville, November 5.
Perry, Spence W. 1991. Interview by author. Tape recording. Jacksonville, February 21.
Rinaman, James R., Jr. 1991. Interview by author. Jacksonville, February 18.
Shorstein, Ann. 1991. Interview by author. Tape recording. Jacksonville, September 18.
Sulzbacher, I. M. 2000. Interview by author. Tape recording. Jacksonville, June 14.
Tanzler, Hans, Jr. 1991. Interview by author. Jacksonville, September 28.
———. 2002. Interview by author. Jacksonville, May 16.
Tolbert, Mike. 2000. Interview by author. Tape recording. Jacksonville, July 11.
Washington, Nathaniel S. 1992. Interview by author. Tape recording. Jacksonville, April 7.
Wilson, Gerry. 1992. Interview by author. Tape recording. Jacksonville, January 15.
Yates, Alton, 1991. Interview by author. Tape recording. Jacksonville, September 25.
———. 2000. Interview by author. Jacksonville, April 21.

Public Records

Bio-Environmental Services Division, Department of Health, Welfare, and Bio-Environmental Services. 1975. *Jacksonville, Florida, Five Year Environmental Status Report, 1970–1975.* Jacksonville.
———. 1978. *Jacksonville, Florida, Annual Environmental Status Reports.*
City Health Department of Jacksonville, Florida. 1963. *Annual Reports and Statistics for 1956–1959.* Jacksonville.
City of Jacksonville. 1971–76. *Bold View Annual Report.* Public Information Office.
———. 1971–95. Budget Message. In *Annual Budget, City of Jacksonville, Florida.*
———. 1984. *Report of the Select Committee to Study Policies and Procedures Related to Police and Public Safety* (Clarkson Report). Jacksonville.

————. 1993. *River City Renaissance: A Vision for the Rebirth of Our City.* Jacksonville.

————. 1994. *Progress Report: Jacksonville River City Renaissance.* Jacksonville.

City of Jacksonville. Community Relations Commission. 1969. A Preliminary Report of the Eastside Civil Disorder. Jacksonville. Mimeographed.

————. 1970. Report of the Task Force on Civil Disorder, October 31, 1969. Jacksonville. Mimeographed.

————. 1971. Chronological Review of the Events During the Civil Disorder, June 16–20, 1971. Jacksonville. Mimeographed.

————. 1971. Preliminary Staff Report on the Prison Farm Incident, August 6, 1971. Jacksonville. Mimeographed.

————. 1984. Committee Report, Hiring Practices Committee, Jacksonville Community Relations Commission. Jacksonville. Mimeographed.

————. 1989. Fact Finding Report of the Jacksonville, Florida, City Council Meeting, September 26, 1989. Jacksonville. Mimeographed.

————. n.d. Hiring and Promotion Practices, City of Jacksonville. Mimeographed.

City of Jacksonville. Mayor's Office of Equal Employment. 1989. *Annual Affirmative Action Progress Report, Fiscal Year 1987/88.* Jacksonville.

————. 1990. *Annual Affirmative Action Progress Report, Fiscal Year 1988/1989: Challenge 1990.* Jacksonville.

Downtown Development Authority. 1987. *Annual Report of the Downtown Development Authority, 1987.* Jacksonville.

Environmental Protection Board, Jacksonville. 1979–1992. *Annual Report.* Jacksonville.

Florida Advisory Committee to the U.S. Commission on Civil Rights. 1966. *Racial and Ethnic Tensions in Florida.* Jacksonville.

————. 1975. *Toward Police/Community Detente in Jacksonville.* Jacksonville.

————. 1996. Jacksonville Briefing Meeting, July 21, 1992. In *Racial and Ethnic Tensions in Florida.* Tallahassee.

Gentry, William C. 1987. Preliminary Report of Special Counsel to the Mayor on Odor Pollution, October 2, 1987. Jacksonville. Mimeographed.

Glover, Jerome. 1971. Report of the Follow-up on Recommendations of the Florida Avenue Task Force Report. In Community Relations Committee, *Report of the Task Force on Civil Disorder, October 31, 1969.* Jacksonville.

Jacksonville Area Planning Board. 1978a. Jacksonville Area Air Quality Control Plan. Jacksonville.

————. 1978b. Solid Waste Sub-element of the 2005 Comprehensive Plan. Jacksonville.

Jacksonville Downtown Development Authority. 1992. Downtown Master Plan Summary. Mimeographed.

Jacksonville Planning Department. 1985. *Evaluation and Appraisal Report 2005 Comprehensive Plan.* Jacksonville.

Jacksonville Transportation Authority. 1993. 1992 Annual Report. Jacksonville.

Mehta, Khurshid K., and James L. Manning. 1988. Dawn of an Improved Environment: Jacksonville's War on Odors. Jacksonville: Bio-Environmental Services Division. Mimeographed.

Mayor's Council on Community Reconciliation. 1992. *Jacksonville Together! Recommendations for Community Healing.* Jacksonville.

Subcommittee of the Jacksonville Community Relations Commission. 1964. First Report of the Hearing of Public Expression. Jacksonville. Mimeographed.

U.S. Department of Housing and Urban Development. 1969. Analysis of the Jacksonville, Florida, Housing Market as of April 1, 1969. In *Report of the Department of Housing and Urban Development, Washington, D.C.* Washington, D.C.

Secondary Sources

Barrows, Robert G., et al. 1994. *The Encyclopedia of Indianapolis.* Bloomington: Indiana University Press.

Bartley, Abel A. 2000. *Keeping the Faith: Race, Politics, and Social Development in Jacksonville, Florida, 1940–1970.* Westport, Conn.: Greenwood Press.

Beeler, Park L. 1973. The Merger Urgers of Jacksonville Are Winning a Quiet Revolution. *The Urban Review.*

Benton, J. Edwin, and Gamble Darwin. 1984. City/County Consolidation and Economies of Scale: Evidence from a Time-Series Analysis of Jacksonville, Florida. *Social Sciences Quarterly,* March.

Bish, Robert L. 1971. *The Public Economy of Metropolitan Areas.* Chicago: Markham Publishing Company.

Brdlik, Mel F. 1972. The New Downtown Means Business. *Jacksonville Magazine,* winter.

Bridges, Amy. 1997. *Morning Glories: Municipal Reform in the Southwest.* Princeton, N.J.: Princeton University Press.

Bullard, Robert D. 1989. Conclusions: Problems and Prospects. *In Search of the New South.* Tuscaloosa: University of Alabama Press.

[Burns, Haydon?]. 1962. The Jacksonville Story on Urban Redevelopment. In *The Jacksonville Workbook for Community Development.* Jacksonville Chamber of Commerce.

Camp, Dresser, and McKee, Inc. 1986. *City of Jacksonville, Refuse-to-Energy Development Program.* Jacksonville.

Carroll, Peter. 1990. *It Seemed Like Nothing Happened: America in the 1970s.* New York: Rutgers University Press.

Carson, Dale, and Donald K. Brown. 1970. Law Enforcement Consolidation for Greater Efficiency. *FBI Law Enforcement Journal,* October.

Carver, Joan. 1973. Responsiveness and Consolidation: A Case Study. *Urban Affairs Quarterly,* December.

———. 1977. Consolidation: Implications for the Black Community. Mimeographed.

Catlin, Robert A. 1989. Blacks in Tampa. In *In Search of the New South: The Black Urban Experience in the 1970s and 1980s,* ed. Robert D. Bullard. Tuscaloosa: University of Alabama Press.

Citizens Advisory Committee on Water Pollution Control. 1966. *Report, Citizens Advisory Committee on Water Pollution Control*. Jacksonville.

Citizens Committee for Better Education in Duval County. 1965. Still Separate, Still Unequal: A Study Specifically Related to Discrimination and Inequities in the Duval County Public School System. Jacksonville. Mimeographed.

Colburn, David, and Richard K. Scher. 1980. *Florida's Gubernatorial Politics in the Twentieth Century*. Gainesville: University Press of Florida.

Community Planning Council of the Jacksonville Area, Inc. 1973. *A Report to the Commission on Goals and Priorities for Human Services*. Jacksonville.

―――. 1974a. Task Force VIII. Equal Opportunity for All. In *A Report to the Commission on Goals and Priorities for Human Services*. Jacksonville.

―――. 1974b. Task Force I. Income and Economic Opportunity. In *A Report to the Commission on Goals and Priorities for Human Services*. Jacksonville.

―――. 1975. Task Force I. Northeast Florida Manpower Consortium Evaluation Report, Summer Employment Program for Economically Disadvantaged Youth. Jacksonville.

Crooks, James B. 1989. The City and Community: Public Policy and African American Rights in Jacksonville, 1964–1989. Mimeographed.

―――. 1991. *Jacksonville after the Fire, 1901–1911: A New South City*. Jacksonville: University of North Florida Press.

―――. 1998. Jacksonville before Consolidation. *Florida Historical Quarterly* 77: 141–62.

―――. 2001. Jacksonville's Consolidation Mayor: Hans G. Tanzler, Jr. *Florida Historical Quarterly* 80: 198–224.

Cummer Gallery of Art. n.d. Jacksonville. Pamphlet.

The Dedication of Fort Caroline National Monument. 1960. *Papers, Jacksonville Historical Society*. Jacksonville.

Defort, Frank. 1987. This Bud's Not for You. *Sports Illustrated*, 2 November.

DeGrove, John M. 1976. The City of Jacksonville: Consolidation in Action. In *Metropolitan Areas, Metropolitan Governments*, ed. Gary D. Helfand. Dubuque, Ia.: Kendall/Hunt Publishing Co.

―――. 1984. *Land, Growth, and Politics*. Washington, D.C.: American Planning Association Press.

DeGrove, John M., and Deborah A. Miness. 1992. *The New Frontier of Land Policy: Planning and Growth Management in the States*. Cambridge, Mass.: Lincoln Institute of Land Policy.

Dennis, Lawrence. 1988. JPA Finds Gold in Its Silver Anniversary Year. *Jacksonville Magazine*, June/July.

Devereux, Sean. 1976. Boosters in the Newsroom: The Jacksonville Case. *Columbia Journalism Review*, January/February.

Doyle, Don H. 1985. *Nashville since the 1920s*. Knoxville: University of Tennessee Press.

Dreier, Peter, John Mollenkopf, and Todd Swanstrom. 2001. *Place Matters: Metropolitics for the Twenty-first Century*. Lawrence: University Press of Kansas.

Dunn, Marvin. 1997. *Black Miami in the Twentieth Century.* Gainesville: University Press of Florida.

Ellis, Thom, III. 1974. Jacksonville Community Planning Conference, a Report, June 12–14, 1974. Jacksonville: Jacksonville Chamber of Commerce.

Environmental Health Study Committee of Jacksonville. 1971. Report of the Environmental Health Study Committee of Jacksonville to the Health Planning Council of the Jacksonville Area. Jacksonville.

Fischer, John. 1971. The Easy Chair, Jacksonville: So Different You Can Hardly Believe It. *Harper's Magazine,* July.

———. 1975. *Vital Signs, U.S.A.* New York: Harper and Row.

Flood Engineers-Architects-Planners. 1983. *Solid Waste Facilities Study for City of Jacksonville.* Jacksonville.

Florida Community College at Jacksonville. 1992. *Jacksonville Vision.* Jacksonville.

Fogelson, Robert M. 2001. *Downtown: Its Rise and Fall, 1880–1950.* New Haven, Conn.: Yale University Press.

Friedan, Bernard, and Lynn B. Sagalyn. 1989. *Downtown: How America Rebuilds Cities.* Cambridge, Mass.: MIT Press.

Gentry, Robert B., ed. 1991. *A College Tells Its Story: An Oral History of Florida Community College at Jacksonville.* Jacksonville: Florida Community College at Jacksonville.

George Peabody College of Teachers. 1965. *Duval County: Florida Public Schools: A Survey Report.* Nashville, Tenn.: Division of Surveys and Field Services.

Goldfield, David R. 1997. *Region, Race, and Cities: Interpreting Southern Cities.* Baton Rouge: Louisiana State University Press.

Goldfield, David R., and Blaine A. Brownell. 1990. *Urban America, a History.* 2nd edition. Boston: Houghton Mifflin Company.

Hallam, George. 1988. *Our Place in the Sun: A History of Jacksonville University.* Jacksonville, Fla.: Jacksonville University.

Harding, C. I., et al. 1967. *Clearing the Air in Jacksonville.* Jacksonville: Air Improvement Committee for Greater Jacksonville, Inc.

Hawkins, Brett W. 1966. *Nashville Metro: The Politics of City-County Consolidation.* Nashville, Tenn.: Vanderbilt University Press.

Hays, Samuel P. 1987. *Beauty, Health, and Permanence: Environmental Politics in the United States, 1955–1985.* Cambridge: Cambridge University Press.

———. 1998. *Explorations in Environmental History.* Pittsburgh, Pa.: University of Pittsburgh Press.

Health Planning Council of the Jacksonville Area. 1971. Toward Environmental Health Quality for Jacksonville, Florida. Jacksonville.

Heaney, Eva. 1965. Jacksonville Takes a New Look at Its Port and Industrial Development. *Jacksonville Magazine,* fall, 17–34.

Helfand, Gary D., ed. 1976. *Metropolitan Areas, Metropolitan Governments.* Dubuque, Ia.: Kendall/Hunt Publishing Co.

Hightower, J. Howard. 1981. Analysis of Survey on the Attitude of Blacks toward the

Police Department. *Jacksonville Urban League's Report on Police/Community Relations.* Jacksonville: Jacksonville Urban League.

Hurley, Andrew, ed. 1997. *Common Fields: An Environmental History of St. Louis.* St. Louis, Mo.: Missouri Historical Society.

Jacksonville Area Chamber of Commerce. 1962. *The Jacksonville Workbook for Community Development.* Jacksonville.

Jacksonville Art Museum. 1993. *History.* Jacksonville. Pamphlet.

Jacksonville Chamber of Commerce. 1992. *Downtown Jacksonville: A Turning Point.* Jacksonville. Mimeographed.

Jacksonville Community Council, Inc. 1984. *Growth Management: A Report to the Citizens of Jacksonville.* Jacksonville.

———. 1985a. *Minority Business.* Jacksonville.

———. 1985b. *Visual Pollution.* Jacksonville.

———. 1991. *Adequate Water Supply: A Report to the Citizens of Jacksonville.* Jacksonville.

———. 1992a. *Life in Jacksonville: Quality Indicators for Progress.* Jacksonville.

———. 1992b. *Young Black Males.* Jacksonville.

———. 1995. *Life in Jacksonville: Quality Indicators for Progress.* Jacksonville.

———. 2001. *Growth Management Revisited: A Report to the Citizens of Northeast Florida.* Jacksonville.

———. 2002. *Beyond the Talk: Improving Race Relations.* Jacksonville.

Jacksonville Council on Citizen Involvement. 1977. *Quality Education and Desegregation in the Duval County School District.* Jacksonville.

Jacksonville Urban League. 1979. *Status of Blacks in Jacksonville, 1979.* Jacksonville.

———. 1985. *Twenty-first Annual Report: Status of Blacks in Jacksonville, 1985.* Jacksonville.

———. 1988. *The Status of Blacks in Jacksonville, 1988.* Jacksonville.

———. 1989. *The Status of Blacks in Jacksonville, 1989.* Jacksonville.

Kallina, Edward F., Jr. 1993. *Claude Kirk and the Politics of Confrontation.* Gainesville: University Press of Florida.

Kerstein, Robert. 2001. *Politics and Growth in Twentieth Century Tampa.* Gainesville: University Press of Florida.

Landon, Jim. 1964. Profile of Jacksonville's Population. *Jacksonville Magazine,* winter, 8.

Larson, J. Edwin. 1964. Insurance Center of the Southeast. *Jacksonville Magazine,* spring, 19–23.

Local Government Study Commission of Duval County. 1966. *Blueprint for Improvement.* Jacksonville.

Lotz, Aileen. 1976. Metropolitan Dade County. In *Metropolitan Areas, Metropolitan Governments,* ed. Gary D. Helfand. Dubuque, Ia.: Kendall/Hunt Publishing Co.

Maness, William H. 2000. *Dear William: The Yeast Is There.* Jacksonville: XLibris Corporation.

Martin, Richard. 1968. *Consolidation: Jacksonville–Duval County: The Dynamics of Urban Political Reform*. Jacksonville: Crawford Publishing Company.

———. 1993. *A Quiet Revolution: Jacksonville–Duval County Consolidation and the Dynamics of Urban Reform*. Jacksonville: White Publishing Company.

McArthur, Robert E. 1976. Metropolitan Government of Nashville and Davidson County. In *Metropolitan Areas, Metropolitan Governments*, ed. Gary D. Helfand. Dubuque, Ia.: Kendall/Hunt Publishing Co.

McGovern, Steven. 1998. *The Politics of Downtown Development*. Lexington: University of Kentucky Press.

Melosi, Martin V. 1981. *Garbage in the Cities: Refuse, Reform, and the Environment, 1880–1980*. Chicago: Dorsey Press.

———. 2001. *Effluent America: Cities, Industry, Energy, and Environment*. Pittsburgh, Pa.: University of Pittsburgh Press.

Miller, Char, ed. 2001. *On the Border: An Environmental History of San Antonio*. Pittsburgh, Pa.: University of Pittsburgh Press.

Miller, D. J., and Associates. 1990. *City of Jacksonville Disparity Study*. Atlanta, Ga.

Miller, Damon C. 1968. "The Jacksonville Consolidation: The Process of Metropolitan Reform." Senior thesis, Princeton University.

Museum of Science and History. n.d. Jacksonville. Pamphlet.

National Association of Counties. 1973. *Consolidation: Partial or Total, an Edited Transcript of the National Conference*. Washington, D.C.

O'Riordan, Cormac. 1990. "School Desegregation in Duval County, 1960–1971." Graduate seminar paper, University of North Florida.

Orum, Anthony M. 1995. *City-Building in America*. Boulder, Colo.: Westview Press.

Patterson, Steven. 1993. "Jacksonville's Downtown Development Authority from 1980 to 1990." Graduate seminar paper, University of North Florida.

Perry, Spence W. 1963. "Riding the Lightning: A Report on Urbanization and Social Attitude Change in the Southern United States." Senior honors thesis, Harvard University.

Portes, Alejandro, and Alex Stepick. *City on the Edge: The Transformation of Miami*. Berkeley: University of California Press.

Research and Policy Committee, Committee for Economic Development. 1976. The Metropolitan Toronto Experience. In *Metropolitan Areas, Metropolitan Governments*, ed. Gary D. Helfand. Dubuque, Ia.: Kendall/Hunt Publishing Co.

Reynolds, Smith, and Hills. 1971. *City of Jacksonville Solid Waste Systems Study*. Jacksonville.

———. 1989. *Siting Process Evaluation—Regional Southeast Solid Waste Disposal Facility*. Jacksonville.

Rosenbaum, Walter A., and Gladys M. Kammerer. 1974. *Against Long Odds: The Theory and Practices of Successful Governmental Consolidation*. Beverly Hills, Calif.: Sage Publications.

RTKL, Inc., and Associates. 1971. *The Downtown Plan for Jacksonville*. Baltimore.

Rusk, David. 1993. *Cities without Suburbs.* Washington, D.C.: Woodrow Wilson Center Press.

Schafer, Daniel L. 1982. *From Scratch Pads and Dreams: A Ten Year History of the University of North Florida.* Jacksonville: University of North Florida.

School Bootstrap Committee. 1963. Summary of the Report of the School Bootstrap Committee, November 6, 1963. Jacksonville. Mimeographed.

Sercombe, Ron. 1963. Mr. and Mrs. Hogan Really Started Something When They Built a Log Cabin. *Jacksonville Magazine,* summer, 9–13.

Sloan, Lee, and Robert M. French. 1971. Black Rule in the Urban South? *Transaction Magazine,* November/December.

Sofen, Edward. 1966. *The Miami Metropolitan Experiment.* Garden City, N.Y.: Doubleday and Company–Anchor Books.

Sollee, Arthur Neyle, Jr. n.d. *The Engineer Speaks: Memoirs Covering Five Decades of Highway Problems in Duval County.* Jacksonville: Arthur N. Sollee.

Southern Regional Council. 1964. Report L-47: The Question from Jacksonville. Atlanta, Ga. Mimeographed.

Stephenson, R. Bruce. 1997. *Visions of Eden: Environmentalism, Urban Planning, and City Building in St. Petersburg, Florida, 1900–1995.* Columbus: Ohio State University Press.

Stone, Clarence J. 1987. *The Politics of Urban Development.* Lawrence: University Press of Kansas.

Swain, David. 1982. Local Public Funding Commitments to Human Services: A Case Study of Jacksonville, Florida. Duplicated.

———. 1982. The Status of Women in the Jacksonville Labor Force: A Statistical Study and Opinion Survey. Jacksonville Urban League. Duplicated.

———. 1983. An Analysis of Consolidated City of Jacksonville General Fund Revenue Sources: 1968 to 1983. Duplicated.

———. 1983. Block Grants Make Little or No Difference: A Local Perspective. *Public Administration Quarterly.*

———. 1983. Neighborhood Opinion on Redevelopment: A Report of Survey Research Conducted for the Jacksonville Urban League. Duplicated.

———. 1985. Perceptions about Political Leadership for the Black Community in Jacksonville. Jacksonville Urban League. Duplicated.

Tarr, Joel A. 1996. *The Search for the Ultimate Sink: Urban Pollution in Historical Perspective.* Akron, Ohio: University of Akron Press.

Teaford, Jon C. 1990. *The Rough Road to Renaissance: Urban Revitalization in America, 1940–1985.* Baltimore, Md.: Johns Hopkins University Press.

University of North Florida Humanities Council. 1993. Symposium: Race Relations in Jacksonville since Consolidation. Typescript.

Walch, Barbara Hunter. 1990. *New Black Voices: The Growth and Contribution of Sallye Mathis and Mary Singleton in Florida Government.* Jacksonville: Barbara H. Walch.

————. 1993. Highlights of Race Relations in Jacksonville since Consolidation. Mimeographed.

Warren, Louise Stanton. n.d. *A House on Hubbard Street.* Jacksonville: Olivette-Crooke Publishing.

Waters, John M., Jr. 1970. The Consolidation of the Jacksonville Fire Protection Division. *Fire Journal,* May.

Watts, David A. 1964. Deepwater Port of the Southeast. *Jacksonville Magazine,* summer, 29–31.

Will, Jeffrey, and Charles E. Owens, et al. 1999. *A Comprehensive Examination of Race in Jacksonville: A Report to the Jacksonville Human Rights Commission.* Jacksonville: Northeast Florida Center for Community Initiatives.

WJXT-TV. 1984. The Smell of Money. Television documentary. Videotaped.

INDEX

Department of Defense, 180
Department of Housing and Urban Development (city HUD), 72, 74
department stores, 131, 131n20
desegregation: of public schools, 24–27
Detroit, Mich.: Renaissance Square, 217, 223
Diamond, Jack, 194–96
Diamond, Rev. Tom, 187
D. J. Miller & Associates, 165–67
Donaldson, Sam, 109
downtown development: before consolidation, 2–7, 75–77; compared with Tampa, 218–21; during Austin years, 192–201; during Godbold years, 125–26, 128–32; during Hazouri years, 170–72; impact of consolidation on, 216–18; planning for, 118–21
Downtown Development Authority (DDA), 75, 192–94; policies under Godbold, 119, 128–32. See also downtown development
Downtown Development Council, 75
Downtown Merchants Association, 129
Durbin Creek, 138, 159
Durden, Judge William, 11
Duval Air Improvement Authority, 15
Duval County: legislative delegation, 40, 46, 71; preconsolidation government, 38
—grand jury: consequences of indictments, 22, 23, 44n20; preconsolidation corruption, 44–45; report on odor pollution, 153
—public schools: desegregation, 24–27; disaccredited, 8–12; governance, 9; reaccredited, 84, 122
Duval County Housing Finance Authority, 145
Duval County School Board: desegregation, 101, 185, 209; expansion of multicultural awareness training, 188; limitations under consolidation, 204; minority set-aside contracts, 165n48
Duval County Taxpayers Association, 11–12
Duval Federal Savings and Loan, 76

Earth Day, 215
East Jacksonville, 88
Edwards, Marvin, 3n6, 198

Edward Waters College, 34; accredited, 122; and civil disorders task force, 87
emergency ambulance service, 84
Emergency Medical Rescue Service, 204
Emmet Reed Center, 49, 66
Enterprise Center, 132
environment: impact of consolidation, 213–16. See also air pollution; solid waste disposal; water pollution
Environmental Protection Agency, 77, 79–80; concerns about floating nuclear power plants, 112; hazardous waste cleanup cost estimates, 180; and clean air standards for Jacksonville, 180; threatens fines, 125, 128, 136; urban sprawl, 184
Environmental Protection Board, 214; and mass-burn facility, 162; objects to proposed southeast landfill, 159
Environmental Science and Engineering, 135
Equal business opportunity program, 189. See also minority business set-aside program
Ernest, Albert, 128

Farmer, Rev. John, 96, 139
Feagin, Robert R., 32–33
Federal Clean Air Act, 80
Federal Solid Waste Disposal Act (1965), 16
Federal Water Quality Act (1965), 14
Ferguson, Ronnie: advocate for minority set-asides, 141; appointed head of Jacksonville Housing Authority, 191; responds to Jacksonville Together, 189; testimony before Florida Advisory Committee to U.S. Civil Rights Commission, 190
festival marketplace. See Jacksonville Landing
First Baptist Church, 122
Fischer, John, 84
Fisher, Dr. John, 46, 53
fleeing felon law, 142, 143
Fletcher, Judge Hugh, 154
Flood and Associates, 77. See also Flood Engineers-Architects-Planners, Inc.
Flood Engineers-Architects-Planners, Inc., 137. See also Flood and Associates
Florida Advisory Committee to the U.S.

James B. Crooks is professor emeritus of history at the University of North Florida, Jacksonville. He is the author of *Politics and Progress: The Rise of Urban Progressivism in Baltimore, 1895–1911* (1968) and *Jacksonville after the Fire, 1901–1919: A New South City* (1991).